STO

Y0-BUD-487

Business in the
Shadow of Apartheid

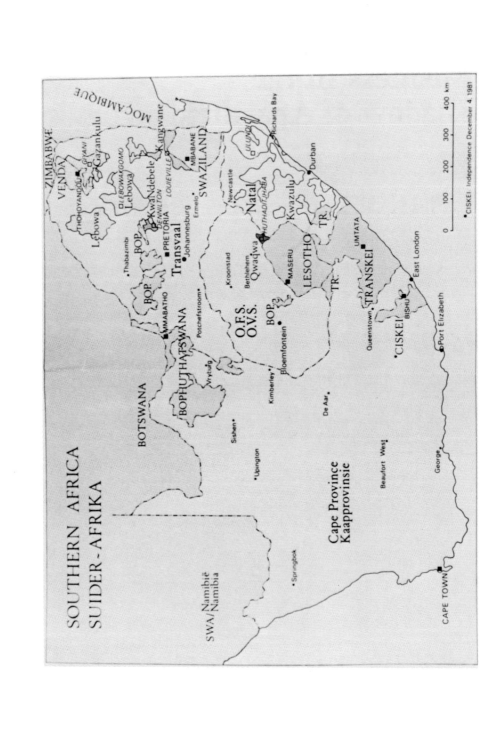

SOUTHERN AFRICA
SUIDER-AFRIKA

MOÇAMBIQUE

ZIMBABWE

VENDA

THOHOYANDOU

GAZANKULU

Gazankulu

Lebowa

GIYANI

LEBOWA/GOMO

KwaNdebele

Lebowa

Thabazimbi

BOP

MMABATHO

BOP

BOP

DENNILTON

LOUIEVILLE

PRETORIA

Transvaal

Johannesburg

Ermelo

Kangwane

MBABANE

SWAZILAND

Newcastle

Natal

Richards Bay

Durban

ULUNDI

BOTSWANA

SWA/Namibië
Namibia

Springbok

BOPHUTHATSWANA

Vryburg

Potchefstroom

Kroonstad

Bethlehem

O.F.S.
O.V.S.

Qwaqwa

PHUTHADITJHABA

MASERU

LESOTHO

Kwazulu

TR.

Bloemfontein

BOP

Kimberley

De Aar

Queenstown

BISHO

CISKEI

TRANSKEI

TR.

UMTATA

East London

Port Elizabeth

Sishen

Upington

Beaufort West

George

Cape Province
Kaapprovinsie

CAPE TOWN

0 100 200 300 400 km

• CISKEI: Independence December 4, 1981

Business in the Shadow of Apartheid

U.S. Firms in South Africa

Edited by
Jonathan Leape
Bo Baskin
Stefan Underhill

Lexington Books
D.C. Heath and Company/Lexington, Massachusetts/Toronto

Library of Congress Cataloging in Publication Data

Main entry under title:

Business in the shadow of apartheid.

Bibliography: p.
Includes index.
1. Corporations, American—South Africa—Addresses, essays, lectures. 2. South Africa—Race relations—Addresses, essays, lectures. 3. Blacks—Employment—South Africa—Addresses, essays, lectures. 4. Industry—Social aspects—Case studies—Addresses, essays, lectures.
I. Leape, Jonathan. II. Baskin, Bo. III. Underhill, Stefan.
HD2922.B87   1985   338.8'8973'068   84-47741
ISBN 0-669-08404-2 (alk. paper)

Second printing, June 1985

Published simultaneously in Canada
Printed in the United States of America on acid-free paper
International Standard Book Number: 0-669-08404-2
Library of Congress Catalog Card Number: 84-47741

Contents

Acknowledgments

This book is the product of a long education. We have many to thank: friends, colleagues, teachers, advisers, and sponsors.

Our education began with a remarkable group of friends we made while studying at Oxford University from 1979 to 1981. It was they who first challenged us to rethink the American role in South Africa. For many thought-provoking discussions and for patient counsel, we are grateful to Hugh Corder, Johann Koornhof, Paul Kumleben, Steven Lukes, Etienne Mureinik, Anthony Skillicorn, Anthony Staak, Peter Strivens, Steve Tollman, and Ilse Treurnicht.

The generosity of the Rhodes Trust permitted two of us to visit South Africa in July and August of 1981, where we interviewed over one hundred people from Nthato Motlana, chairman of the Soweto Committee of Ten, to Piet Koornhof, Minister of Cooperation and Development; from Sam Kikine, general secretary of South African Allied Workers Union, to Harry Oppenheimer, chairman of Anglo-American; from Piet Cillie, chairman of Nasionale Pers, to Helen Suzman, senior parliamentary member of the Progressive Federal party; from an Afrikaner "super-broeder" school teacher in Randburg to a group of black factory workers in a hostel in the Langa township. We cannot thank each of these people individually, but we want to recognize two whose support and guidance, both while we were in South Africa and since then, we will always remember: John Kane-Berman and Steve Tollman.

Upon our return to the United States, we sought to improve our understanding of the American firms with operations in South Africa. We developed a course on the subject at the Yale School of Management. A number of corporate executives helped design and teach the course, including representatives of Citibank, Ford, IBM, Mobil, and Union Carbide.

At the same time, we decided to plan a conference to bring together U.S. executives who make decisions regarding their firms' involvement in South Africa and South African analysts and political leaders. The School of Management agreed to serve as the official sponsor, and many people affiliated with Yale helped us focus and implement our ideas. We want, in particular, to thank Dean Burton Malkiel, Kingman Brewster, Jim Carragher, Richard Eaton, William Foltz, Stan Greenberg, Charles Haight, Geoffrey Hazard, Irwin Miller, William Scranton, and Leonard Thompson.

The advice of our corporate advisory committee, comprised of Wayne Fredericks of Ford, Sal Marzullo of Mobil, John Purcell of Goodyear, James Rawlings of Union Carbide, and Wilfred Koplowitz of Citibank, was invaluable. They generously shared with us the insights and good sense culled from years of thoughtful business experience.

Finally, the conference would have remained simply an idea were it not for generous financial support and hard work. For financial support we thank first The Ford Foundation; William Carmichael and Richard Horowitz provided advice and helpful criticism. We thank also the Carnegie Corporation, where David Hood and Jill Sheffield shared with us their valuable insights. Finally, we thank Yale University, Aetna, Citibank, Mobil, Monsanto, Union Carbide, and Xerox, all of whom provided generous financial support that made the conference possible. We can never thank enough those who volunteered their services, from brainstorming to airport pick-ups, from letter-writing to licking envelopes. Those who sacrificed more than they should have for the sake of the conference include Teresa Barger, Camilla Bishop, Susan Burns, Kathy Cade, Bob Chatten, Howard Costley, Don Hanna, Amie Knox, Sara Lord, Joe Mensah, Hilary Pennington, Peter Schulte, Susan Tanaka, Shey Tata, and Tim Underhill.

Two people played a crucial role in planning and administering the course and the conference. Cindi Cobbs and Tim Knowles were our partners throughout; without their skills and dedication, neither the course nor the conference would have succeeded. We deeply appreciated their contribution and friendship.

The original versions of all but one of the chapters that follow were presented at the conference, "U.S. Firms in South Africa," on September 21–23, 1982. We want to thank all those who were part of the conference as speakers and discussants: Heribert Adam, Tony Bloom, Gatsha Buthelezi, Robert Cabelly, Halton Cheadle, William Cotter, Oscar Dhlomo, Barend duPlessis, Fred Ferreira, William Foltz, Bobby Godsell, John Kane-Berman, Dumisani Kumalo, Richard Moose, Leonard Mosala, Terry Myers, John Purcell, Dan Purnell, Frederik van zyl Slabbert, Frank Wisner, and Griffiths Zabala. We are particularly grateful to our contributors, who painstakingly revised and updated their papers in the first half of 1984.

A small group assisted us along the path to publication. Felicia Green typed the manuscript with care, often catching our mistakes. Several friends improved the introduction with their useful comments: Danny Goodgame, Ann Graybiel, Suki Hoagland, Mervyn King, Jim Leape, Sara Lord, and Tom Ward. Marsha Forrest, Martha Hawkins, and Jaime Welch at Lexington Books coached, corrected, and cajoled us into print. We want especially to thank Mary Pat Morrissey Underhill. To one of us she is a wonderful wife, to the other two a treasured friend who, in that special Morrissey way, always welcomes us in her home.

Finally, we dedicate this book to our parents. From their support and loving criticism we will benefit all of our lives.

Introduction

"I fought with you."
We glanced at each other, unsure of what he meant.

It was midsummer of 1981, and we were in South Africa. On a friend's advice we had left the main highway and taken one of the poorly paved back roads into the Ciskei. An hour later, we discovered what our friend had described to us.

In a sense it was a town, but not a town like any we had ever seen before. Its shape was a perfect rectangle, perhaps a mile long and a half-mile wide, with a simple, easily hurdled wire fence bounding it on all four sides. Within that fence sat row upon row of tiny mud huts—perhaps two thousand of them—which, but for cardboard sheets and wooden planks covering random gaps, had been constructed of the blond, sun-baked earth that carpeted the Ciskei from one horizon to the other.

A dozen barefoot black children had greeted us at the gate and followed us as we walked into the town. The nearer the city center we walked, the larger the crowd that accompanied us. The crowd contained no whites and, remarkably, no young or ablebodied men—only small squealing children, shy teenaged girls, gracious matronly women, and handicapped old men. For the town was a resettlement camp, peopled by children whose fathers, by girls whose brothers, and by women whose husbands and sons labored in faraway cities, places where children, girls, women, and old men were not allowed to live.

Near the center of the camp, we introduced ourselves. Hearing that we spoke English, several giggling young girls pushed forward an older peer who, beneath the weight of public attention, cast her eyes downward and in English demurely asked, "Where are you from?"

Upon hearing us answer "the United States," she leaned over to her side and breathily whispered in Xhosa to a tiny girl who darted away from the crowd and disappeared into one of the sandy mud huts.

Seconds later, an elderly yet muscular black man emerged from the hut. A large man, with salt and pepper hair and a solemn face, he silently stared at us.

"I fought with you," he said, his voice assertive and proud.

As he spoke, the small girl emerged from the hut, clutching in her tiny hands an old, flat tin that long ago had contained tobacco. When she opened the tin, the old man's words became clear: Inside were three tattered combat medals that, more than ten years before we were born, the U.S. government had awarded him for fighting with Americans against the Germans and Italians in the Allied cause of World War II.

This book examines the role of U.S. firms in South Africa. Such an examination raises three general questions, which this introduction addresses: First, why should Americans care about what happens in South Africa? Second, what are the prospects for change? Third, what are the opportunities for American influence?

Why South Africa?

Books like this one often provoke the question: "Why South Africa?" The old man and the Ciskei resettlement camp suggest a few answers.

First, they are reminders that oppression persists in South Africa. But by itself, this does not fully answer the question; for, as offensive as South Africa may seem, it does not monopolize oppression. Indeed, its policies are no more oppressive than those of some other African countries such as Ethiopia and probably much less oppressive than the policies of nations such as Iran, North Korea, and Libya.

So why South Africa in particular? We may think again of the old man and the resettlement camp. For they remind us not just of oppression but of an extraordinary form of racial oppression. They remind us that, simply because they are not white, over twenty million South Africans cannot vote, cannot travel freely, cannot buy their own homes, cannot join political parties, cannot compete for certain types of jobs, cannot generally own their own businesses, and in many instances cannot even live with their own families. As then-Secretary of State Henry Kissinger said in a 1976 speech in Lusaka, Zambia: "The world community's concern with South Africa is not merely that racial discrimination exists there. What is unique is the extent to which racial discrimination has been institutionalized, enshrined in law, and made all pervasive."[1] Other places are oppressive, other places are impoverished, but in South Africa it is "race without exception that defines the ghetto."[2]

The old man and the resettlement camp also remind us that South Africa's brand of racial oppression is the oppression of blacks by whites. The point is not that this form of oppression is more invidious than other forms but that the oppression of blacks by whites strikes a responsive chord within most Americans. It reminds them of their history and to some white Americans seems to provide an opportunity to atone for the wrongs that their ancestors, their parents, and perhaps even they heaped upon black Americans. Thus, one answer to the question "Why South Africa in particular?" is that South Africa, more than other oppressive places, practices the brand of oppression that, given their heritage, many Americans feel morally and emotionally most compelled to oppose.

South Africa's brand of oppression is also that to which history has most prepared Americans to respond. Of course, the racial circumstances in South Africa differ significantly from those in the United States. Nevertheless, America's experience with racism, civil rights legislation, violent and nonviolent political action, black consciousness, multiracial cooperation, and the process of legal and social integration may contain lessons that are valuable to South Africa.

South Africa's form of racial oppression is also that to which the racial composition of the United States requires Americans to be most sensitive. The stands taken by black American leaders such as the members of the Black Congressional Caucus, Andrew Young in his Atlanta mayoral campaign, and Jesse Jackson in his presidential campaign are reminders that American blacks care about U.S. governmental and business policies toward South Africa. The point is not that most black Americans place South Africa high on their day-to-day political agenda but that South Africa reminds Americans of their own black-white cleavage and that, as a result, black Americans view U.S. policies in South Africa as a symbol of white Americans' commitment to racial equality. Should whites and blacks violently clash in South Africa and should either side ask the U.S. for support, many black Americans will view the U.S. response as a barometer of the extent to which U.S. institutions represent black America as well as white America.

This old man and his World War II combat medals remind us also that South Africa's white ruling group, unlike the ruling groups of Iran or North Korea, are, both by history and by preference, Western. Historically, they are part Dutch and part British. Religiously, they are overwhelmingly Judeo-Christian. Politically, they are unequivocally anticommunist, avowedly "democratic," and indirectly dependent upon the Western defense umbrella. Economically, they trade with, invest in, and welcome investments from the West and thereby benefit enormously from the strength of the Western economies. Culturally, they identify themselves as a civilized and economically advanced Western nation.

In short, white South Africans and Westerners are in many respects cut from the same cloth politically, economically, and culturally. Doubtless this shared heritage constrains American actions, but it also provides the opportunity for American influence. Anyone familiar with either the fiercely independent Afrikaner *laager* (the circle of wagons used for defense in frontier days, now a symbol of Afrikaner unity in the face of attack) or the vast abyss separating American political preferences and South African political policies knows that these opportunities do not mean that South Africa is an American client state. We will explore exactly what these opportunities do mean later in this introduction. For now, it is sufficient to recognize that South Africa is different partly because South Africa is susceptible to American influence in ways that Libya, Iran, and North Korea are not. As the Rockefeller Commission stated in its 1981 report, "our inability to deal with every evil on the globe does not mean that we should not act where we have the latitude to do so and where there is a chance that we can make a difference."[3]

The old man in the resettlement camp, who swelled with pride when he told of fighting alongside Americans, also reminds us that many black South Africans feel a kinship with the West. The old man's dwelling place, however, reminds us that he and millions of other South Africans are denied fundamental freedoms and opportunities by a government and a culture that are undeniably Western and capitalist. Unless the West effectively communicates its political principles and makes clear its fundamental opposition to apartheid, anti-Western and anticapitalist sentiment will surely grow not only in South Africa but throughout the continent. Moreover, Western capitalism's detractors will undoubtedly use apartheid to spur the growth of this sentiment: What better example could their propagandists find to illustrate the alleged decadence and oppression of the Western capitalist system?

One final answer to the question, "Why should Americans care about South Africa?" is that the United States has commercial and strategic interests in South Africa. Commercially, more than six thousand U.S. companies do business with South Africa, and over three hundred have operations there. In 1982, U.S. firms in South Africa invested a total of $2.8 billion there, other U.S. firms carried on an estimated $3.1 billion in trade with South Africa, and U.S. banks and other financial institutions loaned South Africa $623 million. That same year, Americans purchased krugerrands worth $363 million, and owned 25 percent of South African gold mining shares (see appendix B). Moreover, the United States has important strategic interests in South Africa's minerals, Cape sea route, and geopolitical position. Certainly, some of these interests may prevent the U.S. from urging reform on South Africa; but certain others should compel the U.S. to urge such reform.

Not the least of these is the United States' interests in preventing what Heribert Adam calls the "Lebanization" of South Africa, that is, the submersion of South Africa in an intractable civil war in which ethnic groups become warring factions, law and order becomes vigilante chaos, superpower competition becomes an ominous sideshow, and the United States becomes a hapless "peacemaker", stuck between antagonists it can neither abandon nor control.

Prospects for Change in South Africa

Americans frequently look to American civil rights experience or recent history in southern Africa in attempting to understand South Africa. The following examination of these analogies shows how they fail to take into account critical features of the contemporary South African situation.

Americans often assume that the civil rights experience of the United States provides an accurate guide for understanding how change can occur in South Africa. The problem, they argue, is one of attitudes. If South African whites can simply be persuaded—through education or exhortation—that blacks are their equals, then integration will follow and apartheid will fall. But the analogy fails because of one crucial fact. In the United States, the problem has been convincing a majority to accept a small minority. In South Africa, the numbers are reversed: A small minority is being asked to incorporate a majority.

The problem is not simply one of numbers. Opening the political and economic system in South Africa to the black majority will involve real losses for whites. At a minimum, it will mean higher taxes, greater economic competition, and less political power. In the extreme, it could mean the confiscation of property, the nationalization of industry, the political domination of whites by blacks, and perhaps even the dilution of the Afrikaner culture. The current political and economic system yields a bountiful harvest for whites; they enjoy the political freedoms and rights of advanced, open democratic societies and a level of affluence that few places in the world can match. Thus, the racial problem in South Africa, unlike that in the United States, is not primarily a problem of attitudes: It is a problem of power.

Americans concerned about apartheid also look to African experience, in particular to the recent history of southern Africa, as a model for understanding South Africa. The white governments in Angola and Mozambique fell in 1974 and the government in Rhodesia-Zimbabwe in 1980; surely, it is argued, it is only a matter of time before the same happens in South Africa. This appeal to the "march of history" masks striking—and ultimately decisive—differences between the situations in Mozambique, Angola, and Zimbabwe and that in South Africa. These differences become clear when one compares the white communities, the black communities, and the conditions affecting guerrilla resistance in each of these four countries.

The white populations of Angola and Mozambique considered themselves Portuguese, and their governments were colonial. In Rhodesia, the whites were recent settlers, most of whom had moved there from England after the First World War. In all three countries, the number of native blacks dwarfed the number of whites. In Rhodesia, for example, there were only 250,000 whites out of a total population in excess of six million: a ratio of 1 to 24.

By contrast, the South African white population dates back to 1652, when Jan van Riebeeck's party of Dutch settlers landed near the Cape of Good Hope. The whites of Dutch heritage do not consider themselves colonialists; they call themselves Afrikaners ("Africans") and strongly believe that South Africa is their country. Moreover, as "Africans," they have no Portugal or England to return to, and as the last "white-ruled" nation in Africa they have nowhere else on the continent to go. The numbers also differ. Whites in South Africa account for five million of the total population of thirty-two million: a ratio of almost 1 to 6. Finally, the ruling whites in South Africa have achieved a degree of internal dominance and international power without equal in Africa.

White South Africa's most obvious source of power is its immense military strength. The size and firepower of the South African Defence Force (SADF) are unmatched in sub-Saharan Africa. The SADF can mobilize a force of 250,000 men. Its arsenal includes combat equipment that is advanced even by Western standards. Some even believe that the South Africans possess nuclear weapons. "Israel has eaten up the Arabs before lunch," then-Prime Minister John Vorster allegedly said in 1967. "We [South Africa] could eat up black Africa before breakfast."[4]

South Africa is as dominant economically as it is militarily. It produces three-quarters of the total GNP of all of southern Africa (south of Zaire-Tanzania) and is responsible for almost nine-tenths of that region's energy consumption. The trade of all southern African countries depends heavily on South Africa (25 percent for Zimbabwe, 37 percent for Mozambique). Yet the dependence is not reciprocal: South Africa relies on the whole of Africa for only 10 percent of its exports and 2 percent of its imports.[5]

The black communities in these countries also differ. In Zimbabwe, nearly all blacks belong to one of two tribes: A majority are Shona-speaking; only 20 percent are Ndebele-speaking. The Shona tribal ties reinforced Robert Mugabe's political organization, the Zimbabwe African National Union-Political Front (Zanu-PF), which was also bolstered by the economic and military assistance of bordering states. Even with these numerical and organizational advantages, however, open elections came to Zimbabwe only after seven years of sustained guerrilla warfare.

In South Africa, by contrast, history divides blacks into nine major tribes. Of these, the largest is the Zulu, which represents only five million of the twenty-three million black South Africans. The white government's policy of "Grand Apartheid" (which assigns each black South African to a "tribal homeland") has entrenched these divisions, and the system of "influx control" (which restricts the movements of black South Africans into and within the so-called white areas) has further divided blacks into what John Kane-Berman calls "rural outsiders" and privileged "urban insiders." These divisions, discussed further below, have been compounded by ideological clashes between black consciousness movements and class-based movements and by personality conflicts between various black leaders. Combined with the severe restrictions placed on black political activity by the South African government, these divisions have hindered the emergence of a unified black political organization.

Even though opinion surveys have since 1976 revealed a steady increase in anger and militance among black South Africans, the military resistance, spearheaded by the African National Congress (ANC), is still minimal after almost twenty-five years of armed struggle. According to outside estimates, ANC forces number only seven to eight thousand (two thousand by South African estimates). They are able to cross the border only in tiny groups of three or four and can increase their forces only very slowly due to the danger of infiltration by the South African secret police.[6] Moreover, while the ANC seems to have been successful in establishing political "cells" in various parts of South Africa, the danger of discovery has prevented them from linking these cells—a necessary condition for concerted action—and from establishing a strong military capability within the country. Shrewd planning on the part of the South African government has further minimized the possibility of armed resistance within the country. "The SADF could seal off every black area in 'white South Africa' within thirty minutes," we were told in 1981. The government has designed black townships to have as few as two entrances, we discovered, so that troops can seal them off easily in the event of an uprising. Finally, the possibility of guerrilla attacks from outside South Africa has recently diminished; Swaziland, in February 1982, and Mozambique, in March 1984, signed mutual security treaties with South Africa pledging to cooperate in the elimination of ANC bases (see chapter 2 for a discussion of these treaties). As yet, guerrilla activity consists only of sporadic attacks on key South African military and commercial installations, such as the May 1983 car-bomb attack on the South African Air Force headquarters in Pretoria, which killed nineteen people and wounded two hundred, and the May 1984 rocket attack on an oil refinery in the port of Durban. While black resistance to apartheid will continue to grow both inside and outside the country, the military threat to the dominance of the white regime seems likely to be only minimal for some time to come.

The Strength of the White Regime

In short, neither the American nor the southern African historical analogies can adequately explain the prospects for change in South Africa. Therefore, we need to explore in greater detail the peculiar features of the South African political landscape. In particular, we need to examine why the white regime in South Africa is so powerful and why the black community has so far offered so little resistance.

The Afrikaners. An analysis of the power of the white regime inevitably begins with the Afrikaners. It is often argued that to understand the Afrikaners one must first understand their history. The Afrikaners' Dutch forebears left Europe long before the Enlightenment and therefore, some have argued, never acquired the liberal attitudes that later shaped political thinking in the West. The Afrikaners' strong Calvinist beliefs, intensified by their frontier experience, bred in them the conviction that they were "a chosen people, analogous to the ancient Israelites, who had a special and exclusive relationship with God and a mandate to smite the heathen."[7] Therefore, when, in the early nineteenth century, the hated British colonial administration tried to enforce equal status for blacks and whites, the Afrikaners responded with outrage, and large numbers of them tried to escape British authority by migrating northward in what came to be known as the "Great Trek." The highly organized and militarily strong Zulus, among others, violently resisted the Afrikaners' migration, thus intensifying the Afrikaners' aversion to the Africans. Ultimately, the Afrikaners triumphed and thereby confirmed their self-image as a chosen people. Later, when the British authorities followed the Afrikaners northward in an attempt to lay claim to the Transvaal's vast mineral wealth, the Afrikaners' bitter rivalry with the British was revived, and their deep belief in the advantages of ethnic cohesion reaffirmed.[8] This cohesion helped the Afrikaners to defend themselves against the economically dominant English, to catapult themselves into a position of political supremacy in 1948, and to defend the position of power and privilege that they had won.

Against this image of the Afrikaners as an historically unique people lingers the memory of a 1981 interview with Piet Cillie, "one of the giants of Afrikaner journalism."⁹ When asked what features of the Afrikaners' history—the pre-Enlightenment immigration, the Puritan self-image as a chosen people, the frontier experience, or the competition with the English—best explained current Afrikaner racial policies, Cillie replied: "None of them. Under similar circumstances, any other people would do exactly the same things we're doing."¹⁰

Cillie's response may ignore some valuable historical and cultural distinctions, but he makes an important point: Afrikaner attitudes and policies are a response not just to a unique historical experience but also to fears that any group might feel under similar circumstances, regardless of its history. Specifically, the Afrikaners fear that if they loosen their political and economic stranglehold and submit to more democratic processes they will ultimately lose their way of life.

Although Africa has produced several laudable democratic achievements in the last thirty years, the Afrikaners take little comfort from post-colonial African experience. They look at black Africa and see the tyranny of Mobutu's Zaire, the recent despotism of Amin's Uganda, and the instability of contemporary Nigeria. In Kenya they see not parliamentary democracy but a one-party state, and in Zimbabwe they see not a multiracial democracy grappling with a difficult political situation but a Shona autocracy capable of ignoring due process for whites. Moreover, their own history of domination makes them fear something similar: That blacks will treat whites in the future as whites have treated blacks in the past.

But the Afrikaner aversion to change is not based solely on such fears. Many whites see power-sharing producing consequences that are far from disastrous but that are simply much less attractive than the status quo. With few exceptions, the Afrikaners remain convinced that the benefits of maintaining their power and privilege through minority rule and apartheid far outweigh the costs. Thus, the central concern of white South Africans, and Afrikaners in particular, has been and still is that of how best to maintain their position as conditions continually change within and around South Africa.

Grand Apartheid. Since coming to power in 1948, the National Party has pursued the goal of maintaining Afrikaner power and privilege through the overarching policy of "Grand Apartheid." Grand Apartheid seeks to make the Republic of South Africa a "white" nation by dividing black South Africans among ten rural reservations and declaring these reservations "independent" countries. The National Party first formalized the strategy in 1959 with the passage of the Promotion of Bantu

Self-Government Act, which abolished the limited parliamentary representation blacks had enjoyed and linked each black ethnic group to a putative "homeland." In this way, the 80 percent of South Africans who are black were allowed political rights only in these underdeveloped, resource-barren rural reserves which together constitute 13 percent of the total land area of South Africa. The goal of Grand Apartheid was and still is to ensure the survival of white supremacy in general, and of the Afrikaner tribe in particular, by denying black South Africans political rights and thus any claim to the common wealth of South Africa.

The Nationalist government's rationale and strategy for pursuing Grand Apartheid have changed over the years. In 1948 the Nationalists were a coalition primarily of laborers and farmers, whose commitment to the policy of Grand Apartheid sprang from a semi-religious devotion to racial purity and separation. In the 1960s and 1970s, however, the once cohesive and comparatively homogeneous Afrikaners became increasingly stratified. Increasing numbers of Afrikaners moved from the countryside into the cities, acquired more education, sought vocational opportunities in the capitalist economy once dominated by the hated English, and gradually lost some of their ideological zeal.

At the same time, South Africa's rapid economic growth created a demand for semi-skilled and skilled workers that the white trade unions, which had erected barriers to black competition, could not meet. Moreover, internal and external pressures to broaden the government's political base increased.

As Heribert Adam points out in chapter 2, the bulk of Afrikanerdom, in particular the group he calls the "ruling technocrats" who now run the party, responded to these changes pragmatically by eliminating protective labor policies and beginning to consider alliances across the color line. Parts of the Afrikaner community, however, rebelled against this pragmatic response. The group Adam calls the "labor racists" refused to accept the changes in labor policy and left the Party in 1969 to form the Herstigte Nasionale Party (HNP). The "orthodox ideologues" refused to accept the need for alliances across the color line and left the Party in 1982 when the ruling technocrats moved toward "sharing power" with coloreds and Indians.

Throughout the period, however, all three groups pursued the same basic objective: the maintenance of Afrikaner power and privilege. Though they quarreled over tactics and though their particular interests clashed, all three groups remained staunchly committed to the continued dominance of Afrikaners and to the strategy, however modified, of Grand Apartheid.

The strategy of Grand Apartheid reflects the dilemma of a white regime that conceives of itself as a "free world" democratic state, seeks the approval and support of the West, but wants to deny basic democratic rights and powers to 80 percent of the population. The strategy is to exploit one of the most vexing questions in politics: How should boundaries be drawn? It reflects the Afrikaners' recognition that if, in the creation of a new political dispensation, a certain group is excluded from citizenship, then that group can make no legal claim to political rights.

Modern democracies exist within specified sets of boundaries. Americans consider it an offense to democracy to deny the vote to a lifetime resident of Mississippi, yet feel no compulsion to submit to a majority vote of, say, the North American continent. The key is boundaries. The Mississippian is a citizen of the United States, a member of the American political community; Mexicans and Canadians are not.

In its policy of Grand Apartheid, white South Africa attempts to exploit this distinction. The white resident of Johannesburg is a South African citizen; the black resident of neighboring Soweto is not. The Sowetan is a citizen of, say, Bophuthatswana, an "independent" state.

It is impossible, however, to conceive of the million people who live in Soweto as anything but South Africans. Most of them have lived there all of their lives, and many have never even seen their "homelands." Seeing the impracticality of this plan and the world's rejection of it, the government has hinted at the possibility of incorporating "urban" blacks into "white" South Africa, but even this modification will not alter the fundamental fact that South Africa *in its entirety* is a nation and Bophuthatswana is not.

Contemporary Israel, Lebanon, Quebec, and Northern Ireland demonstrate that defining a nation can be very difficult. In general, certain minimal conditions must be met. First, a nation requires a significant degree of geographic integrity to facilitate the defense of its interests, the free mobility of its citizens, and the free communication of ideas. Second, a nation needs substantial economic integration—that is, interdependence within its own economy and a degree of independence from other economies. Third, a nation traditionally develops out of a shared history, a collective response to common problems, whether they be external threats or internal crises. Fourth, a nation generally requires a degree of social cohesion. Such cohesion may arise from a common ethnic heritage or may, as in the case of the United States, develop out of shared experience. Fifth, a nation depends upon consent. In general, groups that meet the preceding four criteria cannot justly be excluded from a nation without their consent. Finally, a nation must be recognized by other nations.

Proponents of Grand Apartheid argue that South Africa has never been one nation. Historically, they say, whites have inhabited certain parts of South Africa and blacks other parts. The two groups mixed only when blacks sought the fruits of the prosperous white economy. This, they assert, is no different from the situation in Switzerland, where Germans and Italians work as migrant laborers. Above all, they argue, South Africa is characterized by fundamental ethnic differences. These include not only the differences between blacks and whites but also the differences between Xhosa and Zulu, Tswana and Ndebele, and even Afrikaner and English. "We have no majority in South Africa, only minorities," an Afrikaner schoolteacher told us. Thus, in justifying Grand Apartheid, proponents have sought to exploit ethnic differences above all else.

But ethnicity is just one element of nationhood and frequently an unimportant one. If we consider all the characteristics that make a nation, we see in South Africa not eleven nations but one. Within its traditional boundaries, formalized by the constitution of 1910, South Africa is a geographically unified whole. Few of the "homelands," however, exhibit such integrity. Bophuthatswana, Lebowa, KwaZulu, and the Ciskei are black archipelegoes scattered across the so-called white areas. Most of their "citizens" cannot travel to their own capital without first leaving the homeland and passing through white South Africa.

From the earliest stages of economic development, black South Africans have been an integral part of the South African economy. The mining industry, the driving force of the economy since the end of the nineteenth century, developed because of the abundant supply of cheap black labor. "What an abundance of rain and grass was to New Zealand mutton, what plenty of cheap grazing land was to Australian wool, what the fertile prairie acres were to Canadian wheat, cheap native labor was to South African mining and industrial enterprise."[11] Today, blacks supply virtually all of the unskilled labor and an increasing share of the skilled labor and management in all industries and all regions of South Africa. Moreover, black South Africans account for nearly half of the consuming power in the economy.

At the same time, the "homelands" are completely dependent on the South African economy. With certain exceptions such as the casinos in Bophuthatswana, built to serve vacationing white South Africans, the homelands have little economic activity beyond subsistence agriculture. Overgrazed, overpopulated, and underdeveloped, they are able to supply employment for less than one in six of those entering the work force. As Oscar Dhlomo writes in chapter 6, "these so-called homelands are in fact the depressed regions of our common economy."

The story of the old man in the Ciskei hints at the depth of the shared history of white and black South Africans. The experiences and institutions linking whites and blacks date back to the arrival of the first Dutch settlers in the mid-1600s. Indeed, recent scholarship suggests that segregation and racial discrimination were not the dominant characteristics of South African society as a whole until the last half of the nineteenth century. In 1822, the editor of the Colonial Secretary's report on the Cape Province predicted that the white, brown, and black people of the Cape would gradually meld to form a Creole South African race.[12] A recent historical study of intermarriage found that in the early nineteenth century between one-third and one-quarter of the "white" population had a black or brown grandparent and that over 10 percent and very likely over 20 percent of the "whites" married at that time were married to or living in permanent union with "nonwhites."[13] Of course, the large so-called colored population has its roots largely in the intermarriage of Afrikaners and Africans. Despite the discrimination and segregation that has characterized the last century of South African history, blacks and whites have lived, worked, and even, as the story of the black veteran reminds us, fought side by side.

The overwhelming majority of blacks in South Africa consider themselves South Africans and feel no allegiance to their so-called homelands. The white government has given "independence" to four of these homelands against the wishes of most of their "citizens." Dr. Nthato Motlana, a black leader in Soweto, refers to his assigned homeland as "Bophutha-nonsense."[14]

Finally, the international community has refused to recognize the "homelands" as independent nations. Not a single nation has agreed to exchange ambassadors with the "homelands" or in any way formally recognized their independence from South Africa.

The New Constitution. The most recent manifestation of Grand Apartheid is the new constitution passed by referendum on November 2, 1983. Spokesmen for the government represented the new constitution to the West as a starting point in the movement toward a new political dispensation that would involve all people in South Africa. Indeed, the U.S. State Department welcomed the approval of the new constitution as opening the way to a new political system resting on the consent of all South Africans.

The new constitution is not a step in the direction of reform, however. Rather, it is the National Party's response to the fragmentation of Afrikanerdom and to the need to build alliances, however superficial, across the color line. Before Afrikanerdom began to fragment in the late 1960s, a National Party leader could rely on "the unquestioned trust of his people, who view him as one of their own, regardless of his specific actions."[15] As Afrikanerdom split, however, the National Party lost this "unquestioned trust." To maintain control, the prime minister now must compete for the support of different interests, reinforce his diminished political power with greater administrative authority, or both. The new constitution gives the prime minister this greater administrative authority. Specifically, it replaces many formerly democratic parliamentary procedures with administrative fiat powers; gives to the State President, who is both head of state and head of government (thus absorbing the duties of the prime minister), the power to dissolve Parliament and declare martial law; and, even in ordinary circumstances, enables him to govern with the support of only 30 percent of the members of Parliament, if they represent a majority of the white chamber.

The new constitution is also an attempt to build alliances with Indians and coloreds. It springs from the reluctant recognition that, over the long term, the Nationalists are not strong enough to resist the internal and external pressures associated with excluding over 80 percent of the population from the political system. But, as Heribert Adam argues in chapter 2, this attempt at "power-sharing" shares very little power and therefore builds no new alliances. In short, it lacks legitimacy. Most Indians and coloreds view it as a sham. In the first parliamentary elections, held on August 22 and 28, 1984, the turnout was only 16 percent of those coloreds and Indians eligible to vote—and as low as 3 percent in the more politicized areas around Cape Town. Most blacks view it as a divisive attempt to coopt coloreds and Indians and to entrench their own exclusion.

Some have argued that the government has a plan to incorporate blacks into the political system but cannot reveal it now for fear of a rightwing backlash. But constitutional development is not "on hold" with respect to blacks. On the contrary, the government is actively pursuing a policy of denationalization which is, in John Kane-Berman's words, "expressly designed to exclude any future possibility of incorporation."

The Strategy for Dispossession. Denationalization is the linchpin of what Kane-Berman in chapter 1 calls "a four-pronged strategy to dispossess black South Africans." The four prongs of the strategy, through which the government has given force to Grand Apartheid, are forced resettlement, influx control, financial deprivation of the "homelands," and denationalization. Over the past two decades, the government's resettlement program has forcibly removed two million blacks from their homes in the so-called white areas and transported them to impoverished resettlement camps in their putative homelands. During that same period, the government's influx control system has prevented blacks from leaving the homelands and migrating to the white areas. The government has been revising this system to sharpen the distinction between "urban insiders" and "rural outsiders." Under this revised system, the government has granted certain residential, job, and mobility privileges to a small elite of urban blacks who supply badly-needed skilled labor and even managerial skills to the white economy. At the same time, the government has tightened the controls on all other blacks and imposed unprecedentedly harsh penalties on the employers and landlords who hire and house these outsiders. Thus, while the government grants privileges to urban insiders, it enforces more severely than ever the rules restricting rural outsiders to either unskilled migrant labor or subsistence agriculture in the homelands. As Oscar Dhlomo points out in chapter 6, the government has deprived the so-called homelands of the financial resources necessary for social and economic development. Finally, the government has stripped 7.8 million black South Africans, more than one-third of the total, of their South African citizenship by declaring four of the ten homelands "independent" states. If the government succeeds in granting independence to the remaining six homelands, all black South Africans will have become foreigners—without South African citizenship and therefore without political rights—in their own land.

The Limits of Black Resistance

The political weakness of black South Africans results partly from the white regime's strategy of division and dispossession; partly from the black community's tribal, personal, and ideological conflicts; and partly from the regime's systematic efforts to prevent blacks from developing social, economic, and especially political institutions. Developing such institutions is, of course, a prerequisite to articulating common interests and exerting influence. The government has denied blacks access to white schools and universities, and the Bantu education system has prevented blacks from acquiring even the most rudimentary skills. As recently as 1970, a majority of blacks in rural areas had no formal education. Even today, while less than 1 percent of whites are functionally illiterate in South Africa, the figures for Africans are 30 percent in urban areas and over 60 percent in rural areas (see appendix A). "Job reservation" (the legal reservation of certain jobs for white workers) restricted blacks to manual labor, and thus denied them the opportunity to acquire skills and bargaining power. The "industrial council system" (the industry-wide structure for wage determination dominated by white labor) and the "migrant labor system" (the system for importing low-cost unskilled labor from the rural reservations) prevented blacks from organizing. Finally, the government's repressive security apparatus has snuffed out even the most basic rights of political expression and association.

Since the late 1970s, the government has significantly increased its expenditures on black education and removed many of the restrictions on labor advancement and organization. These changes were a pragmatic response to the shortage of skilled labor in the economy and to the ultimately irresistible demands of black workers, and not to a new liberality on the part of the Nationalist government. While these changes will not soon heal the scars from decades of deprivation, they nevertheless have important implications not only for blacks' educational and economic status but also for the long-term development of blacks' political and organizational skills.

The black community will not easily either overcome the government's strategy of division, dispossession, and denial, or resolve its own tribal, personal, and ideological conflicts. Nevertheless, the black community has the potential to increase its political clout through shrewd strategy development and political organization. For just as Afrikaners are too weak to succeed without political organization and alliances, so also are black South Africans. Of course, building such alliances will inevitably involve risks and require sacrifices, but it will also involve the prospect for much greater political gains than any individual black group could ever capture on its own. The key is strategy development and political organization—something Gatsha Buthelezi emphasizes in chapter 7. The success of the United Democratic Front in coordinating the efforts of over six hundred different organizations to oppose the new constitution and, more recently, to fight the South African government on a range of issues is an example of the potential for collective political action.

What then are the prospects for change in South Africa? The probability of radical change—through the exertion of black power or the fall of the white government—is extremely small. The balance of military, economic, and political power is still far too lopsided for rapid or dramatic change. Indeed, it is still the Afrikaners who control the agenda, and for them the benefits of maintaining power through minority rule and apartheid still far outweigh the costs. As time goes on, these costs will surely rise, and the benefits may fall. For now, it seems likely that, as Kane-Berman argues, South Africa will remain in an uneasy and sometimes violent equilibrium subject to occasional changes and reforms as black South Africans begin to exert their small but increasing influence. It also seems likely that it will be the forces inside South Africa, such as white military strength, black trade unions, Afrikaner party politics, and black political organization, rather than forces outside South Africa, such as pressure from the United States or an alliance with Israel, that will primarily determine the pace of change.

What Can Americans Do?

Americans can nevertheless have some effect on the pace of change in South Africa. There are two sources of American influence: the U.S. government and U.S. firms.

U.S. Government

Recent U.S. initiatives in Central America and the Caribbean basin demonstrate that, when the perceived national interests of the United States are at stake, the boldness of its actions and the extent of its influence can be significant. Should the United States government perceive apartheid to be a serious threat to U.S. interests, it might even intervene militarily. But, few people, if any, believe that apartheid poses such a threat. Thus, armed intervention by the United States is virtually unimaginable.

Another strategy open to the U.S. government is the imposition of economic sanctions on South Africa. As detailed in appendix F, the U.S. government prohibited sales of American computers to the South African army, police, and atomic energy agencies in 1976. In 1978, the U.S. government forbade the sale of any American-made goods or technology to the South African military and police. In 1984, the House and Senate were conferring on a bill (H.R. 3231) passed in the House of Representatives that would impose the most far-reaching sanctions yet proposed. The bill prohibits bank loans to the South African government, forbids the sale of South African gold krugerrands in the United States, and proscribes any increases in private investment in South Africa (see appendix F).

The effectiveness of any sanctions that the United States might impose upon South Africa will depend upon the support they receive from other countries, South Africa's capacity to adapt to the sanctions, and, as Heribert Adam points out in chapter 2, South Africa's domestic politics. Economic sanctions are difficult to enforce against any country, but they are particularly difficult to enforce against South Africa, which has demonstrated that it can get the supplies it needs regardless of sanctions. A March 1984 article in the British newspaper *The Guardian* revealed that South Africa has built a complicated worldwide supply system to protect its international trade in vital materials against comprehensive sanctions. The system operates through Freight Services, the South African shipping agency responsible for breaking the oil embargo against Rhodesia, and involves subsidiaries in nearly every African country and around the world.[16] Moreover, when the international community has successfully enforced economic sanctions against South Africa, the South Africans have been able to adapt to the sanctions. For example, in November 1977, the United Nations Security Council adopted Resolution 418, which imposed a mandatory arms embargo against South Africa that was widely enforced. The embargo was certainly costly for South Africa, but it had the unintended result that South Africa became even more immune to international pressure: South Africa increased its military self-sufficiency from 50 percent in 1977 to 95 percent today.[17] Finally, the effectiveness of sanctions depends upon the role those sanctions play in the competition between political factions within South Africa. In particular, their effectiveness depends upon inter-party Afrikaner politics. As we have already seen, and as Adam discusses in chapter 2, Afrikaner politics are constantly changing. To fail to adapt American foreign policy to these changes is to limit the effectiveness of U.S. actions.

U.S. Business

Americans disagree about the role U.S. business can and should play in South Africa. Some argue that U.S. firms should disinvest, that is, withdraw completely from South Africa, while others believe that firms can more effectively promote change if they remain in the country. Disinvestment is advocated on both moral and strategic grounds. The moral argument is that the profits earned by corporations in South Africa depend on, and largely result from, the state-enforced exploitation of black labor. It is morally indefensible, the argument continues, for American corporations and their shareholders to profit from such an unjust system. The essence of the strategic argument for disinvestment is that the presence of American business can do little to aid the progress of South African blacks but does a great deal to support the white regime. Withdrawal, proponents argue, can hasten the end of apartheid by undermining the economic strength of the white regime, by strengthening internal resistance, or at a minimum by removing the economic stake that may inhibit the United States government from imposing economic sanctions. By contrast, the argument against disinvestment holds that the pressure of American business can significantly advance the interests of black South Africans without becoming a bulwark for the white regime.

The Role of Firms. To understand how firms might influence the course of events in South Africa, it is useful first to examine the nature of firms and their relationship to the political system. We will discuss three basic views of the firm: the "neoclassical liberal" view, the "neo-Marxist" view, and the "pluralist" view.

The Neoclassical Liberal View. The firm, in this view, is simply an economic entity that seeks to maximize the wealth of its shareholders. The firm consists of workers, shareholders, and managers, who contract with one another in a free market and receive an economic return for their labor, capital, and management skills, respectively. Externally, the firm interacts through a set of markets with customers, suppliers, and competitors. In its purest form, this view does not acknowledge the existence much less the importance of social or political factors.

The neoclassical liberal view has, however, provided the basis for the "conventional" thesis on the relationship between economic growth and political change in South Africa. This thesis states, first, that South Africa is a market economy that tends naturally toward the rational use of resources; second, that there is "a contradiction between the rationality of the market and the irrationality of racism, in both its personal form of prejudice and its institutional form of apartheid;" and third, that in this conflict, the rationality of the market is likely to prevail.[18] The proponents of this view predict that businesses will recognize that they can increase profits by meeting the rising demand for skilled workers with the abundant supply of underpaid black labor. Businesses will therefore increasingly employ and train rather than discriminate against black workers. Thus, by pursuing their own economic interests, businesses in South Africa will, according to this view, eventually break the back of apartheid. The ethical implication is that business should go about its business.

The Neo-Marxist View. The firm, in this view, serves its owners' interests and thereby sustains the dominance of the ruling class, of which its owners are members. Within the firm, managers and owners (i.e., "capital") exploit the workers (i.e., "labor") by forcing them to sell their services on terms less favorable than those that would prevail in a free market. Externally, the firm primarily interacts not with the market-place but with the State. The firm cooperates with the State to exploit the workers and promote the dominance of the ruling class.

Proponents of the neo-Marxist view argue that the South African economy is not a "market economy" that allocates goods and services in response to the forces of supply and demand. It is a "labor repressive" economy, in which the prosperity of whites depends upon the repression of black labor. Firms, in this view, are agents of the white ruling class in the exploitation of the black working class. Over time, white prosperity reinforces white domination, and the system increasingly concentrates power in the hands of whites.[19]

Thus, the proponents of this view describe business in both an economic and a highly social and political manner. They predict that, by pursuing their owners' interests, businesses will help ensure the continued dominance of the white minority and the continued oppression of blacks. The ethical implication is that American firms should withdraw from South Africa, for, by doing so, they will undermine the strength of the white regime.

The Pluralist View. The firm, in this view, is an arena in which a multitude of groups pursue their own interests. Within the firm, several groups such as black workers, white workers, South African management, American management, and American shareholders, pursue their interests by bargaining and compromising. Externally, these groups interact with a constellation of other groups, including white customers, black customers, competitors, suppliers, the labor ministry, and the police.

Proponents of this view argue that the firm does not operate in a market economy driven exclusively by the forces of supply and demand, nor is it simply the battleground for two highly antagonistic and unevenly matched classes. Rather, it is a constellation of diverse groups that continually compete or cooperate with one another in pursuit of their own particular interests. A multitude of different coalitions may form: Management and black labor may oppose white labor on one issue, and management and white labor may oppose black labor on another. Thus, proponents of the pluralist view predict only that at any given time these groups will be vying for advantage. Any one of these groups can impose upon the firm costs and benefits that force it to define its interests differently than it would in either a purely market-driven neoclassical world or in a world where the collusive relation between the "state" and "capital" is paramount. The ethical implication is that concerned Americans should use their influence to alter firms' interests to the benefit of black South Africans.

These descriptions are simplifications of the different views held by various students of the role of business and economic development in South Africa. The first two views, the neoclassical liberal view and the neo-Marxist view, represent opposing sides of a fifteen-year-old debate involving many of South African business's most renowned defenders and critics, respectively. The pluralist view represents the informal response to this debate of various South African practitioners who see in South Africa not the irresistible march of economic rationality nor the clash of labor and capital but an enormously complicated dynamic situation that deterministic theories cannot adequately describe.

Evidence. Though the descriptions, predictions, and ethical implications of these three views differ significantly, each explains some aspects of the historical and contemporary role of firms in South Africa.

The neo-Marxist view provides critical insights into the early industrialization and economic development of South Africa. When white South African capitalists discovered huge quantities of gold in the Transvaal reef in 1886, they found that the ore, though abundant, was of very low quality. To mine it profitably, the miners needed low-cost unskilled labor. Consequently, the mines adopted "an elaborate system of labor procurement and control designed to fix the wages of Africans at an ultra-low level and ensure that enough of them would be working for sufficiently long periods to constitute a reliable work force."[20]

To an extraordinary degree, this system relied not upon a free labor market but upon collusion both among the mining companies and between these companies and the government. To recruit labor and to prevent individual mines from bidding up wages, the mines formed a centralized recruiting system and adopted industry-wide maximum wages. The mines also arranged for the local governments to pressure the tribal societies to produce more labor for the mines; to impose a "hut tax" that required rural Africans to earn more cash than their agricultural production could provide; and to adopt land policies that severely restricted Africans' ability to earn a living from the land. To control this labor, the mines helped persuade the government to impose a pass system that vastly facilitated the regulation of black labor and to adopt masters-and-servants legislation which established criminal penalties for labor contract violations such as absenteeism, insubordination, and strikes.[21]

The neo-Marxist interpretation is more ambiguous but still useful in explaining the relationship between business and government in South Africa after the Second World War. The election of the Nationalist government in 1948 created a vast cultural and economic distance between the labor-oriented Afrikaner government and the affluent English-speaking business community. The Nationalist government designed apartheid to strengthen its farm, labor, and civil servant constituencies, not to serve the interests of business. However, English businesses, despite their historical antagonism to the Afrikaners and their sometimes vocal opposition to apartheid, unquestionably benefitted from the onerous security system that guaranteed social and political stability, the influx control system that provided an orderly and abundant supply of labor, and the labor laws and police force that controlled the work force. These repressive labor policies help to explain why black real wages in 1970 were no higher than they had been in 1915.

The neo-Marxist interpretation provides some insight into the relationship between business and government in contemporary South Africa. While the interests of firms have sometimes clearly coincided with the interests of the white regime, the situation is complex. In certain instances, such as when firms have used the South African police to break strikes, the government seemed to be an agent of the firms. In other instances, such as when the South African government has pressured firms to police political activity in the factories and to weed out unauthorized migrant workers, firms have seemed to be agents of the government. In still other instances, such as when the government jailed numerous trade union leaders, the government seemed to be acting in its own behalf but in a way that serendipitously advanced the interests of at least some firms. Thus, while the interests of firms and the government continue to coincide in certain ways, the notion that there is a tight, collusive relationship between them now seems less compelling.

The neoclassical liberal view provides critical insights into the relationship between labor, business, and government, especially in the past ten years. For years, the industrial council system prevented businesses from negotiating separate contracts with each group of workers and thereby maintained an artifically high level of white wages. Job reservation forced businesses to employ highly paid white workers in certain jobs when better qualified black workers would have performed the work for less. The Bantu education system produced a labor force that was dreadfully unskilled and ill-equipped to acquire new skills and thus severely retarded productivity. In the 1970s, however, the increased demand for skilled labor clashed head-on with these apartheid institutions. As a result, a new collective bargaining system that allows direct negotiations with multiracial trade unions is replacing the industrial council system, job reservation has been largely eliminated, and the government has sharply increased its spending on education and training. Many businesses initially resisted and some still resist these changes, in part because they involve certain significant short-run costs including higher black wages and a resentful white work force. In retrospect, however, many business executives believe that these changes have significantly advanced their firms' long-run economic interests. Therefore, in these critical instances, the long-run interests of firms and the long-run interests of blacks coincided.

Finally, the pluralist view highlights the many different groups that influence the behavior of firms. Within the firm, the work force consists not just of homogeneous units of labor or an exploited black proletariat, but of white workers and black workers, skilled laborers and unskilled laborers, migrant "outside" workers and urban "inside" workers, workers involved in European-style trade unions and workers involved in community-based trade unions, white South African employees who resent policies that treat blacks equally and American employees who insist on such policies. Management consists not just of managerial technocrats or agents of the white capitalist class, but of senior managers concerned with financial statements and industrial managers concerned with industrial peace, U.S. international affairs officers seeking to promote equality and South African Conservative Party members seeking to prevent it, white managers and in some places even black managers. Shareholders consist not just of rational wealth-maximizers or members of the white bourgeoisie, but of multi-billion dollar fund managers trying to make their hurdle rates and "one-share" student groups aiming to introduce shareholder resolutions, employers attempting to fulfill a fiduciary duty to their employee pension funds and unions attempting to wrest pension control away from their employers, the Connecticut legislature seeking to respond to the public's opposition to apartheid and the Methodist Church pursuing its social mission. Externally, the firm faces not just an efficient marketplace or an oppressive state apparatus but affluent white customers and poor but numerous black customers, customers who buy quality and customers who boycott, capital-intensive suppliers indifferent toward the firm's industrial relations and labor-intensive suppliers sensitive to sympathy strikes, civil servants from the labor ministry who support collective bargaining and officers from the security police who want to weed out activists.

The pluralist view explains how firms have changed their policies in response to pressure from groups inside and outside the firm. The most widely publicized of these groups have been the anti-apartheid shareholder groups which have used shareholder resolutions to persuade firms to adopt anti-apartheid positions ranging from disinvestment to nonexpansion to trade union recognition. These groups' resolutions rarely receive majority approval but they nevertheless have had a significant impact on many firms' policies. In particular, they have played a major role in inducing firms to adopt the Sullivan Principles (a set of equal opportunity principles for U.S. firms in South Africa developed by the Reverend Leon Sullivan, see appendix E) and to recognize black trade unions.[22] There are three keys to their success. First, there is the "hassle" factor: Many managers are prepared to pay some price, such as an especially large contribution to South African community development, to avoid the embarrassing disruptions of their annual meetings and the high cost of management time associated with fighting such resolutions. Second, shareholder resolutions have forced American managers to focus on their firms' South African operations and on the opportunities to adopt policies that can serve both their own interests and those of black South Africans. Third, over the past several years, a number of large institutions, in particular several public pension funds, have adopted policies that limit investments in the securities of firms with operations in South Africa (see appendix F). If this trend continues, it could have a material effect on the depth and breadth of the market for such firms' securities.

Prominent individuals within firms have also influenced their firms' behavior. The influence of the Reverend Leon Sullivan on the board of directors of General Motors is well known. Less well known but equally important is the role of several chief executive officers who have taken a special interest in their company's South African operations. Moreover, in response to the expression of public concern about U.S. firms in South Africa during the 1970s, several firms created departments of international affairs to serve as liaisons between the U.S. public, the U.S. parent company, and the South African subsidiary. Clearly, some international affairs officers are intended to be little more than buffers between the public and busy executives. Others, however, are talented managers and diplomats who are, on the one hand, sensitive to their firms' interests and, on the other hand, genuinely committed to promoting change in South Africa. Thus, they are able to develop policies that promote the interests of both their firms and black South Africans.

In summary, all three of these views illuminate crucial aspects of the role of U.S. firms in South Africa. The neo-Marxist view highlights the ways in which firms have cooperated (overtly and covertly, intentionally and unintentionally) with the white government to exploit black South Africans. The neoclassical liberal view reveals the important ways in which market forces have led to changes in the apartheid system. The pluralist view shows how the interaction of a multitude of different groups within and outside firms has often influenced firms' behavior.

Strategies for American Influence

What can Americans and American firms do to promote change in South Africa? It is clear from the preceding political analysis that any action must be geared to domestic political circumstances in South Africa. A number of different strategies are available.

The withdrawal of American firms from South Africa could have a dramatic psychological impact on blacks and whites in South Africa. It would surely bolster black morale and might significantly increase the willingness of whites to compromise. Of course, these effects would be lessened if some but not all firms withdrew. Moreover, disinvestment might lead to increased repression if the Afrikaners withdrew into the *laager*.

Disinvestment would also have direct economic effects on South Africa. The withdrawal of U.S. firms would probably undermine the confidence of other foreign investors thereby making it more difficult for the South African government to attract foreign direct investment. This withdrawal would, at a minimum, affect the technology available to the South African economy as a whole and to the South African government, the jobs available to blacks and whites, and, more generally, the pace and nature of economic growth.

These considerations bring us to a point that emerges throughout this book: Different firms are different. Any attempt to use firms to promote change in South Africa must recognize that different firms utilize different technologies, have different relationships with the South African government, employ different numbers of white and black workers, and produce different products. Consequently, different firms have different interests, different constituencies, different opportunities, different degrees of influence, and different degrees of susceptibility to pressure.

The more the interests of individual firms coincide with those of the white regime and conflict with those of black South Africans, the stronger is the case for disinvestment. American firms control large shares of the computer, petroleum, automotive and financial services industries. These industries are vital to the South African economy, and they often involve technology that South Africa could not duplicate on its own. With respect to the companies that operate in these key sectors, that employ few black workers, or, in particular, that supply special expertise or technology directly to the South African government, the case for withdrawal may indeed be compelling. Fluor Corporation, for example, has had contracts in excess of four billion dollars to help construct and maintain coal-to-oil conversion plants that will make South Africa more energy self-sufficient and less vulnerable to an oil embargo; the company is thus providing a service that is critical to the security of the white government and that the government could not easily duplicate. On the other hand, certain American firms, some of which are mentioned below, have taken actions that significantly advanced the interests of black South Africans while doing little to aid the white regime.

Whatever the arguments pro and con, there is little chance that disinvestment will occur in the near future. As the neoclassical liberal view reminds us, firms are primarily economic entities, and for now the benefits of investing in South Africa—where 1983 returns on investment were 43 percent higher for manufacturing and 82 percent higher for mining than the average returns elsewhere in the world—still far outweigh all the costs (see appendix B). Moreover, the political climate in the United States is such that legislated disinvestment is unlikely to take place anytime soon. Indeed, the South African government now regards the threat of disinvestment as so minimal that it has eliminated the exchange controls that formerly all but prevented the withdrawal of foreign capital (see appendix C).

But disinvestment is not the sole strategy available to Americans. To the extent that firms' interests coincide with those of black South Africans, their presence in South Africa may be a force for constructive change. Firms have a strong interest in having a stable and productive work force. Responding to this interest, firms have become increasingly active in supporting housing, education, and training for black South

Africans. As Griffiths Zabala and Oscar Dhlomo make clear in chapters 5 and 6, such social development expenditures may contribute to the emergence of the social, economic, and political institutions that the black community needs to exert political influence. For the same reason, firms have also, although not without some reluctance, begun to recognize and negotiate with black trade unions. "[T]hese trade unions," writes Halton Cheadle in chapter 4, "promise to be a major force in the dismantling of apartheid and the creation of a democratic society in South Africa." Some U.S. firms have taken big steps in this area. In the late 1970s, the Kellogg Company signed a formal agreement recognizing a black trade union; it was the second company in South Africa to do so. In the same time period, the Borg-Warner Corporation agreed to negotiate wages at the plant level with black workers rather than through the government-approved industrial council system dominated by whites. In 1980, the Ford Motor Company agreed to permit full-time black shop stewards in its factories; it was the first company in South Africa to do so.

As the pluralist view suggests, firms are susceptible to pressure from a wide variety of sources. This pressure can focus firms' attentions on community development, the recognition of black trade unions, and other areas where firms' interests coincide with those of black South Africans. But it can also, if appropriately applied, cause firms to redefine their interests to the benefit of black South Africans.

The chapters that follow chart the social, political, and economic landscape facing American businesses that operate in South Africa. The contributors, all but one of whom are South African, examine in depth the role of American corporations in South Africa and their potential for influencing change there.

Part I presents an overview of the political situation in South Africa and the role of U.S. firms. In chapter 1, John Kane-Berman, a leading South African journalist who was recently appointed director of the South African Institute of Race Relations, analyzes recent political and economic developments in South Africa and their effects on U.S. firms. In chapter 2, Heribert Adam, one of the most highly regarded analysts of the Afrikaner community, focuses on the possibilities for outside influence on South Africa, examining the structure of the Afrikaner community and then considering the effects of the 1983 constitutional referendum and the nonaggression treaties of 1984.

Part II presents an analysis of two key aspects of operating in South Africa: industrial relations and community development. In chapter 3, Fred Ferreira, who as director of industrial relations for Ford South Africa has been a pioneer in the field, assesses industrial relations from a management perspective. In chapter 4, Halton Cheadle, a labor lawyer who has for ten years been active in the developing black trade union movement, offers an in-depth analysis of these emergent trade unions. Chapters 5 and 6 look at U.S. firms' opportunities for social development expenditures. In chapter 5, Griffiths Zabala, director of numerous community development projects in South Africa, examines the issues surrounding urban community development. In chapter 6, Oscar Dhlomo, Minister of Education for KwaZulu, analyzes opportunities for rural development.

Part III presents four South African perspectives on the role of firms in South Africa. In chapter 7, Gatsha Buthelezi, Chief Minister of KwaZulu and President of Inkatha (the largest black political organization within South Africa), discusses strategies for liberation. In chapter 8, Leonard Mosala, former treasurer of the Soweto Committee of Ten (a group of leading Sowetans who rose to prominence as the informal spokesmen for Sowetan blacks during the 1976 riots), discusses white power politics. In chapter 9, Tony Bloom, the Chairman of the Premier Group (one of South Africa's major industrial corporations), considers the importance of enlightened self-interest. In the final chapter, Hermann Giliomee, professor of political science at the University of Cape Town and a leading political analyst of contemporary South Africa, discusses the future challenges facing business in South Africa. The differences that emerge among these four viewpoints indicate the distinct perceptions of different groups in South Africa. It is nevertheless important to remember that these four perspectives by no means represent the full spectrum of political opinion. Many groups, reactionary and radical, white and black, are not represented, and many issues are not addressed. A notable and regrettable omission is the position in support of disinvestment. It is against the law for South Africans to advocate disinvestment publicly.

The appendixes offer a statistical summary of South Africa and of the U.S. business presence there; an overview of the movements supporting withdrawal of American corporations, divestment, and the Sullivan Principles; an outline of federal and state actions; an overview of U.S. corporate social expenditures; and an address list of relevant organizations.

The chapters represent a mosaic of perspectives—those of academics, journalists, businessmen, and South African political leaders—which vividly conveys the complexity of the situation. Whatever conclusions one draws concerning the role of firms in South Africa, it is clear that it is difficult to operate within a system that is profoundly and pervasively unjust. Under the system of apartheid, a firm's most basic decisions—whom to hire, whom to train, whom to promote, what wages to pay—become political actions to which black and white workers, and perhaps even the government, will respond politically. With respect to some issues facing firms the "right" policy is clear, although not necessarily easy to implement: Employers should establish wage parity between blacks and whites, provide equal opportunity for promotion, and recognize and negotiate with black trade unions. With respect to other issues, the "right" policy is more ambiguous: Should firms work actively to improve their black employees' standard of living or will that drive the wedge between urban insiders and rural outsiders unacceptably deeper? Should firms continue to raise black wages, many of which still hover at or below the poverty line, or will that contribute to the already massive unemployment of black South Africans and permanently tilt South Africa toward a more capital-intensive economy? Should firms refuse to employ migrant labor, insisting on a relaxation of influx control and resettlement, or will that simply hurt those who already suffer most from apartheid?

U.S. firms can be an obstacle to progress in South Africa to the extent that they supply special technology or bolster foreign and domestic confidence in the white government. But U.S. firms can also foster progress to the extent that they provide education, skills, and organizational leverage to black South Africans. Moreover, the U.S. government can retard or promote progress through policies that affect the conduct or the presence of American firms in South Africa. To assess which public and private actions will do most to promote progress in South Africa one must first understand business in the shadow of apartheid.

Jonathan Leape
Bo Baskin
Stefan Underhill

Notes

1. The Study Commission on U.S. Policy toward Southern Africa, *South Africa: Time Running Out* (Berkeley: University of California Press, 1981), p. 393.

2. Heribert Adam and Hermann Giliomee, *Ethnic Power Mobilized: Can South Africa Change?* (New Haven: Yale University Press, 1979), p. 7.

3. *Time Running Out*, p. 393.

4. Authors' notes.

5. "Destabilization in South Africa: Potgeiter counterattacks," *The Economist*, July 16, 1983, pp. 26–7.

6. Joseph Lelyveld, "Black challenge to Pretoria: rebellion, still puny, is showing more muscle," *The New York Times*, October 12, 1983.

7. George M. Frederickson, *White Supremacy: A Comparative Study in American and South African History* (New York: Oxford University Press, 1981), p. 171.

8. *Ibid.*, pp. 136ff.
9. Adam and Giliomee, *op. cit.*, p. 237.
10. Authors' notes.
11. C.W. de Kiewiet, *A History of South Africa: Social and Economic* (Oxford: Oxford University Press, 1957), p. 96.
12. W.M. Freund, "Race in the social structure of South Africa, 1652–1836," *Race and Class* 18 (Summer 1976):54.
13. *Ibid.*, p. 57.
14. Authors' notes.
15. Adam and Giliomee, *op. cit.*, pp. 69–70.
16. Paul Brown, "South Africa's other secret service", *The Guardian*, March 27, 1984.
17. *The Economist, op. cit.*
18. Lawrence Schlemmer and Eddie Webster, eds., *Change, Reform, and Economic Growth in South Africa* (Johannesburg: Ravan Press, 1978), p. 11.
19. *Ibid.*
20. Frederickson, *op. cit.*, p. 218.
21. See chapter five in Frederickson, *op. cit.*, for an excellent discussion of race and industrialization in South Africa.
22. The Sullivan Principles received general support but also criticism in June 1983 when Bishop Desmond Tutu called on firms to implement what came to be called the "Tutu Principles" or withdraw from South Africa. These four principles differed from the Sullivan Principles in their request that firms actively oppose the oppressive system of influx control that restricts the mobility of black South Africans. In November 1984, Reverend Sullivan revised the Sullivan Principles, calling on firms to "support the end of all apartheid laws" and, in particular, to work for the elimination of influx control. (See appendix E.)

Part I
Overview

1
Recent Political and Economic Developments in South Africa and Their Effects on U.S. Firms

John Kane-Berman

S outh Africa at the moment presents a rather contradictory picture. In the field of labor, a degree of liberalization has taken place that would have seemed unthinkable even five years ago: black workers have successfully won for themselves the collective bargaining rights that were long denied them. Apartheid has been further diluted by the admission of the Indian and "colored" (mixed race) minorities to the parliamentary franchise. At the same time, however, the government has actively pursued a four-pronged strategy to dispossess black South Africans. Through a massive program of resettlement, the government has forcibly removed over two million black South Africans from their homes in urban areas to barren rural reserves called "homelands." With an increasingly restrictive system of influx control, the government has curtailed the flow of blacks from the poverty-stricken rural reserves to the cities, deepening the divide between the privileged black urban "insiders" and the excluded "outsiders." A system of financial apartheid has largely deprived the so-called homelands of the resources needed for social and economic development. Finally, and most important, the exclusion of Africans from the common political system has been entrenched by stripping them of their South African citizenship. Already, one-third of the twenty-three million black South Africans have become foreigners within South Africa as four of the ten homelands have been made "independent."

The South African Economy

In recent years, South Africa has suffered from a deep economic recession. In the heady days after the price of gold reached $850 an ounce (in January 1980), the South African Reserve Bank predicted that an era was dawning

---

The terms "black" and "African" are used interchangeably, although "black" is occasionally used as an umbrella term for those of mixed race ("coloreds"), Indians, and Africans.

in which the economy would be able to grow without suffering the huge current account deficits that in the past have always necessitated harsh deflationary action by the authorities. But as the price of South Africa's biggest export tumbled below $400, this hope of a fundamental change in the structure of the country's balance of payments proved forlorn. The real growth rate of some 8 percent in 1980 was one of the best performances in the world, but the voracious appetite for imports that always accompanies rapid growth in South Africa soon caused the current account of the balance of payments to swing from a surplus of nearly R3,000 million that year to a deficit of nearly R4,000 million in 1981.

Economic recession always causes apprehension in South Africa, because of the country's racial makeup. The brunt of retrenchment, as of unemployment, is borne by black people, particularly Africans. It is at least plausible to argue that one of the underlying causes of the racial violence that began in Soweto on June 16, 1976 and then spread rapidly to 160 other black communities all over the country was the downturn in the economy, and particularly perhaps the decline in available jobs at the very moment when the black school system was putting more and better educated youngsters on to the labor market.

South Africa's record in combating inflation is a good deal worse than those of many other countries. The rate has been in double digits for a decade, rising to a high of 16.5 percent in May 1982 before falling back to 10 percent by February 1984. Some observers nevertheless believe that fighting inflation should take second place to pursuing economic growth in the hopes thereby of avoiding or at least minimizing the chances of political instability arising from high and rising unemployment. The chronic problem of the current account leaves the authorities little room for maneuver, however. Consequently, they are usually reluctant to yield to political or social pressures for countercyclical action to stimulate the economy. The years 1982 and 1983 saw the first absolute decline in South Africa's gross domestic product since the Second World War, with drops of 1.2 percent and 3 percent, respectively.

Foreign investment has, of course, played an important role in South Africa's growth, although several countries now have active groups lobbying against investing in the country. Of South Africa's four main trading partners, only Japan claims to have prohibited investment in the Republic. Sweden is the only other industrial country to have imposed restrictions on investment in South Africa (without actually prohibiting it). Apart from the mandatory arms embargo enacted by the United Nations Security Council in November 1977, official international action restricting business dealings with South Africa has been limited. And in the past year or so, some restrictions have been relaxed. In March 1982 the Reagan administration removed certain items from a list of goods whose sale to the South African military and police forces had been restricted or even prohibited altogether by the Carter administration. The previous year the West German government lifted restrictions it had placed a few years before on the granting to companies of export credit insurance in respect of sales to South Africa. The removal of this restriction apparently made a material contribution to the winning by German companies of some of the major contracts currently being awarded by South Africa's state-owned Electricity Supply Commission (Escom) in its huge program to triple or even quadruple the country's generating capacity by the end of the century. Some years ago, procrastination by the Netherlands government on this very issue of government-backed export credit insurance was the main reason why a Dutch-Swiss consortium lost the contract to build South Africa's first nuclear power station (it went to France instead). The tens of millions of rands worth of business that Escom is handing out to Western companies is an example of the extent to which commercial considerations can overshadow whatever political objections might be voiced to doing business with South Africa, particularly at times when slack conditions at home compel companies to compete eagerly for overseas contracts. According to one report, Escom in 1981 handed out more contracts for electricity generating equipment than all the power utilities in the United States put together, prompting one South African newspaper to comment that an "international battle" was underway as "the world woos Escom." Apart from the Germans and a French-German consortium, American and British firms won large Escom contracts, with the Japanese and the Swiss among the other nations competing.

If South Africa industry can look forward to having enough electricity in the years ahead, it certainly cannot expect to have enough skilled workers to keep the machines going. A few years ago ministers used to say that the skills shortage was "critical." Now they use words like "chaos" and "catastrophe" to describe the shortage of skilled labor. The skills shortage exists alongside an abundant supply of unskilled people. By constraining economic growth it also helps to keep unemployment high. At the same time, it contributes to inflation and exacerbates balance-of-payments problems, since South Africa's inability to produce enough to meet domestic demand during boom years causes the excess demand to be diverted abroad. In the view of the then Minister of Finance, Owen Horwood, the boom of 1979–1981 came to an end mainly because of "the shortage of skilled and semi-skilled labor and the absorption of most of the surplus production capacity." The chief executive of a motor manufacturing company went so far as to say that growth in 1980 could have been nearer to 11 percent "had it not been for shortages of skilled labor." In 1984 the then Minister of Manpower, Fanie Botha, said that the shortage of high-level manpower would lead the economy into catastrophe in the next economic upswing.

Engineers of every description, accountants, managers, draftsmen, data processors, bank tellers, artisans of all kinds, and of course people to teach other people how to do all these jobs—all of these are in very short supply. The skills shortage has its origins in several factors, but chiefly in the policy adopted in the 1950s of gearing African education to the assumption that blacks should be employed in laboring jobs, better educated blacks being seen by the new National party government as more likely than illiterate people to demand equality.[1] The stunting of African education by a policy of starving it of all but the barest minimum of public funds was complemented by other factors that prevented blacks from being trained for or employed in any but laboring jobs. These factors included an employment color bar laid down by the government, reserving specified skilled and semiskilled jobs for whites; restrictions demanded by white unions—and agreed to by their employers—in terms of which the official color bar was extended to a wide range of other jobs; and sheer racial prejudice on the part of managers against allowing blacks to perform any but the most menial tasks.

Some of these barriers are now being overcome. The official industrial color bar has been phased out everywhere except in the mines (where its relaxation is being discussed); union-employer color bar agreements are similarly being relaxed; and prejudice, though still widespread, is beginning to break down. The practices that effectively barred blacks from being indentured as apprentices and employed as artisans in the "white" areas, which contain all the country's main industrial centers, have been abandoned, and the recruitment of black apprentices is now taking place.

With these relaxations of the industrial color bar has gone another sensible development: the government's recognition of the foolishness of its earlier policy that Africans must be no more than hewers of wood and drawers of water. Though it still lags far behind expenditure on white education, public spending on black school and post-school education has been substantially increased.[2] The Department of Education and Training, which is responsible for black education in the "white" areas in South Africa's segregated education system, has been attempting to remedy some of the defects of the past, paying attention not only to the education of schoolchildren but also to that of adults (through night classes for example) who never previously had the chance of obtaining schooling. In Soweto in particular, efforts have been made to eradicate some of the factors that led to the bitter explosion in June 1976. The improvements there may be one of the reasons why subsequent attempts to organize school boycotts in that township were largely a failure.

One of the most important advances in my view is that the government, since April 1, 1979, has accepted responsibility for building schools, including secondary schools, in the African townships in the so-called white areas. Previously these heavy capital costs were borne by the African communities themselves, a particularly nasty piece of apartheid since none of the other races was expected to build schools for its children. The State having assumed responsibility for building black schools in the "white" areas, it has been possible to make a start with compulsory education for blacks, though this is being done gradually and with some effort to avoid actual coercion, the Department of Education and Training evidently being concerned to avoid being accused of enforcing a seriously unpopular system of segregated education on the black population.[3]

The efforts to improve black education, which some of the government's critics are loathe to recognize, have all taken place inside the structure of apartheid, however. The continued enforcement of segregation throughout the country's schooling system is a major grievance among black people, and one that is likely to ensure a more or less permanent state of tension in the segregated black schools and universities until the government abandons this central prop of its ideology.

A government white paper published in November 1983 accepted many of the recommendations for educational reform proposed by the main committee of the Human Sciences Research Council's investigation into education in South Africa, under the chairmanship of Professor J.P. De Lange. However, the government stipulated at the same time that the country's education system would remain racially segregated. Several private schools have become partly desegregated under a more or less blind official eye, but freeing children in state schools from apartheid is not among the policy adjustments the government has been talking about.

In 1973 the government relaxed its earlier prohibition on the industrial training of Africans in the "white" areas. It also introduced tax incentives for employers to train their black employees. More recently, sixteen centers have been opened in the "white" areas to enable blacks there to obtain the theoretical training that apprenticeship regulations require. However, the continued enforcement of segregation at vocational and technical levels has irritated many companies—especially "when blacks are refused entry to half-empty technical colleges," as one businessman complained. Desegregation of technical institutions would, of course, be an encouraging beginning, but the crisis in South African education goes too deep to be capable of remedy simply by advances at the vocational level. One is talking not merely about a shortage of carpenters or welders that can be overcome by crash courses, but about huge segments of the African and so-called colored populations that are basically uneducated. It seems as if more and more people in the private sector are coming round to the view that the shortage of technical skills among blacks in South Africa cannot be remedied until the basic education system for blacks is drastically improved, an improvement that some do not believe is really possible as long as the country's policy is apartheid first and education second. This, at any rate, is how I interpret the following remarks made recently by the chairman of one of South Africa's largest industrial and mining conglomerates.

> We employ 193,000 people, of whom 130,000 are black. A survey carried out two years ago showed that 60 percent of them had had less than six years' formal schooling and were either partly or completely illiterate. It was clearly self-illusory to talk of training them in technical skills. And so we were forced to introduce literacy and numeracy classes staffed by professional black teachers, to take them to a stage where they would be able to undergo training. We are all aware that the problem starts long before the university stage. Our basic educational system is wrongly structured and as a result its final product is totally inadequate either in numbers or in quality. When knowledgeble people call for a common educational system for all race groups in this country they are not raising a political issue. They are, in fact, expressing the view that there is no other way that the educational system will be able to provide the level of skilled manpower we shall need in the future— indeed that we require at this very moment.[4]

The Rise of Black Trade Unionism

The upward shift in the occupational color bar and the admittedly slow and often tension-ridden advances in black education are two of the most important developments taking place in South Africa. A third is the rise of black trade unionism. This is important not only in itself but also because of numerous lessons that can be learned from it that are relevant to other fields. The term "black unions" is not entirely accurate, since many of the unions in question have it as a firm policy that membership should be open to all, irrespective of race or color. I will stick to the term, however, because most of these unions speak mainly for black workers.

The emerging independent black union movement—independent because these unions are free of control by the established white labor movement—is now ten years old and comprises some 300,000 workers organized into about thirty unions. Black unionism in fact dates back much earlier than ten years ago, but the authorities succeeded in the 1950s in virtually destroying it by issuing a series of orders banning union officials from attending gatherings, visiting factories, and entering black townships. The formation of a new group of unions in the early

1970s, which was closely associated with a series of wildcat strikes in Durban in 1973, was therefore really a rebirth.

The Durban strikes, which actually followed a major strike by Ovambo contract workers in Namibia at the end of 1971, were an event of the greatest significance. Not only did they give great impetus to black unionization, they also put black labor practices in South Africa firmly on to the international map, where they have stayed ever since, as more than one company has found to its discomfort. South African newspapers began reporting closely on labor issues, often with material showing employers in an unfavorable light, and a leading British paper provoked uproar by publishing a series of articles exposing the "starvation wages" it alleged British subsidiaries in South Africa were paying.

This led to the adoption in 1974 by the British government of a code of conduct designed to encourage British firms in South Africa to improve their treatment of their black employees; it also led to the appointment of a special attaché to the British embassy in South Africa to assist them and monitor how they were doing. The United States followed with an official appointed to encourage better labor practices among American companies in South Africa, and the Reverend Leon Sullivan introduced a voluntary code of practice for them. (Although most major American companies in South Africa claim to be following the Sullivan Principles voluntarily—and some have gone even further—efforts have been made in the United States to make the Principles legally enforceable.) Subsequently, the British code was tightened up and embraced by all the member countries of the European Economic Community.[5] Only Whitehall and Washington appear to have made any serious attempt to monitor their subsidiaries' labor practices, however.

If the two officials of these governments helped to encourage the new black union movement, the same cannot be said of the South African authorities. Although the prime minister himself, then B.J. Vorster, implicitly criticized the low wages that had sparked off the Durban strikes, the government sought to undermine the unions by promoting in their place a system of works and liaison committees with very much less power. But the new generation of African workers was not to be denied the union rights enjoyed by white, Indian, and so-called colored workers, and somehow their unions survived. The government then made a frontal attack in an obvious attempt to repeat the success it had had in destroying the unions in the 1950s. At the end of 1976 it served banning orders on about thirty people, both black and white, involved with the black union movement. Still the unions managed to survive. Finally the government had no choice but to reconcile itself to the fact that this new phenomenon had come to stay. A commission of inquiry into labor legislation (the Wiehahn Commission) was appointed to devise an industrial relations system to cope with it.[6] In the first part of its report, published on May Day 1979, it recommended the removal of racial discrimination from industrial relations and, consequent upon that, the granting to African employees of the same rights as other workers had long enjoyed to form and join trade unions that could be officially registered with the government. In legislation initially enacted in that same year but substantially revised in 1981, Parliament gave effect to that recommendation.[7] It was a great victory for black South Africa, probably its greatest so far.

It is important to note that trade union rights were not something handed to black workers on a plate by a government that had suddenly decided to reverse its policies. They had to be fought for and won. A united front of government and employers had to be taken on and beaten. This was achieved not only by a good deal of bravery in the face of intimidation, but also by planning, organization, and hard work. Black political activity in South Africa is sometimes weakened by its emphasis on mere reiteration of demands and denunciation of apartheid, to the exclusion of more mundane organizational work. But not the black union movement, whose success was rooted in the fact that very large numbers of black workers, many of them no doubt illiterate, organized and mobilized for united action.

Another important point worth noting is that most companies, irrespective of whether they were multinational or local, were uncertain as to how to deal with the new phenomenon. Frequently when black union officials appeared in the factories, managements' responses were to call the police or to dismiss anyone seen associating with them. A few companies responded to black unions by entering into working agreements with them, but most tried to impose the government's rather ineffective works and liaison committees instead, not infrequently provoking strikes in the process.

In partial explanation of the rather reactionary corporate behavior then prevalent, it should perhaps be pointed out that black unions were in a kind of legal no-man's land. They were not prohibited by law, but neither could they be officially registered and in any case the government's hostility to them was obvious. However, even when the post-Wiehahn legislation provided for registration, many companies persisted in their attempts to undermine the independent black unions by trying to channel black workers into so-called parallel unions set up by the established white labor movement with the purpose of controlling black unionization.

In the last few years, the generally hostile attitude to black unions has been giving way to a more pragmatic and liberal approach and a steadily growing number of companies of all nationalities has been entering into recognition agreements with them. The management-labor negotiations that are taking place more often are the closest thing South Africa yet has to multiracial decision-making.

Why then rake over the old bones? The business sector's previous difficulty in dealing imaginatively with a new challenge invites the question how it will respond to future issues. One of these is the government's plans to tighten up influx control and involve employers more closely in enforcing it. Another is its constitutional program involving denationalization of African South Africans. The riots in Soweto led companies to pay much more attention than in the past to problems in the black townships in the "white" urban areas. The Urban Foundation, set up in the wake of the urban violence, is a product of the business world's greater concern with the living conditions of its black employees. The school built by American companies in Soweto also reflects acceptance by businessmen of responsibilities outside the factory gates, as do the initiatives taken by U.S. companies in Port Elizabeth, for example, to deal with problems in black housing and education. But what about the rural areas? It is at least possible that as great a crisis is building there as the one that exploded into the open in the urban townships eight years ago. Will business be able to stand aloof? Can it stand aloof from policies now being implemented that are likely to precipitate this crisis? We will return to these questions in due course.

The fact that the black union movement had to fight for its place in the sun has stood it in very good stead. Had black unions simply been granted registration rights without a struggle, they would in all probability today be not very different from many white, colored, and Indian unions, which are the rather tame bureaucratic affairs one would expect unions to be that relied on pigmentation rather than organization to protect their interets. Many of them would almost regard it as unbecoming to go on strike.

The black unions, by contrast, were generally not able to rely on company pay-clerks to collect their dues for them by deductions from worker pay-packets; they had to engender and retain rank-and-file loyalty by devising structures and procedures that could deliver results worth paying for. Of course, they made mistakes. Sometimes they spread their limited money and manpower too thinly over too many factories to be able to serve the membership properly, with the result that disillusioned workers dropped out of the unions at one end almost as rapidly as eager recruits were joining at the other. But by trial and error they learned to cope, for example, by pulling in their horns and going not for mass recruitment but for consolidation of strength and organization in one factory before moving on to the next. It was a question of the survival of the fittest in a tough marketplace where the rules had been made by their opponents.

The relevant point here is that the black union movement that employers face today has been shaped by the strategies it had to adopt to survive. Hence, for example, the great emphasis many of them place on decentralized democratic structures and the cultivation of leadership on the factory floor. One consequence is the strong demand for committees of shop stewards to have the right to negotiate about wages at factory level, a procedure that runs counter to the system to which many companies have long been accustomed in their dealings with white unions, which is that wages and working conditions are determined by umbrella bodies, known as industrial councils, which in some cases cover an entire sector on a national basis and thus make for uniformity.

For historical and other reasons, the preferred formula of managements, which is simply to slot the black unions into the established system, is not acceptable to many of these unions. If the 1970s were taken up with black labor's struggle for official acknowledgment of its right to organize for collective bargaining purposes, it looks as if the 1980s are being taken up with devising the institutional forms and procedures that this bargaining will take. This is unlikely to be easy. It has already occasioned a number of bitter disputes. I think it is fair to say, though, that unions and management show a better understanding of each other's point of view on this issue than was the case a year ago.

The extent of black unionization is still very limited when measured against an African labor force of almost seven million, so that for many companies the challenge of organized black labor power is only just beginning. But the official recognition of black bargaining rights has at least made the position of multinationals somewhat easier in two respects.

First, it is now easier for them to comply with the clauses in the various codes of labor conduct urging them to deal with representatives of black labor organizations. The earlier reluctance of most companies to deal with unregistered unions threatened to undermine the already limited legitimacy of the codes and so probably caused an increase in pressures by antiapartheid lobbyists for companies to cut their business ties with South Africa.

Second, the more constructive manner in which more companies, including multinationals, are now dealing with black unions has probably contributed to a climate in which there does not appear to be majority support within South Africa for disengagement by foreign companies.

The external mission of the African National Congress (ANC), the black political party that went underground after it was proscribed in 1960 and whose exiled military wing has been prosecuting a campaign of insurgency against the South African government for nearly two decades, has long lobbied hard in foreign countries for economic sanctions against South Africa. Its stance against foreign investment has found some echo inside the country, notably among some church organizations and the Labor party (one of the main parties among "colored" people). There also appears to be support for the idea among sections of the black intelligentsia, although fear of prosecution and political victimization has no doubt inhibited frank public expression of their viewpoint.

But even allowing for this, it is fair to state that at the present time there is not majority support among black people in South Africa for the withdrawal of foreign investment. An opinion survey in which people were able to express their views anonymously and which also showed substantial, if ill-defined, support for the ANC gave some indication of black attitudes in 1981. In answer to the question "Should foreign firms stop doing business?" 49 percent of people surveyed answered "no," while 36 percent answered "yes." This finding corroborates one made in 1980 by social scientists at the University of Natal that the majority of blacks regard jobs as a great priority and do not support disinvestment as an ideological stance. Moreover, officials of some of the major black trade unions report that they have heard no demand from their members for disinvestment. Chief M. Gatsha Buthelezi, who as president of Inkatha Yenkululeko Yesizwe (the National Cultural Liberation Movement) heads the largest black political organization in the country's history, has also stated that he has heard no demand from his membership for disinvestment in South Africa.

This perhaps gives foreign companies a breathing space, but one that may be filled with a variety of challenges beyond those involved in industrial relations and black job advancement. Chief Buthelezi has pointed out that foreign capital not only means more jobs but also contributes toward South Africa's economic power and so helps "prop up white military might, which is used by our white countrymen to maintain the status quo." Obviously, many people who, like Chief Buthelezi, believe that foreign companies can play a role of "constructive engagement" in South Africa find themselves in rather a dilemma when they consider that there must be a large number of multinationals among the 1,000-odd private-sector firms involved in South Africa's armaments industry.

It is relevant to note in this context that the South African Federated Chamber of Industries (FCI) felt it necessary in 1982 to warn companies with foreign connections against becoming publicly identified with the South African Defence Force. At issue was an army logotype that would apparently be available for companies to display on their products if they donated funds for army recreation centers. "This is fine in the case of a local company catering for a local white consumer," the FCI said. "But in exporting, companies could run into difficulties from the marketing point of view. They can anticipate an unsympathetic attitude from overseas quarters. The second area of concern would be the black market. Companies displaying the logo would find opposition from certain sectors of the black community which do not support the South African war effort."

The rise of the union movement has generated fear in some quarters and delight in others that Africans now possess an instrument they can use to make political demands. Businessmen fear they will become the hapless victims of a dichotomous government policy that grants economic but denies political rights. Far from accepting the former as a substitute for the latter, or at least being content with them for the time being, blacks, they fear, have had their expectations aroused and will pile on the pressures for political enfranchisement. Factories, as Fred Ferreira, the industrial relations director of Ford Motor Company in South Africa, writes in chapter 3, could become political battlegrounds.

It would be unrealistic to expect that the mood on the shop floor will be immune to the numerous problems afflicting black township dwellers: the chronic and worsening housing shortage, pass raids, seemingly never-ending rises in bus fares, the high crime rate, to name but some of the most obvious. Recalling the 1976 upheavals is perhaps again instructive. They occurred at the end of the period of relatively large rises in real wages that the Durban strikes generated, a time, however, when the authorities in Soweto were succeeding in their intention of reducing the rate of black housing construction in accordance with the policy introduced in the late 1960s of using the housing shortage as a lever to prise black people out of the townships in the "white" areas and redirect them to the homelands. The frustration of families with more money to spend but little chance of spending it on the first thing most families think of buying, a house, was no doubt very great. Disruptive action by factory workers was the exception rather than the rule in 1976, but with the black work force now apparently in a generally more assertive mood, there is concern among businessmen in South Africa that township problems could easily overflow into their factories. As workers compare conditions in the workplace to their squalid home environments, their sense of relative deprivation increases. Frustration at the system then erupts through the only available outlet: action on the shop floor.

Where do industrial relations problems end and township problems begin? When does frustration about a housing shortage turn into a demand that one's employers go and see the government about it? When does resentment about pass raids turn into determination to join a general strike? On this continuum we do not know at what point we are at present located, or even in which direction things may be moving. Certainly issues have arisen beyond the factory gates that have led to action inside them. The wave of strikes all over the country in 1981 over a government plan to make pension funds compulsorily transferable is one example. Anger among workers in the eastern Cape at the fact that the granting of constitutional independence to the Ciskei "homeland" would result in many of them losing their South African citizenship was another. A wave of anger at the death of a trade union official in detention in February 1982 was yet another. Strikes in reaction to issues like these may occur in the future more often than in the past.

But whether the union movement will become involved more systematically in political campaigns is not quite the same question. In a broad sense, the rise of the union movement is a political development and the satisfying experience of achieving gains through united action is unlikely to stop at employment conditions. But it seems as if there has been a tendency for some people to jump to conclusions about unions and politics. Academic and newspaper commentators who recently have saddled the unions with responsibility for what they see as the coming political struggle seem to ignore the possibility that black politics may be more complex. It may, for instance, be the case that black workers see their unions as essentially industrial organizations which should not jeopardize what they can achieve in that field by moving into others and so inviting a ferocious clampdown by the State.

Also, I do not think it is true to say, as some of these commentators do, that blacks have no political vehicle and therefore no choice but to employ their unions in this role. One of the most critical issues confronting South Africa at the moment is the government's plan to hand over the Kangwane "homeland" as well as a portion of KwaZulu to Swaziland, thereby denationalizing about 800,000 black South Aricans—that is, depriving them of their South African citizenship. The campaign against this plan is being led by the leaders of the two communities most directly affected, Chief Gatsha Buthelezi, of KwaZulu, and Enos Mabuza, chief minister of Kangwane. In concert with the official white opposition, the Progressive Federal party, they have mobilized one of the most broadly based political campaigns the country has seen in years, with Inkatha playing the decisive role in mobilizing black opposition.

Although the very same issue, denationalization of Africans, was at stake in the hiving off the Ciskei by constitutional separation from South Africa at the end of 1981, the black unions were unable to mobilize a campaign against it of any consequence, partly because the security police threw several hundred unionists into detention without trial. This is not to criticize the unions, but to make the point that they are not necessarily the best-placed organizations to fight every issue damaging to black people. The most deprived people in South Africa are to be found in the "homelands" in the large resettlement camps established to accommodate Africans removed from "white" areas in terms of the policy of geographic apartheid. As we will see below, these people are effectively excluded from the labor market. There is thus little that trade unions can do for them.

When the government banned all the organizations in the "black consciousness" movement in October 1977 in what was apparently an attempt to crush the remnants of the Soweto revolt they were accused of inspiring, there was a feeling in some circles that the black unions would have to take over their roles. There was, however, strong antipathy among union officials to any notion that they should hand over the unions to politicians.

The bulk of the black union movement would probably resist strongly any attempts by any other organizations to interfere with them. Of course, the more democratic the internal workings of a union are, the more difficult it will be for anyone to intervene from outside. Unless its nature changes, then, the bulk of the black union movement in South Africa is not easily amenable to externally induced politicization. Politics could still come from inside, however. So far, although more than one union has been pushed into a strike (on a labor issue) by decision of its membership against the advice of its officials, there does not appear to have been much pressure for more direct political action. So although particular circumstances may result in political strikes from time to time, it would probably be at least premature to suppose that a general shift by the union movement or even major segments of it toward more systematic political involvement is underway.

It is worth noting that black people in South Africa apparently do not see the black union movement as a political vehicle. One of the most comprehensive surveys of black opinion done in South Africa in recent years was that conducted for the Buthelezi Commission, a commission of inquiry appointed in 1980 by the KwaZulu legislative assembly. According to Professor Lawrence Schlemmer, a social scientist at the University of Natal who wrote a detailed report on the survey's findings, "hardly any respondents indicated that they expected trade unions to acquire political goals." The finding is particularly interesting because the same people who also gave rise to the finding that there has been a general shift toward militancy among black people. "At this stage, at any rate, it would seem as if trade unions are perceived by black South Africans as having a role specific to the industrial context and not in a wider political sphere," Professor Schlemmer observed. Asked "Which organization or parties black people like yourself think will be important in their lives?" the vast majority of respondents mentioned obviously political bodies like the African National Congress, Inkatha, or various "black consciousness" groups. Barely 1 percent cited trade unions. People whose opinions were sought were referred to the strikes in Durban in 1973 and then asked when they thought mass strikes would happen again. Slightly more than half said they expected labor unrest very soon. But only 8 percent of the sample said that labor unrest would occur again on the 1973 scale if certain political goals were not achieved. Observed Professor Schlemmer:

> In no single sub-group in the population, not even the most highly politicized, did the proportion associating political goals with labor unrest exceed 11 percent. The great majority of people mentioned wages, working conditions, occupational advancement, and education as the areas where changes needed to be made to prevent unrest ... There is very little evidence from the results quoted above that a new political dimension is entering the sphere of labor problems and labor issues among rank-and-file people.[8]

Although blacks in general may not see trade unions as political vehicles, this does not mean that they are unaware of, or would be unwilling to use, their strength as workers in a political cause. In the survey just referred to, blacks in KwaZulu-Natal were asked the following question: "If a particular well-respected leader of the African people wished to show his strength to the government and in a big speech one day he were to ask black workers to stay away from work for two weeks, what would happen?" Twenty percent said almost all workers would stay away, while 49 percent said many, though not all, would. In other words, seven of every ten people would join the strike. A breakdown of the positive respondents indicated particularly strong support for such a political strike among "the better educated and more politicized people." However, rural people who held land also indicated that there would be widespread response to such an appeal. If the same respected leader were to "ask people not to buy from certain shops," the survey wanted to know, what would be the result? Sixty-four percent indicated that almost all of the people would obey the request. Again, the survey found, the positive response would not be limited to the more politicized or better educated groups, or to youth or urban people. These results are particularly interesting in view of the fact that Chief Buthelezi has repeatedly stressed the potential of strikes and consumer boycotts as nonviolent weapons.

The most recent attempt at a general strike was in May 1981, when leaflets purporting to have come from the African National Congress were handed out calling for a three-day strike against the official celebrations for the twentieth anniversary of South Africa's becoming a republic. There was no response, one trade unionist commenting that black workers could not be expected to go on strike simply because they were handed leaflets urging them to do so. Consumer boycotts have had mixed results in the past few years. At least two organized by black unions and supported by a number of other organizations have been important contributing factors in capitulations by the companies with whom the unions were in dispute. But several others have failed as a result of poor planning or the absence of substitutes for the products boycotted. Convincing threats of boycotts have also succeeded in persuading companies to reverse decisions, notably one that Inkatha implicitly threatened to call against a financial institution that stopped opening accounts for illiterate people on the grounds that they were blocking up banking halls.

It is sometimes pointed out that by 1985 blacks will account for more than half of the total consumer spending in South Africa, that they already constitute nearly three-quarters of the work force, or that by such-and-such a date most artisans' jobs will be filled by blacks. Nobody denies that these changes taking place in the racial structure of the economy represent potential power for blacks. But it is no more than potential power. Whether this potential is translated into actuality depends on the mobilization of people on a systematic and sustained basis, which necessitates institutions and networks geared for that purpose and able to devise tactical strategic objectives. There is still a vast amount of groundwork to be done in laying the foundations for such mobilization, however.

Opinion polls in the last few years have suggested that there is growing support among blacks for the African National Congress. The most recent survey revealed that it was the most popular organization on the Witwatersrand and that in Natal its support was second only to that of Chief Buthelezi. However, it is not clear from the polls what the content of ANC support is: Is it identification, among older blacks in particular, with a tradition of nonviolent protest against apartheid dating back three-quarters of a century? Is it identification, especially among younger blacks, with the renewed campaign of insurgency that the external mission of the ANC has been waging in South Africa since 1975? There are no clear answers to these questions, although the polls reflect a growing (though still minor) tendency among blacks to talk about revolution. Many blacks have applauded some of the incidents of insurgency and sabotage, whose targets have included police stations, railway lines, government buildings, and energy installations. In May 1983 nineteen people were killed and more than two hundred injured when a carbomb exploded in a busy street outside South African Air Force headquarters in Pretoria. In May 1984 an oil refinery in the port of Durban was severely damaged in a rocket attack. The ANC claimed responsibility for both these attacks.

Will South Africa then follow the pattern of Angola, Mozambique, and Zimbabwe, where guerrilla warfare eventually destroyed minority rule government? It should not simply be assumed that a domino theory applies in southern Africa. The Republic is very much more powerful than any of its neighbors, and it has also demonstrated that it has abundant political will to take preventive and retaliatory military action against insurgents in these states and indeed to take diplomatic and military steps to destabilize their governments. Most of these countries have said they will not allow the ANC to operate military bases there. One of the first foreign policy announcements Prime Minister Robert Mugabe made after he took over the leadership of Zimbabwe in March 1980 was that such bases would not be allowed. On March 16, 1984, the South African and Mozambique governments signed a nonaggression treaty, the "Accord of Nkomati," in which each promised to curb guerrilla movements operating against the other. It was shortly afterward revealed that South Africa and Swaziland had signed a nonaggression treaty on February 17, 1982, though this had been kept secret. The agreements were followed by strong action by the Mozambique and Swaziland authorities to curtail the activities of the ANC. But even if such difficulties did not succeed in preventing the ANC from pushing what is at present a low-intensity campaign to higher levels, it would be wrong to assume that the fundamental stability of the South African government would be jeopardized. (See chapter 2 for a detailed discussion of the implications of the nonaggression treaties.)

Whether the use of violence against a system of government perceived by many to be a form of institutionalized violence is justifiable is of course a moral question. But what is often overlooked is that it is also a practical question. Chief Buthelezi has put the point forcefully. "Perhaps the belief is that sabotage and armed insurgency will soon create instability and chaos," he told a meeting of black civic politicians in October 1981:

> I believe we could be headed for a situation like [that in] Northern Ireland, in which a system lives with sabotage and violence for decades without collapsing. Violence is a terrible fate and, apart from my moral objections to it, our people will lose much, much more than those supporting the government, before victory is achieved. Brothers and sisters,

our people can fight and if necessary they will fight. If fighting was a strategy that could bring change soon, we would be part of that action now. Our judgment, however, is that at this point it would be a war which cannot be won.[9]

A state of what I have elsewhere called "violent equilibrium" or a perpetual stalemate like that in northern Ireland is a frightening prospect.[10] It automatically invites the question: Is nothing being done by the authorities to avoid such a situation? The South African government has shown over the past few years in the field of industrial relations, and also to a somewhat lesser extent in that a black education, that it is capable of pragmatism and compromise. I want now to turn to other areas of policy and attempt to assess whether they also reveal signs of reform.

The New Constitution

On November 2, 1983, the white electorate overwhelmingly endorsed a new constitution. The Republic of South Africa Constitution Act, No. 110 of 1983, which replaces the constitution of the Union of South Africa of 1909 and the constitution of the Republic of South Africa of 1961, was almost universally condemned by Africans. The new constitution was more than five years in the making and split the National party in the process. It gives Indian and so-called colored minorities a parliamentary franchise and seats in a multiracial cabinet. This represents a dilution of purist racial ideology although both the structuring of the new legislature and the fact that whites number 4,675,000, "colored" people 2,715,000, and Indians some 850,000 will probably ensure that the white monopoly of political power in Parliament remains entrenched. Moreover, far from being a "step in the right direction," as some observers believe, the new constitution, by excluding Africans from the new parliamentary franchise, is an attempt to entrench in the political system what has come to be known as "Grand Apartheid." The government's constitutional proposals gave rise to two new political groups in 1983, the United Democratic Front, a loose multiracial association of community, women's, religious, youth, and other groups, and the National Forum, a somewhat smaller organization.

However, the new constitution should not simply be rejected out of hand because it does not go far enough and apparently does not cater to the political demands of Africans. We are operating in a real, not an ideal, political world, where we do not always have the luxury of being able to choose what we want, but instead usually have to settle for less, certainly in the short term. So rather than dismiss the new constitution without further ado, I want to raise the question whether it does not perhaps at least represent a foundation on which to begin building the kind of common and nonracial political society that would fit in with South Africa's common and increasingly nonracial economy. In other words, we need to recognize that compromise has a place in politics and attempt to evaluate the constitution in a pragmatic way—with the proviso that in doing so we do not lose sight of the kind of society that we should be working toward.

That society should be based on five principles:

1. Common citizenship and nationality
2. The right of all adults, irrespective of race, to have a voice in central political institutions, including Parliament
3. A judicially protected bill of rights guaranteeing political freedoms and habeas corpus
4. The elimination of racial discrimination—not simply its replacement, as is the government's intention, by discrimination on the basis of citizenship and nationality
5. The right of workers to collective bargaining

Only the last principle now obtains in South African law. To insist that the other four be incorporated in a new constitution immediately may be justifiable, but it is a demand that nobody at present can even begin to think of enforcing, whether by democratic or by insurrectionary means. Without losing sight of the ultimate goal, which is a society based on these principles, I would suggest that we need an interim yardstick against which to assess the new constitution. This should be whether or not it does, or can, take us in the direction of the utlimate goal. This yardstick may seem rather unexacting to those who argue that an immediate transition to majority rule is the only acceptable political path for South Africa. Unexacting as it is, it does have the advantage of catering to the situation where change has to be brought about in stages because it cannot be achieved overnight.

How does the new constitution measure up to these rather modest criteria? It does not. It fails the test. It furthers none of the political goals just defined, but in fact undermines them. Some of them it undermines not by default, but by design. Far from taking the South African peoples down the road toward a common society, it seeks to execute a constitutional U-turn and take us farther away from it. South Africa's rulers seem hell-bent on repeating the mistake of 1910 by imposing on South Africa yet another constitution that is unacceptable to the great majority of the country's population of some thirty-one million. The debate as to whether or not the "executive president" that is in store for South Africa will be a dictator or not seems to have overlooked the point that imposing this constitution on South Africa is itself an act of dictatorship.

It has been argued that, by letting Asians and "colored" people into Parliament, a principle has been conceded that gives Africans a foot in the door. However, part of the government's intention in letting these two minorities in is to help it pile up more pressure from the inside to keep the door closed. Moreover, ministers have made categorical statements that Africans will never be allowed in. The government is sometimes accused of not having a policy for Africans. In fact, of course, it has a very clearly defined policy on black political rights and has been steadily implementing it since 1959, when the Promotion of Bantu Self-Government Act gave effect to its basic principles. This piece of legislation abolished the limited parliamentary representation (through whites) that blacks had enjoyed until then and sought instead to identify each black "ethnic" group politically with its putative "homeland" in the rural reserve areas.

Since these foundations were laid, the policy has been elaborated, refined, and steadily implemented, but never deviated from. The best testimony to this is the fact that, to date, 7.8 million black South Africans—more than one-third of the total of nearly 23 million—have been denationalized and turned into foreigners. This act of depriving them of their South African citizenship takes place automatically when the "homeland" with which they are supposedly politically linked by historical tribe affiliation becomes a constitutionally separate state from the rest of South Africa. Of the ten homelands, four have so far become constitutionally independent states. It so happens that of the 7.8 million people who lost their South African citizenship when these four homelands became "independent," more than 3.3 million actually live not there but in the 86 percent of South Africa that is officially designated as the "white" areas. But as far as their political rights and citizenship status is concerned, this makes no difference. In the eyes of the government they are foreigners and have no claim on political rights in the "white" areas. It is the government's intention that all the other six "homelands" will also become independent, the net result being that there will then not be one single African in South Africa with South African citizenship.

This continuing process of removing the South African citizenship of Africans is as much a part of the government's program of constitutional change as is the new tricameral Parliament. They are two sides of the same coin. The argument that allowing Asians and "colored" people into Parliament gives Africans a foot in the door tends to overlook the fact that the coin is two-sided. This is why the contention that the new constitution is at fault for failing to include Africans, though valid, is based on a false premise. Africans have not been omitted from the new system so much as deliberately placed outside it. The government has not neglected to provide a constitutional future for them; it is providing a separate one through its policy of hiving off the "homelands" into constitutional "independence."

This is where the "hidden agenda" argument breaks down. This comfortable argument goes along the lines that the government has a plan to bring Africans into the new system but cannot at this stage reveal it for fear of right-wing reaction. For this agenda to be valid, the constitutional status quo in respect of Africans would have to be retained until the day when the time to include them was ripe. In fact, constitutional development for Africans is not static or in limbo, but fully operational, as the program of denationalization shows. This process is taking us farther from the goal of a common society. Indeed, incorporating Africans into central political institutions in South Africa would be incompatible with the continuing policy of turning them into non-South Africans by denationalizing them. The present policy of denationalization is in fact expressly designed to preclude any future possibility of incorporation. The logic of this basic incompatibility is apparently being overlooked by those who believe the new constitution is open-ended with regard to Africans.

It seems likely that Africans will strongly condemn any Indian or "colored" leaders who participate in the new tricameral Parliament and multiracial cabinet. This is one respect in which the new constitutional proposals are a recipe for greater racial tension. Another is the fact that they are a reconfirmation of black exclusion. The Union of South Africa was constituted in 1910 as a white supremacist state. Since then the black demand for political rights has been repeatedly denied. Now, however, South Africa has had a lengthy process of constitutional deliberation in which black views were among those sought and listened to. The end of it turns out to be not merely another denial but a somewhat more elaborate response, a new constitutional system that admits others who have also been asking for political rights but excludes Africans, telling them they do not even have the basic qualification of citizenship. In other words, we have moved from a situation where whites were simply saying "no" to a request, to one where they are telling black people they no longer have the right even to voice it, that they are out of court. Ever since their land was taken by military conquest, blacks have been third-class citizens in South Africa. That was traditional apartheid, the policy of every government South Africa has had since union. The program of political apartheid now being implemented seeks to remove citizenship altogether.

It can, of course, be argued that the denationalization process has been under way since 1976 (when the first homeland, the Transkei, became a constitutionally separate state) and that the new constitution makes no difference in this respect one way or the other. But this argument overlooks the fact that the new constitution elevates political apartheid from ordinary legislation into fundamental law. Political apartheid until now has existed side-by-side with the 1910 constitution, which predated it, and thus could—and did—operate without it.

The new constitution, by contrast, is based on political apartheid. The exclusion of Africans from the parliamentary franchise is upgraded from being a defect, as it was in the 1910 constitution, to being the very precondition for the operation of the new constitution. The Minister of Constitutional Development and Planning, Chris Heunis, has thus contended that it it is impossible to include Africans in the new Parliament because doing so would upset the racial ratios. If they were included, he said, the ratios would be 36 Africans to 9 whites to 5 "colored" people to 2 Asians. Even if only urban Africans were included, the ratios would be 16 to 9 to 5 to 2.

Further steps are already being embarked upon to complete the process of constitutional restructuring now underway. Having politically pulled black and white apart through the denationalization program, the government finds it necessary to put them back together again for certain purposes. A structure is required within which the joint white-Indian-"colored" political system can consult the "foreign" blacks since their respective territories (the "white" areas and the "homelands") are so closely intertwined geographically and economically. This structure is the so-called confederation of states. It is founded on two cardinal principles: black denationalization and sovereignty of member states.

Denationalization and confederal restructuring together exclude from discussion black political rights in the institutions of what was once merely the "white" areas of South Africa but is now legally a foreign country. As each "homeland" becomes constitutionally "independent," all its African citizens lose their South African citizenship and thus their claim to political rights in South Africa. Political apartheid is no longer merely an exclusion of black people from the parliamentary franchise, but a matter of constitutional structure and interstate agreement.

The government has made it clear that the key element in how Pretoria and the homelands come together is that there must never be a central executive authority over all of them. The homelands must never have any say over Pretoria's policies. This, of course, touches on the crucial difference between a federation and a confederation, the former founded in common nationhood and a central authority with specified powers over all the component provinces or states, the latter consisting, in the government's definition, of "sovereign independent states" with no central authority.

In contrast to the constitutions of 1910 and 1961, the new constitution makes it all but impossible to extend the franchise to Africans. Even if the political will existed, any attempt to undo the process of separation and move back toward common nationhood would involve difficulties almost unprecedented in political history. How, for instance, would one set about negotiations between the eleven separate sovereign states that the government has in mind?

When there is no agreement among the population of a country on political starting points like citizenship and the franchise, sensible statesmanship would seem to indicate that options should be kept open and flexibility maintained. But Prime Minister P.W. Botha will go down in history as the man who did exactly the opposite. Clearly, Mr. Botha hopes that his twin scheme of change entrenches African exclusion from the parliamentary franchise so firmly that the near impossibility of reversing the situation will lead to a general acceptance of the new dispensation. The opposite consequence would of course be that the persistence of African demands for representation at the center of power, with a constitution unable to accommodate them, will ultimately lead to the overthrow of the political system.

A Strategy for Dispossession

The process of denationalizing Africans is the constitutional prong of a four-pronged strategy for dispossession. The other three prongs are influx control, population removals, and financial apartheid.

The pass and influx control laws, whose main purpose is to limit the number of Africans in the so-called white areas to the minimum compatible with the labor needs of the economy, date back to the nineteenth century. Current developments in this field can best be understood by referring to the report of the commission of the inquiry into the utilization of manpower (the Riekert Commission).[11] Published only a week after the reformist Wiehahn Report on industrial relations, the Riekert Report was a comprehensive blueprint of urbanization policy for the future and, in its divisive thrust, an entirely different kettle of fish.

In essence, what Piet Riekert, a former economic adviser to the prime minister, recommended was the division of the African population into two groups: those with official permission to live and work in the "white" urban areas on a continuous basis, and those without. Elsewhere I have used the terms "insiders" and "outsiders" to describe these two categories.[12] The former would appear to number about one in four adult blacks. In the hopes of providing a more contented work force in the main industrial areas, Dr. Riekert proposed—and the government accepted—that this privileged class of "insiders" should be able to change jobs and places of residence more freely than in the past. They would also be eligible to purchase houses in the townships in the "white" areas on ninety-nine-year leases.

Alongside the advances in black education and training in the "white" areas, it is obvious that these reforms are part of a strategy designed to remove some of the grievances that gave rise to the township riots in 1976. Add in the other major change—the recognition of black trade unions—and it appears that the government, with the support of the business community, is attempting to lay the foundations of a black labor aristocracy in Soweto and other black townships in the so-called white areas. Increased powers of municipal self-administration were introduced in these townships by the Black Local Authorities Act, No. 102 of 1982. Restrictions on black business and professional men are being lifted in an attempt to foster the rise of a black middle class.

Some critics on the left view these changes as an attempt to build up a class of blacks with a vested interest in political stability, buying them off with privileges in the hope that they will back the whites in any future confrontation with the dispossessed and the unemployed. Other observers believe that if this is the intention, it will not succeed, because the beneficiaries will not be satisfied with material gains but will become even more insistent on political rights.

Nobody is entitled to criticize these "insiders" if they are able through good fortune or some other means to escape certain aspects of apartheid. But the reverse of the Riekert coin is that the price of their privileges is being paid by the rest of the black population, against whom the government, in accordance with the Riekert proposals, is erecting higher and higher barriers to keep them out of the "white" areas. These "outsiders" are all those people, probably three-quarters of the country's adult Africans, who do not possess in their pass or reference books the rubber stamp exempting them from the general prohibition that bars all Africans from remaining in the "white" areas for more than seventy-two hours at a time. Their situation is becoming steadily worse as they are squeezed between economic recession and tougher influx controls.

One of the chief ingredients of the government's plan to stabilize the position of urban "insiders" was that they should get preference over jobs. Not only can they change employment more freely than in the past, but employers in the urban areas are required to satisfy the labor bureaus that no "insider" labor is available before they can get permission to hire "outsider" labor from elsewhere. Much of any additional black labor that may be required by economic growth in the major industrial areas can be found, so the government appears to believe, in smaller towns in the "white" areas. The pass laws have already been changed to allow this labor to move from these smaller towns to the cities. In other words, net increases in labor demand are expected to be met more from within the "white" areas than by recruiting from the "homelands" under the migratory labor system. Although the "homelands" will remain labor reservoirs of last resort, their role appears to be undergoing a change from primarily that of labor reservoir to that of confinement area to which unemployment can be exported.

People from the "homelands" are finding it more difficult to obtain jobs in the urban areas. Until a few years ago, employers often did not bother whether their black workers were authorized to live in "white" areas, but simply hired them anyway, paying nominal admission-of-guilt fines if they were caught with "illegal" people on their payroll. But one of the chief concerns of the Riekert Commission was to stamp this out, and the maximum fine payable by employers was accordingly increased from R100 to R500. In the past few years, employers have been firing or refusing to hire black workers whose passes are not in order.

The government is now proposing to tighten the pass laws even further, giving effect to Riekert's proposals that "outsiders" should be smoked out of the "white" areas by attacking them at their place of residence as well as their place of employment. It has been proposed that those employers still recalcitrant enough to employ outsiders should now face a maximum fine of R5,000 or a year in jail, or both. Their personnel registers will be subject to inspection by the authorities. In addition, anyone found accommodating an "unauthorized" black person on their premises after ten o'clock at night will be liable in the first instance to a fine of R500 or six months in prison and thereafter to a fine of R20 for each night that the offense continues. By thus denying "unauthorized" black people both employment and shelter, the government hopes to drive them out of the "white" areas altogether, householders and employers having to play a much more active role in enforcing the pass laws than they have been required to do in the past.

These proposals, published in an earlier version in October 1980 but then withdrawn for study and amendment after a public outcry, were reintroduced in Parliament in 1983 by the Minister of Cooperation and Development, Piet Koornhof, as the "Orderly Movement and Settlement of Black Persons Bill." After the Bill was tabled again in early 1984, the government announced that it was withdrawing it and that an Urbanization Bill would be prepared for introduction to the new Parliament. If these proposals are ultimately enacted, they will be the most drastic and comprehensive piece of apartheid legislation since the pass laws were extended in the 1950s to include women. They must also be one of the cruelest and most massively disruptive laws currently being considered by any government anywhere.

Dr. Koornhof's bill is not an aberration. It is an expression of the well-established policy that the number of black people in the "white" areas must be kept to the minimum compatible with the labor needs of the economy. The purpose is, of course, to keep the margin by which whites are outnumbered as narrow as possible. This is proving a more and more difficult task since the "homelands" are seriously overcrowded and incapable of providing jobs for the people supposed to live in them. The government appears to take the view that black people who leave them without permission to seek work in the towns are political recalcitrants with ulterior motives. In fact, they are simply making the perfectly rational economic decision of going to look for work where it can more easily be found, in the large industrial areas of the country, where the great bulk of industrial development takes place.

Though they may argue about actual numbers, South Africa's demographers are agreed that large-scale black urbanization will take place during the remainder of this century. The social and political implications of this are obviously great, prompting the government to embark on desperate measures to try to stem the expected tide. The aim of the proposed new pass legislation is to do this by reducing the relative attractiveness of the cities by using measures that are designed to destroy whatever chances officially unwanted black people have of obtaining work by day and shelter by night. The police alone cannot handle so enormous a task. Hence the help of businessmen and householders is to be enlisted under threat of crippling penalties for those who do not cooperate. Attempts are at the same time being made to revitalize the government's program of industrial decentralization, which until now has been a failure. A new set of incentives for businessmen shifting operations to decentralized areas came into effect on April 1, 1982.

A crucial element of the overall apartheid policy is the government's massive population removal program.[13] Following the laws in 1913 and 1936 that imposed territorial apartheid on the whole of South Africa, dividing it up into the "white" areas, comprising 86 percent of the land, and the ten black "homelands," which together make up the remaining 14 percent, the government has been pursuing a policy of clearing as many black people as possible out of "white" areas. While the pass and influx control laws are essentially designed to prevent black people from coming into these areas, the population clearance program is directed at mass removal of entire communities and sectors of the population. Its targets fall into four main categories:

1. Black peasant communities living on islands of land, officially known as "black spots," in the "white" areas who are being cleared out of those areas and moved into the "homelands" under the government's "homeland consolidation" plans
2. Certain black urban communities living in townships adjoining "white" cities and towns but which are being demolished and their people shifted into a nearby homeland, whence they must commute daily to work in the white areas
3. Black people removed or displaced from white farms in terms of laws abolishing squatting and the labor tenant system
4. Blacks officially described as "unproductive people" and defined as "those who because of old age, weak health, unfitness, or other reasons are no longer able to work"

No comprehensive official statistics of the number of people removed or displaced are available. But if (incomplete) removal figures revealed by the government are read with census statistics and various other data, it appears that the number of Africans removed or displaced so far is between two and three million, with another million awaiting eviction. Although the government sometimes claims that removals are voluntary, there is persuasive evidence of force being used. In a number of areas to which removals have taken place, lack of proper sanitation and water supply has led to outbreaks of cholera, only one of a variety of diseases characteristic of displaced communities.

Displaced people are usually economically worse off than before. Peasant farmers removed seldom get adequate farmland in compensation because there is very little such land available in the overpopulated "homelands," and laborers generally find themselves farther from employment centers. Once removed into a homeland, a person is forbidden by law to leave there to search for work outside. He may work outside only if he has been recruited from inside the homeland by a government labor bureau or a licensed private recruiting agency. However, as I have already noted, the entire thrust of post-Riekert urban areas policy is that black labor must be localized and stabilized in those areas, employers being able to import black people from outside only as a last resort and then only for a maximum of a year at a time and furthermore only in a specified job category that cannot be easily changed.

People removed to the homelands thus get locked into a system of structural unemployment in large, densely packed settlements where there is little opportunity to make a living even out of subsistence agriculture. In addition to the resulting problems of poverty-related deficiency diseases, a structural deterioration in the environment takes place through overpopulation, overstocking, and overgrazing, while the land around the removal areas becomes steadily denuded of vegetation as people move farther and farther out in search of firewood. Reports from universities, semiofficial commissions of inquiry, and even government agencies, point to the resulting incidence of permanent damage to the land and soil erosion. South Africa is said to be losing 400 million tons of soil a year through erosion.

The "homelands" are all more densely populated than the "white" areas despite the fact that the latter contain all the heavily populated industrial centers. The average population density of the so-called white areas in 1978 was 20.5 people per square kilometer. With the sole exceptions of the Bophuthatswana homeland, where the figure was 31.75, and the Transkei, 55.1, all of the homelands were at least three times as densely populated as the white areas, with the figure for KwaNdebele being 84.6 and that for KwaZulu 98.9 per square kilometer (1980 figures).

Although the South African government claims that the blacks of South Africa are better off than those elsewhere on the continent, the homelands are in fact poor even by African standards. Gross national product (GNP) per capita ranges between R257 (1977 figures) in the case of QwaQwa to R418 in that of KwaZulu. This places the poorest homelands in the same economic bracket as Angola and Lesotho, and the middle-range homelands alongside Egypt, Senegal, and Ghana. The richest is on the same level as Zambia, while all of them are poorer than Botswana, Swaziland, Nigeria, the Ivory Coast, and the Congo, to say nothing of even richer countries like Algeria or Mauritius (1978 figures).

In fact, the homelands are worse off by African standards than these comparisons suggest, for they are based on gross national *income* figures, an abnormally high proportion of which consists of money sent into the homelands by migrants working outside. In the case of Bophuthatswana, for example, more than half of GNP is made up of migrants' remittances. The gross domestic product (GDP) of their homelands ranges from R84 to R204, placing their productive and income-generating capacities on much the same level as Tanzania, the Sudan, Zaire, Somalia, and Ethiopia.

Two additional sets of statistics can be mentioned, to give an indication of the fiscal resources available to the homelands from taxation of their citizens and grants from Pretoria. KwaZulu, which, as we have seen, is the richest homeland in terms of GNP per capita, had a budget for fiscal 1982–83 of R401 million, which implied government expenditure per head of population in KwaZulu of R126. Lesotho, recognized as one of the poorest countries in the world, had a budget of R265 million, allowing for government expenditure per head of R202.

The other telling figures relate to jobs. In 1973 to 1975, when South Africa's real GDP grew by an annual average of more than 5 percent, the homelands experienced an average annual increase of 100,100 in the number of people entering the labor market. Of that number, 28.4 percent found jobs in the homelands, and 36.8 percent in nearby "white" areas. Of the remaining third, perhaps one in four obtained a job as a migrant worker in the "white" areas.[14] The rest would have remained jobless, joining the one million or more people already unemployed in the homelands.

Let us now pull these various threads together. The "homelands," poor even by African standards, are unable to provide work for more than one in three work seekers even when the economy is booming. They are so densely populated that the opportunities for even subsistence farming are limited and may be declining. Their administrations have even fewer financial resources than a country like Lesotho. The South African authorities are aggravating their problems by displacing or forcibly removing more and more people into them in their efforts to purge the "white" areas of officially unwanted blacks.

At the same time, following the Riekert Report, the work force of the main industrial areas of the economy is being "stabilized" and the access of "outsiders" to jobs there progressively reduced. The recruitment of workers as migrants is being cut down. Now, to give further effect to the Riekert proposals, very much tougher pass laws have been drawn up to prise officially unwanted people out of the "white" areas.

Is not a vicious circle being created? More and more people are being displaced into "homelands" that not only cannot accommodate them but whose ability to do so is declining, forcing more and more people to leave in desperation to look for work outside. In other words, the pull of economic opportunity in the industrial areas is accompanied by an equally strong set of factors pushing people out of the homelands. So the government tightens up the pass laws in an attempt to force them back, but once forced back they simply increase the pressure on scarce resources and so strengthen the factors pushing people out again.

There are indeed growing signs that the homelands may be reaching the bursting point. White farmers in the Transvaal, Natal, and the eastern Cape are complaining of blacks moving on to their land without permission. They have asked for footpaths leading out of the homelands to be blocked off and for the boundaries between the homelands and their farms to be patrolled by the army. Discussions are now being held between Pretoria and the four homelands that have become "independent," with a view to erecting border fences. There have been calls too for controlled border posts between the "white" areas and the independent homelands.

Roadblocks and border posts were in fact set up in August 1981 to prevent people returning to Cape Town, whence they had been evicted to the Transkei and the Ciskei by police who set fire to their shelters and then rounded them up with guard dogs. Earlier attempts to remove these officially unwanted people from the city had run into problems when they arranged to defend themselves on charges of pass law violations, thus preventing the normally very rapid processing of such cases through the courts. Extra staff had to be brought in to assist the authorities. When they found they still could not cope, a decree was gazetted giving them powers to deport the people concerned as "aliens" without first charging them in the courts. This was done by a convoy of buses in the night. However, so determined were the two thousand or more deported people to return to Cape Town, where they or their husbands or wives had jobs, that during one period of five days 229 buses enroute from the Transkei to Cape Town had to be apprehended while police and pass officials checked their occupants' passes. At one point six hundred deported women besieged South African officials in the Transkei and held them hostage until police were summoned to rescue them.

It seems that the desperation of the deportees to return to Cape Town was matched only by the desperation of the authorities to keep them out. The action of the government provoked a group of businessmen in Cape Town to issue an unprecedented statement expressing concern, while a number of foreign ambassadors proposed making a protest to the government (a proposal abandoned under pressure from the U.S. government). During this series of events, one woman miscarried and one lost her child from double pneumonia.

I have sketched this rather grim episode in an effort to draw attention to the crisis that seems to be building up in the rural areas as influx control and resettlement policies progressively cut millions of South Africans off from access to the mainstream economy. Whether these people, whose number runs into millions, will accept this fate remains to be seen. But it is at least possible that the government's attempts to confine steadily increasing numbers of blacks to the homelands will be a cause of racial conflict in South Africa in the years ahead.

The plight of these "outsiders" in the "homelands" is doubly tragic. Not only are they the victims of ever-tightening influx control laws, but they suffer political discrimination at the hands of a number of Western aid agencies who are willing to offer aid in the "white" areas but refuse for political reasons to do so in the homelands. This policy has the effect of reinforcing the Riekert "insider-outsider" division and withholding assistance from the very people whose need is greatest. The divisive Riekert policy is also being unwittingly fostered by a range of liberal institutions, among them opposition politicians and newspaper commentators who repeatedly urge upon the government that urban blacks must be given political rights but seem to forget that homeland blacks also lack political rights.

It is necessary to beware of agitating only for the incorporation of urban blacks into central political structures because there could surely be nothing more unjust or dangerous than to grant one-half of the black population political rights and not the other, especially when the single most important factor determining whether blacks in South Africa are rural or urban is not choice, but the pass laws. It is of course correct to point to the absurdity of a policy that demands that blacks in "white" areas exercise their political rights exclusively through the homelands. But the fact that it may superficially seem less absurd to expect homeland dwellers to exercise their political rights exclusively through the homelands does not make that policy any less objectionable. The objection to the policy of hiving off the homelands into "independence" and in the process denationalizing their putative members would not be one jot less cogent if only people living in them lost their South African citizenship. The man who has lived his entire life in the remotest corner of KwaZulu surely has a claim on South African citizenship and the parliamentary franchise that is exactly equal to the claim of a man who has lived in Soweto all his life. The fact that the man in KwaZulu may have a vote for the KwaZulu legislative assembly is no more a substitute for the parliamentary franchise than is the fact that the Soweto man may have a vote for the Soweto community council.

I have tried in this chapter to identify the main currents of government policy, indicate where it is being altered or reinforced, and also show how the various strands fit together. It should also be apparent that some of the major thrusts of policy are highly contradictory of one another, while others are deeply divisive.

At a constitutional level provision has been made for a common political system for whites, Indians, and "colored" people, from which Africans are not only being excluded but their exclusion entrenched by stripping them of their South African citizenship through the hiving off of the "homelands" into constitutional separation from Pretoria. Although this denationalization policy is designed to make all black people into foreigners and hence remove the very foundation of their claims to political rights, a certain class of them in the "white" urban areas is being granted economic and social privileges, including home (though not land) ownership, greater freedom to change jobs, and first claims on any vacancies. More money is being spent on the education of the children of this class of insiders. This category of people is defined mainly in terms of sustained employment or long residence in the white urban areas. People fortunate enough to be eligible for lawful employment in the urban areas may now also be promoted to more senior jobs and bargain collectively through trade unions.

In other words, for this category of Africans a steady process of economic integration is underway. The implication of this growing economic integration alongside continuing constitutional separation is that the "white" areas will contain a steadily mounting proportion of denationalized people in their midst, occupying strategic jobs, with steadily increasing consumer power, higher and higher levels of income and education, and increasing power on the factory floor—all at the same time as they are becoming increasingly alienated politically not only from whites, but also from Asians and "colored" people seen by them to be cooperating with whites in practicing political apartheid against them. The increased urbanization that is facing South Africa, which may indeed be the dominating social and economic development between now and the end of the century, will dramatically heighten the contradiction between social and economic forces on the one hand and constitutional policies for Africans on the other.

While policy regarding insiders is contradictory, policy toward outsiders is deeply divisive. Against them, territorial apartheid is being implemented with ever increasing stringency. People whose labor is not required by the central economy are being removed from the urban areas by tougher and tougher influx control laws, while rural areas and smaller towns are being systematically purged of black people by massive population removal and displacement schemes. Once removed to the "homelands," these millions of dispossessed people join other "outsiders" for whom the government is progressively disclaiming responsibility. Although they have been allocated only 14 percent of South Africa's land, the ten homelands contain half the African population and about 40 percent of South Africa's total population.

The political and physical dispossession to which I have referred is accompanied by a process of financial dispossession, one of the least publicized but most insidious forms of apartheid. Once a homeland becomes a constitutionally separate state it inherits responsibility for tackling huge backlogs in housing, education, health, welfare, and social infrastructure. The economic and financial resources of the homelands are far too limited for them to be able to cope with these backlogs. Of course, whether "independent" or not, the homelands have part of their public spending financed through the central exchequer in Pretoria. But that is not the point. The government has taken to referring to grants to homeland administrations as "foreign aid." The former secretary of information, Eschel Rhoodie, once claimed that, per capita, the "transfer of wealth" in South Africa from whites to blacks is much higher than any nation achieves through foreign aid programs. This claim rests on a number of false assumptions, one of which is that all corporate taxation, including taxes generated by 80,000 whites and 600,000 blacks in the mines, is somehow "white" money. Another false assumption is that anything spent in the homelands out of the central exchequer, to which people of all races contribute, is a reflection not of black people's rights but of Pretoria's generosity. On Dr. Rhoodie's argument, white school-children in the Transvaal, whose education is financed by taxpayers of all races via the central exchequer's grant to the Transvaal provincial administration, are getting no more than their due, but any funds channeled to children in, say, the Bophuthatswana or Lebowa homelands for their education is "foreign aid." It is relevant to note in this context that the ten homelands now have responsibility for the education of two of every three African schoolchildren in South Africa.

Homelands that seek constitutional separation from Pretoria not only assist in the denationalization of South African citizens, but also by that very process forfeit their claim to a say in how the financial resources that they help to generate will be used. After all, the only means by which the ordinary citizen has a say in what happens to his taxes is his franchise for the legislature that enacts the country's budget. It should be borne in mind that "independence" for the homelands also means independence for Pretoria. In fact, this is what the whole process is really all about—freeing Pretoria from any legal claim that the "independent homelands" or their denationalized South African citizens may make on what was once their mother country but has now become a foreign state. Constitutionally, these homelands and their citizens are reduced to the same status in Pretoria's eyes as Malawi or New Zealand or any other foreign country.

It seems unavoidable that companies, local and foreign alike, will have to face up to some of these issues. The almost unanimous endorsement that the business community gave the Riekert Report was unfortunate. In addition to encouraging the immediate enactment (in 1979) of drastic steps to tighten up the pass laws, it gave a general stamp of employer approval to the whole new blueprint regulating the black labor market. Some sections of business have taken to having second thoughts, however. A number of business organizations, among them the U.S. Chamber of Commerce in South Africa, have been lobbying against the Orderly Movement Bill; their objections may have been among the reasons why enactment of this bill has been delayed. Foreign companies involving themselves in such lobbying will, of course, be facing up to the government on some of its most basic policies. But it is unclear how anyone committed to what is popularly known as "constructive engagement" can avoid this.

Just as groups like the Urban Foundation are working to improve living conditions in the urban townships, there is now an urgent need for much more attention to be paid to the grave problems in the homelands as well. Chief Buthelezi is one of the few black leaders, and probably the only one with a mass following, who has stated that he is willing to support those who argue that foreign companies should be "constructively engaged" in South Africa. He has also said that their aims do not go far enough, for they seek success "where it is most easily obtained," in "short-run equality and improvements in the workplace." In September 1980 he told the Reverend Leon Sullivan, author of the Sullivan Principles for American subsidiaries in South Africa, that Inkatha was "concerned that the economic progress of blacks in South Africa should not be measured only by the performance of a few dozen large multinationals." He added:

> Perhaps the most critical need of the black rank and file in South Africa is for more employment opportunities. Another critical need is for industry, which has long benefitted from the African rural areas as (a supplier) not only of labor, but of services and security for the families of laborers, to plough back some of the surplus value of that labor into the rural labor-supplying areas.[15]

Although it is probable that the government may succeed in persuading some of the six remaining non-independent "homelands" to accept "independence," Inkatha and the KwaZulu legislative assembly have vowed that KwaZulu will never take this step and so cooperate with the government in denationalizing South Africa's six million Zulus. Chief Buthelezi has accordingly demanded business support for the black claim to a voice in national politics and also urged the private sector as a whole to tell the government bluntly that its confederation plans are unworkable and that any plans it may have to forge an alliance between itself, business, and the black middle class are also unacceptable. Given the increasing racial divisiveness of the government's political policies, how can the private sector avoid taking up challenges like this from Chief Buthelezi and other black leaders?

A wide spectrum of business leaders recently threw its support behind a commission of inquiry set up by the KwaZulu legislative assembly to devise a form of multiracial government for Natal and KwaZulu as a political and economic entity within South Africa. The commission—known as the Buthelezi Commission, although Chief Buthelezi was not himself a member of it—reported early in 1982.[16] It found that the principle of multiracial regional government was acceptable to a majority in each racial group in the province, including the minority white, Indian, and "colored" groups.

The Buthelezi Commission was historic in more ways than one. It was the first black initiative of its kind. Racially, politically, and in the breadth of interest groups that comprised it, the commission was the most widely represented constitutional commission in the country's history. It did not produce another document listing the evils of apartheid but a careful study seeking practicable alternatives to the problems that would face any government in South Africa no matter what its ideological position. And through the involvement of some of the leading corporations and business organizations in South Africa, it elevated "constructive engagement" to new heights. It took engagement beyond the conventional areas of industrial relations and wage levels into the realms of economic planning and development, social policy, urbanization, and, of course, politics.

Most important of all, the Buthelezi Commission showed that political compromise between the races in South Africa is still possible. The changes in industrial relations, in which several American companies played a leading role, which have taken place in South Africa in the past few years illustrate the same point. I believe that American firms in South Africa have the responsibility and the opportunity to keep the situation open to such cooperation.

Notes

1. See Muriel Horrell, *Bantu Education to 1968* (Johannesburg: South African Institute of Race Relations, 1968); Edgar H. Brookes, *Apartheid—A Documentary Study of Modern South Africa* (London: Routledge and Kegan Paul, 1968); pp. 44–59; John Kane-Berman, *Soweto—Black Revolt, White Reaction* (Johannesburg: Ravan Press, 1968), pp. 183–91.

2. See Kane-Berman, *Soweto*, pp. 183–91, and chapter on education in *Survey of Race Relations in South Africa 1983* (Johannesburg: South African Institute of Race Relations, 1984).

3. For more detail on changes in black education see *Financial Mail*, January 7, 1977, April 18, and December 25, 1978, and May 18, 1979, as well as *Times Educational Supplement*, November 21, 1980 and January 30, 1981.

4. For further details on skill shortages see Business International, *Apartheid and Business—An Analysis of the Rapidly Evolving Challenge Facing Companies with Investments in South Africa*, (Geneva: Business International, 1980), pp. 79–118; Business International, *A Fresh Look at South Africa* (Geneva: Business International, 1982), pp. 95–101.

5. For details of the codes see *Apartheid and Business*, pp. 52–71.

6. Departments of Labour and of Mines, *Report of the Commission of Inquiry into Labour Legislation (Part One: Key Issues)* (RP 47/1979).

7. Industrial Conciliation Amendment Act, No. 94 of 1979, and Labour Relations Amendment Act, No. 57 of 1981.

8. For a comprehensive survey of black political attitudes see Buthelezi Commission, *Volume VI—The Report on the Attitude Surveys: Popular Response to Current Politics and Alternatives in the Region of KwaZulu and Natal* (1982).

9. Speech to a Meeting of the Urban Councils Association of South Africa, October 1981.

10. See Business International, *Apartheid and Business*, pp. 219–20.

11. Republic of South Africa, *Commission of Inquiry into Legislation Affecting the Utilization of Manpower (excluding legislation administered by the Departments of Labour and Mines)* (RP 32/1979).

12. *Financial Mail*, May 11 and May 18, 1979.

13. John Kane-Berman, "Population removal, displacement and divestment in South Africa," in *Social Dynamics* (Cape Town), pp. 28–46; *Forced Removals in South Africa* (Cape Town: Surplus People Project, 1983); *Resettlement—Papers Given at 51st Annual Council Meeting* (Johannesburg: South Africa Institute of Race Relations, 1981); and chapter on African removals in *Survey of Race Relations in South Africa 1983*.

14. For statistical and other information on the South African homelands, see Bureau for Economic Research, Cooperation and Development (Benso), *Statistical Survey of Black Development, Part One: RSA/Self-governing National States* (Pretoria, 1982); *Part Two: Independent States (TVBC Countries)* (Pretoria, 1982). See also the chapters on the homelands in *Survey of Race Relations in South Africa 1983*. For information on GDP and GNP figures for African states, see various issues of the *Bulletin* of the African Institute in Pretoria.

15. Internal memorandum prepared by Chief Buthelezi for discussion with Rev. Leon Sullivan, September 1980.

16. Buthelezi Commission, *Volume I—The Main Report* (1982).

2
Transforming Apartheid: The Interplay of Internal and External Forces

Heribert Adam

Afrikaner Nationalism Reexamined

Among the sober assessments of U.S. interests in South Africa by the Study Commission on U.S. Policy toward Southern Africa (the Rockefeller Commission), one finds a rare lapse into wishful thinking. It is the contention that the option of major economic sanctions against South Africa "must be kept in the U.S. policy arsenal."[1] Since this distinguished body recommended against U.S. expansion and new entry into South Africa (but also against disinvestment), the commitment of U.S. and European firms in South Africa has grown substantially. U.S. investment alone increased by 13 percent in 1981 and by 6.5 percent in 1982. The 1200 British companies followed by 375 American and 350 West German firms with a total foreign investment of R30 billion in 1982 seem to confirm the South African propaganda of stability and growth. These interests constitute an effective veto block against meaningful disengagement.

Furthermore, while much of the public focus has turned on Western investment in South Africa, the increasing South African investment in North America has hardly been noticed. Via a Bermuda subsidiary, Anglo-American alone is said to have had 108 separate investments in the United States and 36 in Canada in 1981.[2] This diversification into North American mining and mineral companies allows the conglomerate to circumvent currency restrictions and provides a profitable outlet for accumulated assets in a region politically much more stable. The links of mutual interests forged between South Africa and America are nevertheless similar to the much more highlighted Western involvement in South Africa.

I am indebted to the SSHRC of Canada for a Research Grant and to Hamish Dickie-Clark and Kogila Moodley for criticism.

In short, the expectation of effective sanctions by Western interests against South Africa at present remains totally unrealistic, quite apart from the two separate questions as to whether they are desirable and, if so, can be implemented. Interestingly, conservative and socialist administrations in power follow identical policies. Mitterand could not be more business-minded on South Africa than Giscard d'Estaing. The world recession gave the preservation of domestic employment clear priority over moral concerns. Western Europe, whose standard of living is largely based on expanding trade relations, is prepared to deal with the devil as long as it provides mutual benefits. Social democrats in European governments have not been able to enunciate satisfactorily the difference between trade with the Soviet Union and trade with South Africa.

While the fate of governments depends on economic performance, they in turn depend on freedom of the private sector that is interested solely in profit margins. What is often underestimated is the ready willingness of international business to cultivate whoever can best guarantee access to high profit margins in the region and above all stability regardless of ideology, let alone color. Gulf Oil has no problems with the Cubans guarding its installations in Angola. Investment decisions depend on long-term predictability. After the due posturing has been performed, South Africa, from the view of the crucial outside powers of whatever outlook, seldom poses a moral dilemma, but merely necessitates an assessment of risk.

Multinationals can be expected to disengage when the South African connection becomes a serious nuisance, negligible in the overall balance sheet of foreign investments, and, above all, threatened by real instability. In the meantime the official policy "neither to encourage nor discourage" South African involvement merely reflects that there is no policy at all, except maintaining the status quo. The central recommendation of the Rockefeller Commission, that the existing engagement should be maintained but no new involvement undertaken, amounts to a corresponding avoidance of the issue: either foreign investment is beneficial to black advancement—in which case, it should be increased—or alternatively it is harmful and therefore should be withdrawn.

For some South African interest groups stability and economic growth also rank top on the agenda. These priorities are enhanced by if not dependent on, international legitimacy. Here South African domestic and external interests merge. It is this common platform which gives outside intervention some limited leverage in influencing internal events. However, the possibility of outside interference tends to be grossly overrated. The behavior of Israel, which is much more dependent on outside forces than the more self-sufficient South Africa, should warn against the danger of overestimating external pressure.

If external intervention is to have any impact it must be geared precisely to the domestic situation in South Africa. Instead of the fine tuning required, many of the good intentions are dissipated because of false perceptions of the target groups. Almost the entire academic and journalistic literature on South Africa rests on the false assumption that groups under pressure close ranks. South Africa is said to have developed into a garrison-state with its defenders displaying a fortress mentality of stubborn intransigence. As a *Foreign Affairs* article recommending forty-one different sanctions put it, "The history of South Africa has been characterized throughout this century by movement in one direction— into the *laager*, into a defensive structure founded on the progressive consolidation of white power through the legal separation and subjugation of blacks."[3]

But a ruling group rarely is a monolithic block. Undoubtedly, white power has been entrenched. However, in this process it has also created contradictions which at the same time have developed into a serious source of cleavage as well. Not only are there always unintended consequences of State policy, but, more important, the benefits and costs of any given policy affect different sections unequally so that they gradually come to perceive their interests differently. Changing perceptions lead to new alliances and splits, far removed from the static image of South African politics so frequently portrayed. Intra-Afrikaner conflicts at present overshadow the black-white cleavage, so that P.W. Botha can say that he has more in common with a "colored" than with Frederik van Zyl Slabbert, Afrikaner leader of the liberal opposition Progressive Federal Party.

It is to these issues of a divided ruling class that any outside intervention must be sensitive. Whether a South African government will be receptive or hostile to any specific outside interference does not depend on its intrinsic worth or the reputation of its source but its use in the party-political infighting. Generally speaking, domestic politics determine foreign policy stances more often than outside influences shape internal policy, unless they directly affect the crucial domestic power struggles.

Likewise, it must be recognized that whatever a U.S. administration does or does not do vis-à-vis South Africa, depends on its perception of its domestic U.S. constituency. While it may be impossible to separate the moral from the political, it is safe to assume that much of the public indignation of the United Nations or of Western governments and nongovernmental institutions about South Africa represents moral posturing for ulterior purposes, rather than effective attempts to bring about change. To bathe in the purity of sanctimonious condemnations, particularly when they do not cost anything, merely fulfills the need for legitimation.

Competing Ideologies

While much of the literature does indeed distinguish between enlightened (*verligte*) and reactionary (*verkrampte*) outlooks, important recent developments are obscured by this simplified notion of good and bad. At present four competing definitions of Afrikaner policy vie for hegemony among the divided volk. They may be labeled (1) the labor racists, (2) the orthodox ideologues, (3) the ruling technocrats, and (4) the critical moralists. Each ideological outlook and policy prescription derives from a distinct constituency within the Afrikaner ranks. Behind a common communal rhetoric, quite different priorities emerge. This analysis assesses the strategies propagated by the four groups in order to cope with their different perceptions of crises, their potential or actual political clout, and their susceptibility to outside influence.

The Labor Racists. The *labor racists* of the extreme right-wing Herstigte Nasionale Party (HNP), which split from Prime Minister Vorster and the National Party in 1969, were left out in the political cold when in the 1970s the government favored business interests over conflicting white union demands on job reservation and labor conditions. To be sure, in the Afrikaner State the worker section has at no time been the dominant voice. But with the working-class whites historically constituting up to a third of the Afrikaner voters, organized Afrikaner labor exercised virtual veto power on crucial issues of black labor. The ethnic mobilizers of the Broederbond (the elite, highly political and once secret Afrikaner fraternal organization), themselves of "good financial standing" as a criterion of admittance, nevertheless integrated the poorer brothers ideologically and politically. With the increasing stratification of Afrikanerdom in the 1960s and 1970s, the declining percentage of white manual workers generally, together with the imperatives of new labor policies on the mines, the white workers were dropped from State protection.

Why did this Afrikaner class coalition fall apart, despite its strong ideological coherence? Why did so strong an ethnic bond as belonging to a powerful Afrikaner nationalist movement in the end prove so weak that its alleged invincible unity disintegrated precisely when the challenge to Afrikaner rule deepened? Among the many, necessarily simplified, answers one aspect stands out.

During the boom of the 1960s and early 1970s two shifts in traditional labor practice became imperative: Capital-intensive production increased, which demanded a stable, urban, semiskilled (black) work force, contrary to the traditional policy of relying mainly on rotating, cheap migrant labor; and skilled (white) workers, protected by the color bar, were mostly upgraded into the technical/supervisory positions of mechanized production. At the same time they were not able to fill the increasing demand for skilled technical manpower. By insisting on the color bar and blocking African advances, the white workers became a decisive stumbling block to economic growth. This obstacle could not be removed by the employers alone without the collaboration of the state. The defeat of the mine workers union in their last strike together with the decline of the South African Confederation of Labor and its associated unions, signaled the demise of the traditional protective labor policies.

On the political front, the Afrikaner establishment succeeded in purging the followers of Albert Hertzog from its crucial political institutions, particularly the Broederbond. In the bitter infighting, many of the present members of the Conservative Party who then held prominent positions in the Nationalist establishment, played an active part. In the 1972 purge of HNP sympathizers from the Broederbond, each member had to sign an oath confirming that he "was not associated with the HNP either through membership or cooperation, and if I was associated, I undertake to end this association immediately." The HNP leadership has not forgiven the then Broederbond chairman Andries Treurnicht and his supporter Prime Minister John Vorster for this expulsion from Afrikanerdom's most influential organization. This history accounts for a variety of contemporary personal incompatibilities in addition to the different class base of the two groupings on the political right of the National Party. Despite the obvious advantages of avoiding a split vote now, it is not at all certain that the two camps will form an electoral pact against the Nationalists. If the Conservative Party and the HNP were to form such a pact, the Government might well be defeated in the Transvaal and possibly in the country as a whole.

However, in such an event the Progressive Federal Party (PFP) could well hold the balance of power, provided white democracy still exists. Its abolition in South Africa is not as easy as the example of authoritarian-corporate regimes in Latin America suggests. Any minority government in South Africa cannot ignore legitimacy. The temptation to expand the executive State into a technocratic dictatorship would still have to accommodate substantial sections of the white right wing and liberal sections alike. Any further absorption of political power by the present government would be fiercely resisted by the combined right-wing whose collaboration in the civil service and the army would prove essential.

In the meantime, the leader of the HNP, Jaap Marais, who is a superior orator, can claim the purity of having castigated the dictatorial tendencies and the sellout of the National Party long ago, while his competitors remained opportunistic accomplices in the crime of destroying Afrikanerdom. It is obvious that any outside influence on this parochial section of Afrikanerdom remains minimal.

The Orthodox Ideologues. In contrast to the openly racist rhetoric of HNP leader Jaap Marais, Andries Treurnicht and his lieutenants in the newly formed Conservative Party (CP), avoid openly reinforcing grass roots, racist sentiment. They cultivate respectability. Their main constituency lies in the lower echelons of the vast Afrikaner civil service, comprising 40 percent of all economically active Afrikaners and what Marxists would call the "petite bourgeoisie," the lower middle classes. Conscious of their newly acquired white-collar status, they do wish to keep aloof of "lumpen ethnics." Their vague party program mixes pre-Vervoerdian ideology with calls for a colored and Indian homeland in order to ensure white self-determination and avoid power-sharing. Thus it distinguishes itself by completely ignoring the reality of an interdependent economy, let alone the political wishes of the subordinate population. Contrasting "sharing of power" with an advocated "division of power" remains meaningless in the absence of any workable blueprint to achieve it.

It is ironic that the catchword of "power-sharing" precipitated the split. As is explicitly admitted, power-sharing will take place only at the symbolic level. The nominated colored and Indian "leaders" enjoy the style but not the substance of office. Complex constitutional arrangements ensure that Afrikaner Nationalists still dominate the system completely. There is not even a hypothetical possibility of temporary loss of power, since potential alliances between coloreds and Indians and the white opposition is ruled out. In fact, the proposals do not weaken but substantially strengthen the ruling group's hold on political power by legally replacing traditional democratic procedures with administrative fiats.

One reason for the nevertheless wide appeal of conservative ideology lies undoubtedly in the occupational position of many of its adherents. Most civil servants are sheltered from economic reality by job security and state protection. The prospect of competing with members of former outgroups is perturbing. Moreover, the labor control board officials, the Afrikaner policemen or teachers of Christian-National education, who are themselves subaltern actors in a system where they receive the orders from above, were previously rewarded, in part, by their conviction that they were serving a cause. With the old apartheid certainty in disarray and the meaning of their work in question, they cling to a glorified past order with great zeal, regardless of its consequences.

The past ideological mobilization through Christian-National indoctrination in separate schools for Afrikaans-speaking white children now backfires on the technocratic Nationalists. Teachers, who are comparatively poorly paid and 70 percent of whom are women, constitute a latent support group of the orthodox ideologues, particularly in the Transvaal. In an ironic reversal of an earlier cherished practice, the Minister of National Education, Gerrit Viljoen, now feels obliged to caution teachers against bringing party politics into education, "which could cause alienation between parent and child."[4] The sectarian nature of white education is best reflected in the existence of two teachers' organizations in the same province, the Transvalse Onderwysersvereniging (TO) and the (English) Transvaal Teachers Organization (TTO), whose main complaint focuses on the nepotism and indoctrination of the Afrikaner-dominated educational bureaucracy.

An equally powerful multiplier effect in molding sectarian attitudes still falls to the Afrikaans clergymen. By no means as ideologically homogeneous as the church front would imply, it was nevertheless the house meetings of dominees to which Treurnicht, himself a former cleric, devoted much time. The effect led one government minister to wail against "theological racism which will destroy this country."[5] When two Afrikaner churches, the leading Nederduitse Gereformeerde Kerk (NGK) and the smaller Hervormde Kerk, were finally expelled from the "World Alliance of Reformed Churches" at its Ottawa meeting in 1982, the expected soul searching in South Africa was awaited in vain. The action was simply rationalized as another part of the international "total onslaught" against the country. Pleas by more enlightened ministers for a unified and desegregated church were rejected as "untimely" by the majority and the conservative church hierarchy.

The churches, like other ethnic organizations, are constantly criticized for failing in moral and spiritual leadership by adopting a noncommittal, self-righteous stance on politically divisive issues. However, given a divided membership and with the conservative flock in the clear majority, vested organizational interests in preserving unity win out over moral duties. The increased factional politicization of the constituency after the split of the National Party paradoxically results in an apparent depoliticization of the official organizational stance of its auxiliary institutions. Even an overtly political organization such as the Broederbond is now politically so paralyzed that it denies that there are any differences within itself. The choice such organizations face is either to split or confine themselves to uncontroversial, cultural issues. For the time being, the crucial support institutions of Afrikaner nationalism, unlike the National Party, opt for formal unity and factional infighting over institutional influence. This gives the political arena added weight for determining the fate of the nation.

What makes people susceptible to one or the other of the competing explanations of reality remains one of the most vexing questions in the social sciences. The Marxist answer of class interests breaks down when people in the same class position adopt opposite ideologies. Whatever makes equally wealthy farmers in the Transvaal or teachers in the Free State, who have identical material interests, nevertheless define their political interests so differently escapes economic reductionism.

The past politicization of the Afrikaner civil service with wide discretionary power, based on the underlying consensus of the incumbents, would also seem to backfire now. No longer do all officials automatically implement all orders from above; they now interpret them according to their own vision. The admission by ministers that their own staffs are undermining official policy is not merely a rationalization of inertia. Intradepartmental conflicts, for example, between the Department of Manpower and the Police about how to deal with newly legalized union activities, increasingly create problems for administrative efficiency. The unofficial involvement of South African intelligence officers in the Seychelles, the continuing efforts of South African State employees to destabilize Zimbabwe and Mozambique, and various other incidents indicate that state officials increasingly act without orders from above. The continuing death of detainees in policy custody, despite the worldwide outcry after the assassination of Steve Biko, would seem to suggest that the technocratic top is too weak, if not unwilling, to put its house in order. The reluctance to persecute the individual perpetrators may well be also due to the fear of appearing soft on security, thereby providing the right with another cause. In short, deracialization means detribalization of the South African civil service, with a depoliticized professionalism of adherence to rules replacing the exercise of discretion.

In this area in particular, Western governments have a clear interest and duty to press Pretoria to respect international law. If the incipient tendencies toward a Lebanization of southern Africa were to accelerate, U.S. interests would be directly affected. U.S. intelligence, for example, must be as interested in protecting Zimbabwe's Prime Minister Robert Mugabe from his opponents operating from South Africa, since it is keen to unravel Soviet influence in the region. The same applies to the domestic dimension of human rights violations. The apartheid opponents in unions and civil rights groups clearly need and deserve all the outside support they can get from forces equally interested in evolutionary development. As necessary as it is to protect the victims of apartheid, it is equally crucial to impress on black nationalist activists an important lesson from comparative conflicts in divided societies elsewhere. Once a civil war has escalated to a higher level of mutual violence, the few legal and moral restraints in committing atrocities break down easily. Self-styled vigilante groups do not recognize any legal conventions but operate to seek revenge and "teach lessons."

While South Africa has been spared the death squads of the Latin American model so far, the extension of the unrestrained killing of suspected dissidents remains a distinct possibility, should the legitimacy of an authority erode. At that stage the ground may well be prepared for the takeover by an extreme dictatorship with widespread popular approval, based on the sentiment that Marx once described before Napoleon took power: "Better an end with terror than terror without end." At present the ruling establishment perceives of itself as accountable at least to its domestic constituency and world audience. But compared with the potential of repression in modern, scientific barbarism, the bungling, paternalistic autocracy of Afrikaner nationalism could pale into mere authoritarian dilettantism. Particularly where an official war legitimizes extraordinary measures, there are few moral precepts that bar large-scale atrocities or even genocide.[6]

Traditional democratic theory insists on a depoliticized military combined with the clear supremacy of civilian authority over strategic issues. How well the barracks are under the control of an elected government and parliament is considered the threshold between democratic and military rule. However, in white South Africa, as in Israel, this distinction does not apply. Increasingly, the entire society becomes militarized. In these states, the boundaries between politicians and the military are fluid, personnel is interchangeable and both spheres merge. Rather than the politicization of the military of the Latin American kind, the militarization of the polity characterizes the beleaguered ethnic state.

The Ruling Technocrats. While Andries Treurnicht and the Conservative Party attempt to sell a fiction (partition), the ruling technocrats articulate a pretense: power-sharing. A few handpicked coloreds and Indians with no mandate from their community cannot negotiate on their behalf. First through the President's Council and now through the new tri-cameral parliament, these colored and Indian "representatives" provide a symbolic presence in a permanently white Nationalist-dominated government. They have little legitimacy among their group. The imposition of ethnicity, in contrast to the concept of self-chosen group membership, remains deeply offensive to stigmatized people separated into racial parliaments. Above all, the exclusion of more than 70 percent of the population from the central government makes a mockery of rational conflict resolution by further polarizing a divided society. The tragic effect of it all is that any consociational arrangement will be so discredited by "sham-consociationalism"[7] that a constitutional compromise will be impossible when it is really needed.

Nevertheless, the new constitution has been widely acclaimed in the Western press as a step in the right direction, too cautious and insufficient yet, but with the political inclusion of urban blacks inevitable at a later stage. P.W. Botha's difficulties with his right wing are sympathetically recognized, and orthodox ideologues have, as never before, legitimized continued Western applause for Pretoria's "daring venture of change."

There are three main arguments why the constitutional reforms amount to a step backward in terms of evolutionary change and stability. First, the symbolic admittance of coloreds and Indians is paralleled by an accelerated exclusion of blacks from the central political institutions. The denationalization, resettlement, and consolidation of Bantustans continues unabated. Blacks have not been left out of the political process for the time being to be included later but have been deliberately assigned roles outside the State. Formerly, as second-class citizens, they at least had claims to full citizenship; now, as foreigners, they have no legal claims whatsoever. In addition, the artificial cleavage between urban blacks and migrants is being reinforced in terms of differential political and residence rights. Second, the political incorporation of middle groups at the expense of blacks deepens existing distrust among the subordinates and further poisons race relations. Between coloreds and Indians on the one side and blacks on the other as well as among the Indians and coloreds themselves, splits between collaborators and the majority who oppose it polarize the communities and foster attitudes hostile to seeking consensus and compromise. Third, the newly admitted participate in a constitutional charade that further wastes valuable time. It makes a mockery of the sense of urgency which is needed to achieve an acceptable settlement for the majority population. In short, the changes exacerbate rather than resolve the problem.

The criticism of the ruling party, therefore, ought not merely admonish its cooptation policy, but should also focus on the fact that the party is not rational enough to adopt a policy of genuine conflict minimization. While the President's Council's Report relies heavily on the international authorities on consociationalism, particularly Arend Lijphart, it blatantly ignores the author's preconditions for a successful power-sharing model, such as mutual veto power, freedom of political activity for all interest groups, representativeness of group leaders and relative equality of available resources of the competing groups.

What are the prospects of achieving the ruling technocrats' envisaged depoliticization of ethnicity in South Africa? With almost the entire Afrikaans news media backing the government and a well-oiled party machinery at its disposal, the National Party may well hold its present level of 40 percent support among all white voters. According to a nationwide opinion survey for *Rapport* in August 1982, based on the assumption that all parties had nominated candidates, the figures were:

NP — 43 percent; PFP — 20.2 percent; CP — 14.5 percent; NRP — 7.1 percent; HNP — 2.4 percent. This distribution was roughly supported in four by-elections in November 1982. Even without ideological tribal appeal, the National Party still can reward supporters through patronage and can ostracize heretics.

The greatest asset of the government, however, constitutes the latent support of the (English) business community. The much publicized Carleton meetings in 1980 and the follow-up Good Hope conference in 1981 between the business and government elite ratified the new alliance between the state and private capital. Afrikaner Nationalists are known to have successfully approached the former despised *Engelse geldmag* (English high finance) for campaign contributions in order to keep the common orthodox opponents in check. Ultra-right folklore changed the National Party initials (NP) into "New Progs," the false symbol for Jewish-capitalist-internationalist integration policies under the guidance of South Africa's Rockefeller, Harry Oppenheimer, former chairman of the Anglo-American Corporation. However, it was through the advances of Afrikaner business that English business impressed on the government the need to recognize the failure of traditional apartheid. While the denationalization of blacks and the creation of "independent" states still continues, the changing manpower needs and the creation of new labor relations through legal unions has removed one previously contentious area of uncertainty.

Technocratic considerations of a settled urban labor force notwithstanding, the present rulers are obsessed by black numbers. The redefinition of nationality by administrative fiat, as well as the proposed land deal with Swaziland all aim at elevating the nonblack section of the population into an official numerical majority, should universal enfranchisement become necessary. The major stumbling blocks to these designs remain KwaZulu and Chief Gatsha Buthelezi's adamant refusal to contemplate independence for the numerically strongest ethnic group. Nationalist thinking in South Africa cannot envisage that people would not necessarily vote along ethnic lines. And yet all the surveys of nonwhite opinion indicate that the ideological cleavages among the subordinate castes remain as varied as among the ruling group. Given a universal franchise, nonracial parties of liberal reconciliation and gradual, moderate, social-democratic policies would clearly come out on top of ethnic-racial appeals in South Africa at present. Surprisingly, a majority of 70 percent of blacks still prefer a liberal-conservative economic value system of individual entrepreneurship, peaceful negotiations, and compromise, to Marxist alternatives. It is the government policy of political exclusion that causes rapidly increasing support for militant options, albeit often more out of frustration than conviction.

With official intervention perceived as undue interference into sovereign affairs, it is the private sector that has the greatest leverage to improve black living conditions. Nonetheless, the managerial structure of most firms reflects the domination in the wider society. Despite labor codes, the economic environment has not become deracialized. A few desegregated toilets and cafeterias are displayed, but more important aspects are ignored. Particularly in hiring, training, and assigning supervisory roles, multinationals and local firms alike hardly deviate from established practice. The preferred method to deal with the skills shortage is to step up recruitment of British immigrants. Company assistance in black education, the training of union leaders or the defense of civil rights activists has been confined to a few far-sighted business leaders. On the whole, corporate involvement in the political reform process in South Africa has been minimal. Organized business has followed the government lead rather than taking the initiative of seriously putting controversial policies on the agenda of the state.

On the other hand, the legalization of black unions and strikes has led a generally more sophisticated management for the first time to negotiate earnestly and to recognize the stabilizing role of the emerging union power. Some progress has also been made in the move toward nonracial wages. Nonetheless, the political issues inevitably spill over into the factory floor, although the rank-and-file members have frequently displayed great shrewdness in separating militancy about direct interests from mobilizing calls for more abstract goals. While the number of strikes and stoppages steadily increased to about three hundred in 1981, no industrywide strikes have yet taken place and only 10 percent of the black work force is in fact unionized. Most industrial action resulted from traditional paternalism and highhandedness on the shop floor. The distrust between workers and management has grown to such proportions that even enlightened labor policies become suspect of manipulation. Too often business takes the easy way out by accepting the role of auxiliary policeman—a role the government would like the private sector to accept in enforcing pass laws and political supervisions. With many firms tacitly obedient to government policies regarding influx control, the recent prime victims of the recession have been the migrants and squatters without Section 10 rights to urban residency. No labor code applies to the accelerating rural poverty. In contrast to many Marxist analyses, which stress the Bantustans as sources of cheap labor, the Bantustans' role as dumping grounds for superfluous labor now stands out. In addition to the political advantages for Pretoria, it can thus avoid the social costs of increased structural unemployment by abandoning the state's responsibility for people across "international boundaries."

South African business as well as foreign companies have been silent beneficiaries of these schemes. In addition, many foreign firms still lag behind internationally acceptable labor practices. U.S. firms obey the Sullivan Principles to varying degrees, but compliance is not mandatory and monitoring together with sanctions for violators could be stepped up. While the ruling group is not willing to repeal any racial legislation for political reasons, it can at least be pressed to allow much more de facto rights for the formerly excluded. Desegregated institutions in the nonpolitical field (factories, universities, professional and leisure organizations) also constitute de facto power, regardless of the franchise.

While the technocrats attempt to disassociate the economy from the polity, the disenfranchisement of the black population inevitably means the politicization of ethnicity and the progressive delegitimation of the free enterprise system. An emergent African middle class that is not even allowed freehold tenure at their place of residence and prohibited to set up shop in the white cities will be an unlikely candidate for embourgeoisement. While the fragmentation between the relatively privileged black urban dwellers and the unemployed rural population may indeed increase, so may the selected radicalization of the countryside. For the polity as a whole, the presence of a formidable rightwing will undoubtedly also aid in repoliticizing the economic issues and bring ethnic ideology back to the agenda of the state. The pragmatic technocrats will have to address not just budget balances and profit margins, but also the basic questions of justice and values.

The Critical Moralists. The outcome of the ideological debate about the nature and future of Afrikanerdom depends also on the *critical moralists*[8], who have a dormant and unorganized constituency. With the politicization of the Afrikaner cultural institutions through the split in the National Party, the dissenting theologists, Polstu students (Afrikaner students formally committed to a peaceful transition to a multiracial South Africa), and atomized Afrikaner intellectuals do play an important role in redefining Afrikanerdom. Only an extreme stereotypic view of Afrikanerdom can come to the conclusion: "Afrikaners do not produce critical self-analysis."[9] Various writers, academics and even journalists in the government-supporting press have set a process in motion which permanently challenges the claims to legitimacy of the powers that be. Unlike English liberalism, which in its quest for universal values denigrated Afrikaner ethnicity, the critical moralists speak as Afrikaners from the inside. Most will not join or even vote for the Progressive Federal Party with its image of anti-Afrikaner Jewish-capitalist, despite its authentic Afrikaner leader, Frederik van Zyl Slabbert.[10] Their political ideals are nevertheless close to the PFP program and strategy. They are involved in rewriting Afrikaner history by separating Afrikaner cultural achievements from oppresive Afrikaner politics. If a reconciliation between African and Afrikaner nationalism is to be achieved, this demystification of their historical role constitutes an important step. On the contemporary scene the critical moralists act as catalysts of new visions when "Afrikanerdom's ideology is what each day's problems demand."[11] This yeast in the ideological dough is hardly appreciated by the Afrikaner establishment; for example, its proponents are ostracized and frequently excluded from academic rewards. Consequently, they deserve the attention that the international community showers on this rare species. It is to be hoped that the outside observers descending on the few dissenters in Stellenbosch and Potchefstrom are not misled into confusing the voices of the critics with the might of the status quo.

Comparative political history suggests that a ruling group seldom anticipates a challenge to its rule by early compromise. More often than not, a ruling group is able only to react to events and not to control them. Its past success becomes the seeds of its doom. And yet what Afrikanerdom has set in motion so far seems more than "only desegregating the deck chairs on the Titanic."[12] Human groups can also learn historical lessons. They can "adapt to circumstances in unanticipated ways."[13] History is open-ended, and, within constraints, people do have choices. Instead of suffering predetermined doom, they can prevent it through alternative policies. Particularly in a society in which socialization stresses conformity to group values rather than individual autonomy, wise political leadership can redefine goals rather than merely lagging behind popular sentiment. Political leadership can be the variable that ensures that the conservative attitudes of individuals are not translated into public policy. In a crunch, enlightened self-interest rather than certain doom is likely to appeal to most ordinary citizens, as the lesson of Zimbabwe has shown again. This has not happened for large sections of white South Africa, because they have not been exposed to a real crisis. Contrary to survival propaganda and conventional wisdom of widespread anxiety, whites, on the whole, have been sheltered from the prospects of losing power. For Afrikanerdom the crucial question remains whether a learning process can anticipate the consequences of continued minority monopoly, or whether an irreversible crisis is needed to drive this lesson home.

How can meaningful change in this situation be effected from outside? Contrary to widespread advocacy, this analysis has argued that sanctions are not only unlikely to be adopted but, even if adopted, would be unlikely to have much effect on the domestic policies of the South African government. Assuming all the recommended measures were to be carried through—government insurance of exports abandoned, the flow of trade, credit and capital investment curtailed, diplomatic and military cooperation ceased, tourism discouraged and South African Airways landing rights lifted, refugees and liberation movements assisted— all these acts would minimally affect the battle for hegemony among South Africa's oligarchy and its relations with its subject population. To be sure, it would boost the morale of the disenfranchised majority, but this alone would scarcely provide it with the means to reverse the power relationship.

In short, South Africa has developed into an integral part of the Western global economic system. Therefore, it is naive to pretend that one part is willing to sacrifice another with which it has beneficial relations at all levels. Such a policy lacks a sufficient constituency at present, save those who posture about the abhorrence of apartheid. In light of this objective constellation inside and outside South Africa, the ritual discussion of the emotional question as to whether all-out sanctions would facilitate or hamper the case of majority rule, remains futile and academic.

Apart from the small measures sketched, there is, unfortunately, very little outside actors can do that will decisively influence this drama of "violent evolution."[14] To pretend otherwise, means adopting an unrealistic, frequently hypocritical stance, or, alternatively, participating in the inconsequential shouting of misguided activists.

Constitutional Engineering

On November 2, 1983, white voters in South Africa decided by a two-thirds majority in a nationwide referendum to approve a new South African constitution. The new political dispensation still excludes the 70 percent African population from participation in central political decision making but includes symbolically the 10 percent so-called coloreds and 3 percent Indians in separate Parliaments. White control has been streamlined into a more technocratic, expanded executive state with greater powers for the ruling National Party and the office of the State president. The coloreds and Indians now play the minor role of educating whites in nonracism.

Three racial parliaments constitute an extension of apartheid. There would be nothing wrong with ethnic representation if the group members were to identify with these labels. But in South Africa, ethnicity is imposed by the government, regardless of the feelings of the people. For example, there are no voluntary "coloreds", for "colored" is simply a legal racial category created by the Afrikaners. And yet these brown

Afrikaners are not allowed to sit in the same parliament and vote on the same roll, because this would jeopardize National Party control and offend traditional sentiment. Therefore, the new constitution lacks legitimacy, the most vital precondition for making it work.

The majority of white South Africans, however, pride themselves on having voted for progressive constitutional change. In their perception they have agreed, for the first time in history, to share power with people of color. The modest beginning is said to lead inevitably to more change later. A "step in the right direction" is better than the status quo that would have been assured had the die-hard racists won.

Much of the support for the flawed constitution came, somewhat hesitantly, from traditional critics of apartheid policies, particularly in the English business sectors and parts of the English press.[15] Their reasons are an interesting case of self-delusion.

While hardly anyone praised the constitution as a likely recipe for future stability, it was supported as an apparent improvement on the status quo. Had the government lost the referendum, it would have had to compromise to the right and not to the left.[16] F.W. de Klerk, the likely successor to a discredited reformer, P.W. Botha, would attempt to reunite Afrikanerdom. Foreign investors would view a "no" vote on the referendum, for whatever reason, as a refusal by white South Africa to change.[17] After all, the cautious move toward a more representative government represented progress, surely to be followed by later political inclusion of the black majority. These assumptions are clearly fallacious.

Could the Pretoria regime renege on its step toward modernizing racial domination? Could it afford to go back into the *laager* in 1984? The answer depends largely on a proper understanding of the nature and functions of its constitution.

Constitutions generally recognize but do not create political rights. Effective constitutions mirror the sociopolitical conditions in a country, but are not responsible for them. Above all, constitutions reflect power relationships. A constitution regulates the diverse interests of competing groups through a mutually accepted social contract but does not in itself determine the strengths of these groups. Given that constitutional change occurs in response to the need to accommodate new social forces, a return to the old order is not in the cards. The traditional apartheid order simply fails to meet the requirements of an interdependent, advanced capitalist economy. The stretched manpower needs and the legitimation crisis of Pretoria are not to be solved by perpetuating the status quo.

The strength of the ultra-right in South Africa notwithstanding, a return to the status quo and simultaneous economic stability would simply be impossible. To be sure, the Conservative Party still speaks for a substantial white section, but this section represents a declining constituency and a failing ideology. The white, lower income groups and racist ideologues fear the competition of a rising black stratum and, therefore, need to rely on government protection. With this policy they are at odds with the powerful technocratic, free-market dynamics at work at present. Regardless of the outcome of the referendum, South Africa would have had to come to grips sooner or later with its economic advancement and political lag, even under an ultra-conservative regime.

The option of stalling reform, therefore, no longer exists. If it were tried, it would aggravate the inherent contradictions of the already outdated South African political order to such an extent that no sane government could keep itself in power and remain part of an international economy. Real isolation, not just rhetorical condemnation as at present, would be the consequence. The price of a stalled reform would be a declining domestic economy with much more serious instability. With the hopes for reforms dashed, there would be an internal and external loss of confidence of such depth that the various latent cleavages would break open to an uncontrollable extent. Political optimism and belief in evolutionary progressive development, however slow, forms an essential part of the psychological glue that holds the deeply divided society together.

If the illusion of genuine reform provides the necessary climate for business as usual, it must be reinforced by more legitimate political arrangements. "Power-sharing" and "more representative government" triggers such approval. "For the first time in South Africa's history whites will share power with people of color," is the congratulation offered by the newspaper with the highest circulation.[18] But by all standards of power-sharing, the newly included middle-groups have no constitutional power to win any issue, either alone or in a coalition, against the will of the white group.

Do the three racial Parliaments constitute a more representative government? The two additional houses have little legitimacy among their constituents because they are based on racial membership. The key decision-making procedures are so firmly controlled by the white party in power that any "loyal opposition" is reduced to a democratic fig leaf rather than a potential alternative government. Authoritarian corporatism, not democratic openness, characterizes the new rules.

The new politics will still be devised by non-African group representatives, albeit no longer whites only. Coloreds and Indians determining the political role of the majority population in cahoots with the ruling section can only aggravate intergroup tensions, particularly between the majority and the newly coopted middle-groups. As long as the cooptation policies are not backed up by the repeal of racial legislation, colored and

Indian participants in the new deal cannot deliver and are widely discredited as collaborators. It is particularly the expanding colored and Indian middle class that is offended by the continuous racial classification. These professionals—lawyers, doctors and teachers with wage parity with their white colleagues—have now reached a measure of material equality that sharply contrasts with their second-class political status. No "colored," for example, is a voluntary "colored." This continuous status inconsistency has alienated the educated urban leadership from the political system. This resentment expresses itself both in apathy and militant repoliticization as a spillover from the white political debate. A newly founded United Democratic Front seeks to unite all apartheid foes outside the official political channels rather than working within the constitutional rules. Does the constitution allow for later African inclusion? The newly approved rules are predicated upon further African denationalization in "independent" homelands. Even if limited powers of self-government are granted to urban councils, Africans will not be involved in central decision-making. Therefore, the "yes" vote amounted to a vote for the continuation of the Grand Apartheid designs of African denationalization.[19]

It is true, though, that the reform process once started may develop its own dynamic. Although Prime Minister Botha has reiterated that there is no hidden agenda, he could hardly say otherwise in light of right-wing accusations of him as sellout. Regardless of intentions, there are always unintended consequences. The pressure for African inclusion may build up sooner than the regime realizes at present. Given a less ideologically oriented caucus, more pragmatic policymakers will eventually be forced to recognize reality, particularly when interacting with a wider circle of interest groups and ideological outlooks in the new dispensation. Technocrats are not immune to learning lessons about the rising costs of maintaining privilege. However, what is at issue are not intentions or the goodwill of constitution makers. The tragedy lies in the fact that the new rules invite more conflict rather than minimize it. They waste precious time in letting excluded forces build up outside the political system rather than anticipating the pressure before the dam bursts with dire consequences for all.

Whether any informed outside observer can believe in the viability of such questionable stabilization policies, as the chairman of Anglo-American argues, remains questionable indeed. His predecessor, Harry Oppenheimer, came to the opposite conclusion by announcing his intentions to vote "no." The split among big business about the scope and direction of political reform remains one of the intriguing aspects of the referendum.

It also showed the official opposition, the Progressive Federal Party, under its leader Frederik van Zyl Slabbert, as more principled than its critics will give it credit. This party, often denounced as the political arm of English business, did not waver, despite assumed majority support among its supporters for the new deals and most leading English business-men deserting their political home. On this issue the PFP leadership in-deed articulated the long-term interest of white security against the short-term views of their traditional supporters.[20] These were blinded by their newfound access to the corridors of political power.

It was Afrikanerdom, however, that has split most traumatically over the sham constitution, despite the National control being firmly con-solidated. "Power-sharing," the euphemism for the pragmatic adjust-ments, was interpreted by the far right as compromising Afrikaner sovereignty, the thin edge of the wedge with which big business would want to sneak in color-blind profit interests rather than guarantee tradi-tional white protection. Ironically, this accusation is not without some truth.

The irony lies in the severe constraints which Afrikaner political culture imposes on any serious technocratic attempt at conflict manage-ment. The present regime indeed fears the ultra-right as a much more immediate threat to its power base than the left. Given its ethnically bound constituency, it cannot open itself sufficiently to the tainted liberal spectrum without disintegrating as an Afrikaner party. It cannot embrace genuine reforms without jeopardizing its basic Nationalist sup-port structures. Given the cold war that the limited reforms caused in all Afrikaner institutions, Prime Minister Botha, indeed, probably "went as far as he could." Many English speakers, themselves as conser-vative and as solid beneficiaries of apartheid as the ruling section, wanted to give the government credit for its "courage" and not lose such a valuable ally. Herein lies the main explanation for the size of the "yes" vote on the referendum. However, accepting the ethnic limits of reform politics, the regime cannot go as far as necessary in order to thwart serious future conflict. Unless a new constitution is freely negotiated by representatives of all major interest groups rather than imposed by one section, it aggravates confrontation by forcing the excluded group to seek redress by other means. In the meantime, compromise and modera-tion become discredited as "leading nowhere."

How aloof many white South Africans still are from such basic prem-ises of conflict management is shown in the reasons of many "progres-sive" academicians for their support of the new dispensation. They made the point that an all-inclusive democratic system "will only be achieved if the actual beginnings of mixed government show responsible leadership, an overriding willingness to cooperate and a deeply felt dedication to eradicate prejudice and fear."[21] These condescending preconditions imply that the newly included still have to prove their worthiness before they can expect further concessions. This insistence on proper behavior views political conflicts that a constitution is supposed to regulate, in terms of paternalistic rewards, contingent on the learning experiences of rulers. All-powerful as they may be, real power-sharing will not arrive in South Africa because the excluded have demonstrated nonthreatening conduct. On the contrary, only realistic threats and pressures force enlightened rulers to compromise. The South African conflict is not about the eradication of prejudice and fear. These will always exist among mobilized competitors. How the conflicting claims and perceptions can be channeled into mutually acceptable bargaining procedures remains the fundamental issue of successful constitution-making.

The new constitution, based on black exclusion rather than incorporation, will only lead to a further rejection of the rules of the game. By politicizing the majority population and feeding its resentment of racial privileges, the constitutional engineering of Pretoria ironically hastens the downfall of institutionalized racism. When even avowed political moderates, such as Chief Buthelezi's Inkatha, vehemently reject the new deal, the arrogant dismissal of such black opinion by both government and business and by many progressive critics of apartheid, bodes ill for the proclaimed sophisticated techniques of evolutionary incorporation.

Economic Recolonization

The peace accord between Mozambique and South Africa in March 1984, the withdrawal of South African troops from Angola, and the prospect of an internally acceptable settlement of Namibia heralded a new constellation in the region. The economic recolonization of the Frontline States by South Africa can be compared in its importance with the political decolonization after the coup in Lisbon ten years earlier. Why have implacable socialist governments in the Moscow camp suddenly agreed to switch sides? Why does South Africa suddenly show itself willing to abandon an aggressive and belligerent policy toward her black neighbors after it stalled on detente and Namibian independence for years?

Popular answers to the first question have stressed the debilitating effects of South Africa's military destabilization efforts, the three years of a severe draught, the depressed world market for most commodity exports in a global recession and the obvious administrative disintegration of Mozambique and Angola as a consequence. Indeed, grossly underdeveloped by the most negligent colonial power from the start, Angola, and even more so, Mozambique never had the chance to recover after most of the non-African entrepreneurial and professional intelligentsia had left the strife-torn area. Assistance from the Eastern bloc proved no substitute. The emphasis on military aid by Moscow and its satellites could not hide the fact that the socialist bloc could not, or would not, come to the economic rescue. Tied in to the South African economy by manifold historical links (electricity supplies, railway and harbor connections, migrant labor remittances), Mozambique was worn out when it decided in favor of pragmatic survival rather than ideological martyrdom. Internal peace, accompanied by South African trade and tourists will, at least, fill the empty shops with food and the bankrupt state coffers with hard currency.

Long before the Mozambiquan surrender, Luanda had been driven to negotiate with the South African occupant. At stake was the freedom of the South West Africa People's Organization (SWAPO), with the ruling Movimento Popular de Libertacao de Angola (MPLA) under the increased pressure of the South African-supported forces of the Uniao Nacional para a Independencia Total de Angola (UNITA). Unlike the MRM mercenaries in Mozambique, however, Savimbi's UNITA movement can fall back on widespread popular support. A MPLA-UNITA coalition government seems the only way to pacify the country.

For South Africa, the spoils of a Southern African Economic Market promise to be huge. First, a formal economic hegemony proves far cheaper than a costly military dominance. There are clear limits to aggressiveness that an inflation-ridden economy with severe skilled manpower problems can bear without eroding the affluence of the ruling minority.

Second, the rapprochement means the final demise of the Southern African Development Coordination Conference (SADCC), set up by the black governments to lessen the dependence of their economies upon the Republic of South Africa. The bloc was an economic response to a political problem. It had to fail where only a political solution to an economic disparity could be the answer. The accord represents the recognition of this contradiction. On the other hand, it merely ratified what had taken place anyway in the form of an increased incorporation of the frontline economies into the South African orbit. Zimbabwe's trade with its SADCC partners had fallen since its inception in 1980, and the intention of pruning long established economic linkages for political reasons was doomed from the start.

Third, Angola provides the plum for an expanding South African monopoly capitalism short of export markets and enticing investment opportunities. As Stanley Uys has pointed out, South Africa will become the *economic* vehicle for Western influence in a region where socialist blueprints have failed so obviously.[22] Pretoria has succeeded in offering herself as an economic shield against communism where the West could not accept her military and political alliance before. It would not be surprising now to see the apartheid prime minister visiting the White House or a reelected Reagan descending on Johannesburg after attending the independence celebration in Windhoek.

Whether this unprecedented legitimacy of Pretoria extends to its domestic policy, as is frequently alleged, however, remains doubtful. The moral opprobrium of neo-apartheid may well increase. The crusade to extend the external stability to the internal South African scene could heighten. The external rapprochement has been interpreted as setting Pretoria free to pursue internal repression even more vigorously. However, far from giving the government a free hand, it binds the white rulers to tread more cautiously for fear of upsetting this delicate accord. This awareness is clearly reflected in some Afrikaner editorials: "South Africa [must] be doubly careful . . . we cannot afford a Biko or a repetition of 1976."[23] These unintended consequences of pursuing external legitimacy then benefit anti-apartheid activists internally, rather than undermine their legitimate opposition. With the external perception of threat diminished as an excuse, domestic policies will come under increased scrutiny. South Africa has succeeded in reestablishing a *cordon sanitaire* at her periphery only to find herself exposed more intensely at the core, where the real battle for control or power-sharing is taking place.

The accord also has been wrongly viewed as a severe setback for the African National Congress. To be sure, expelled from support bases in Mozambique, the organization will be hampered in carrying out acts of sabotage in South Africa. But committed guerrillas may still operate from farther afield or from inside the country. The new strategic situation may well force the ANC to rethink its military preference. Under this dubious strategy, the ANC attacked where the enemy was strongest and itself the weakest. A more political opposition, using unions and other legitimate organizations, may concentrate on areas where the apartheid defenses are weakest and the democratic opponents prove strongest. The journalistic focus on security considerations notwithstanding, so far Pretoria has never really been concerned about the occasional ANC incursions emanating from Maputo. In fact, South African propaganda exaggerated and utilized the ANC threat or the Cuban presence in Angola to mobilize white support at home. When the South African army bombed ANC shelters in Maputo or Lesotho, its prime motive aimed at placating domestic right-wing opinion. "Going soft" on the enemy would have undermined P.W. Botha's constituency, 82 percent of the white voters having approved of an aggressive policy of retaliation.

It was the clear demise of the right-wing ideologues, as evidenced in the November 1983 constitutional referendum that gave the ruling technocrats the confidence to pursue a pragmatic policy of economic recolonization rather than military destabilization. As long as the present regime was threatened by its conservative ideologues, it could not entertain Namibian independence and controversial constitutional reforms simultaneously. A SWAPO flag over Windhoek would have caused a backlash in the Republic, fanned by returning Afrikaner civil servants in the same way as Rhodesian expatriates backed the conservative racist parties in South Africa. The referendum alleviated this fear, particularly since the National Party can now count on a greater percentage of support in the English community than among Afrikaners.

Pressure from Washington is not to be overestimated. Afrikanerdom has rarely yielded to vague sticks but merely embraced the many carrots of "constructive engagement." But contrary to Marxist propaganda, Western capitals became increasingly concerned about the potential instability in the region, created by Pretoria's military aggression. Disintegrating black governments could have paved the way to a "Lebanization" of Southern Africa. In a political vacuum the various guerrilla armies would have operated outside governmental control and opened the avenue for external interference. The regional settlement has foreclosed this potential instability in the interest of all three parties: South Africa, the Frontline States, and Western capitals.

The envisaged package is enticing for all parties, even SWAPO and, indirectly, the Soviet Union, who would not lose face. With a gradual Cuban withdrawal, already agreed upon by Dos Santos and Castro, a SWAPO government in Namibia reappears on the horizon. With the release of the respected SWAPO founder, Herman Toivo Ja Toivo from its jails, Pretoria gambled that Sam Nujoma will finally have found his rival. In the end, economic coexistence under Pretoria's hegemony may indeed emerge from the diplomatic maneuvers as unexpectedly as the Zimbabwean reconciliation was brought about by the Lancaster agreement. Nelson Mandela and the ANC, however, need not fear being left out. Any lasting peace on the periphery will depend on the stability of the core. Namibia could be the model and forerunner for a South African "solution." How a moral consensus with the representative leader of the excluded black population can be established in the Republic of South Africa itself will be the final test case for the reform from above under pressure from below.

So far, the South African state that so successfully engineered external detente has not found an acceptable formula for internal pacification. The regime is at a loss as to how to incorporate politically at least its urban blacks without losing control. The answer clearly lies in all-party negotiations of representative leaders from all communities about mechanisms of power-sharing that exclude one group being dominated by another. In as far as the external accord has removed the false threat of being besieged, it may also have helped to ease the necessary process of domestic rapprochement.

Notes

1. The Study Commission on U.S. Policy toward Southern Africa, *South Africa: Time Running Out* (Berkeley: University of California Press, 1981), p. 426.

2. Th. W. Lippman, "A South African empire reaches to U.S.," *Washington Post*, April 11, 1982.

3. Clyde Ferguson and William R. Cotter, "South Africa: What is to be done?," *Foreign Affairs*, January 1978, pp. 253–274.

4. *The Star Weekly* (Johannesburg), October 9, 1982.

5. *The Star Weekly*, September 18, 1982.

6. For example, an academic supporter of Treurnicht, Professor Hercules Booysen, warned, "This country can be put on fire, not only by blacks, but by whites too." Apartheid, he argued, has given whites a false sense of security. If that system is taken away, violence could erupt. (*New York Times*, July 25, 1982).

7. A term coined by Theo Hanf who elaborates on the idea in Theo Hanf et al., *South Africa: The Prospects of Peaceful Change* (London: Rex Collings; Bloomington: Indiana University Press, 1981). For the best up-to-date-assessment of the Botha politics see, Hermann Giliomee, *The Parting of the Ways* (Cape Town: David Philip, 1982). For a perceptive, critical review of recent developments see also Lawrence Schlemmer and David Welsh, "South Africa's Constitutional and Political Prospects," *Optima* 30, no. 4 (June 1982): 210–231, and John Kane-Berman, "A Sharp Step Backwards," *Frontline* 2, no. 9 (August 1982).

8. Johan Degenaar, the political philosopher at Stellenbosch, first used the term "morally-critical Afrikaner."

9. Peter Lambley, *The Psychology of Apartheid* (London: Secker & Warburg, 1980), a singularly unhelpful and opinionated account to understand the mentality of a ruling group by an English psychiatrist.

10. The PFP is still largely an English-speaking, upper-middle-class organization. In the last general election, 1981, only 5 percent of Afrikaners, but 25 percent of Afrikaners with university education voted for the PFP.

11. *The Economist*, May 22, 1982.

12. Ferguson and Cotter, *South Africa*, p. 274.

13. George M. Frederickson, *White Supremacy: A Comparative Study in American and South African History* (New York: Oxford University Press, 1981), calls this "one of the more general lessons of history" (p. 281).

14. A notion coined by former U.S. ambassador in South Africa, Bill Edmondson.

15. The influential Johannesburg *Sunday Times* and *Financial Mail*, for example, backed a "yes" vote while the Durban *Sunday Tribune* and the Cape *Times*, owned by the same group, advocated a rejection of the proposals. The Afrikaans press, as well as the government-controlled radio and television, of course were unequivocal in their stance. This despite the large ultra-right opposition in Afrikaaner ranks, comprising up to 40 percent of the total Afrikaner vote, particularly in the most populous Transvaal.

16. Johan van der Vyver, leading Human Rights advocate and Law Professor at the liberal University of the Witwatersrand, in the Johannesburg *Sunday Times*,

October 16, 1983. Similarly, Alan Paton earlier, who retracted after severe criticism by his liberal friends.

17. Gavin Relly, Chairman of Anglo-American, *Sunday Tribune* (Durban), October 9, 1983.

18. *Sunday Times* (Johannesburg), October 2, 1983.

19. A point stressed by John Dugard, *Sunday Times* (Johannesburg), October 16, 1983.

20. For a popularized survey of the arguments of all political parties, including the black groups see: [no author] *Yes, No. Your Guide to the New Constitution* (Lange-Lucus Publishing, 140 Oxford Road, 140 Melrose, Johannesburg, n.d.). The 100-page booklet ends with an excellent overview by Hermann Giliomee of the history and interests behind the various white fractions. In another article ("The English in Disarray," *Eastern Province Herald*, September 6, 1983), Giliomee describes the reluctance of the English-speaking establishment to make up its mind publicly. This initial confusion, however, has given way to numerous individual partisan announcements by leading English speakers, mostly in support of the constitution.

21. Marinus Wiechers, *Sunday Times* (Johannesburg), October 9, 1983. Wiechers, a law professor at University of South Africa, was also a member of the Buthelezi Commission.

22. Stanley Uys, *The Guardian*, March 3, 1984.

23. Die Vaderland, March 5, 1984.

Part II
Operating in South Africa

3
Industry and Labor: A Management Perspective

Fred Ferreira

The Social and Political Background

One cannot discuss industrial relations in South Africa today without first examining the political and social-community issues that impinge on labor, for these issues have become totally intertwined with industrial relations in this country—probably more so than in any other democratic country. An industrial relations practitioner in South Africa must, for this reason, acquire knowledge and skills in areas beyond the borders of traditional industrial relations.

Because the current government of South Africa has denied blacks political rights, outlawed black political organizations, and banned their local leadership, blacks' frustrated aspirations have been concentrated in virtually the only forum in which they are officially permitted to express their opinion: the trade unions. Industrial relations in South Africa is therefore bedeviled by social-political issues and inevitably takes on the racial overtones of a black-white struggle. Such tensions have been compounded by the fact that historically management positions were limited to whites under a job reservation system. Hence, a lopsided system has evolved with whites constituting most of the management and black the workers. This segregation of the workforce further complicates industrial relations.

Industrial relations in South Africa has undergone changes unparalleled in other spheres of black living. Since the Wiehahn Commission reports, the government has introduced significant labor reforms, including the recognition of black trade unions, the abolition of the job reservation system, the admission of blacks to apprentice training, recognition of the principle of freedom of association, and the introduction of a unitary labor law. These reforms not only opened channels for articulating black views on labor issues; they also raised expectations. It is folly to expect that such a segment of the South African social structure as important as labor could be isolated from reform without affecting the broader political and social ideals of blacks more generally.

Naturally, then, labor began to use the legitimate structures that were created for them to achieve other, including political, ends. And because the position of black labor is politically determined, we must expect that political issues will continue to affect labor issues.

There is profound disagreement in South Africa over what constitutes the appropriate political dispensation.

The ruling National party has tried to entrench the right of self-determination for whites under a new constitution incorporating the coloreds and Asians, but excluding blacks, who account for 71 percent of the population of South Africa. (See the introduction and chapters 1 and 2 for a discussion of the new constitution.) At the same time, increasingly impatient and radical black opinion is demanding nothing short of majority rule within a unitary political system.

The level of black discontent has been rising steadily since the Soweto riots of 1976. Professor Lawrence Schlemmer of the University of Natal found, in repeated surveys of black men on the Witwatersrand, that the proportion responding to carefully prepared and tested questions by declaring themselves to be "angry and impatient" with life, increased from 39 percent in 1977 to 44 percent in 1979 and 56 percent in 1981. Professor Schlemmer's basic question may over- or underestimate political anger; what is significant, however, is the trend.

Discontent is increasing and, moreover, is not limited to black youth. Comparative studies conducted by Professor Schlemmer since 1972 have shown a marked shift in the political thinking of rank-and-file blacks, both urban and rural. In 1972 the dominant political sentiment was apathy. The white structure seemed massive and immovable, and the main response to it was helpless acquiescence. Ten years later the mood has changed. In 1972 blacks were far less concerned with politics in daily affairs than were whites; today they are significantly more politically conscious than any other racial group in South Africa.

Formerly, although blacks sought improvements in their circumstances, they were not particularly interested with comparing themselves to whites. Now, possibly because they have attained a degree of affluence, or because it appears within their reach, equality with whites takes pride of place. When faced with a choice between a higher material gain with continued inequality or a lower gain coupled with equality between black and white, eight of ten opt for the latter. The most significant change in attitude, however, is that black people no longer see the white system as immutable. Perceiving possibilities and opportunities, they are no longer apathetic; they have much more determination and confidence even though they often conceal it.

In the absence of any vehicles for political expression, blacks often bring broader political and community concerns to the workplace. There such issues compound true workplace grievances such as wage levels, and lead to work stoppages, strikes, and demands for participation in the decision-making process of the employer.

The most important community issues affecting industrial relations are education for the worker and his children, housing availability and quality, job security, and police harassment. Each of these issues is tied to the inferior treatment of blacks in South Africa.

There is a great disparity between black and white education whether measured by the amounts spent per child (R192 for blacks versus R1,385 for whites), the teacher-to-pupil ratio (blacks 1:43, whites 1:18), the curricula, or the quality of facilities. (See appendix A.) Additionally, about 60 percent of black teachers are considered to be underqualified, having no university education or any other recognized professional qualifications.

There is an undisputed housing shortage among blacks, and the red tape associated with obtaining and purchasing a home under the ninety-nine-year leasehold program is formidable. Freehold remains a mirage.

Job security for most blacks is complicated by the enforcement of measures leading to a system of migrant labor. The problem is compounded by management attitudes. Labor has been regarded historically as a management tool, a "unit of production" that can be picked up and dropped at will, and regulated through influx control legislation in an attempt to match supply with a fluctuating demand.

It is estimated that one in six South Africans are somehow associated with the police system as informers, collaborators or active sympathizers and support a harassment pattern ultimately leading to interrogation, detention, and bannings. Because management is viewed as exploitive and desirous of control of labor, management connivance with the security police is often assumed.

These are the issues invariably transferred to the workplace, where they become part of the grievances arising there, such as the level of wages, the opportunities for skill training and promotion, job security, union recognition, and discrimination. Although statutory job discrimination is rapidly being dismantled, its spirit is still very much alive and often manifested in aloofness and paternalism on the part of managements.

Black labor found in the trade union movement a vehicle to articulate their demands, and having no other legitimate way of protesting, began viewing the employers, particularly the multinationals, who are perceived as being more visible and susceptible to international pressures, as powerful potential agents for change. It was but a short step for workers to transfer their political and social-community frustrations to the shop floor, where it was easier to identify a target—the employer—and to exert pressure.

Additionally, South Africa's chronic shortage of skilled workers and the government's acceptance of the need to abolish occupational color bars and provide increased training opportunities for blacks have placed powerful bargaining resources in the hands of black workers.

Trade unions at present embrace only about 10 percent of the total black labor force in South Africa. However, against the sociopolitical background just sketched, this percentage is bound to grow. In light of the political and social issues involved, it is also likely that community-based unions will flourish more rapidly than others. Community-based unions aim at forging links between workers and the community or community organizations, to gain both material and moral support for the worker. These unions therefore facilitate the interaction between the community and the workplace and create greater solidarity, which is a potent—and essential—force to black labor when launching sympathy strikes and consumer boycotts of products produced by offending companies.

Another feature of community-based unions is that generally they shun the official bargaining machinery because utilization of this system could be perceived as acceptance of the status quo. This aloofness from the system, which affects those registered unions that are vying for the same potential membership, places the industrial council system under stress. Consequently, some councils have shown a willingness to reform and are increasingly likely to accommodate a dual system by accepting decentralized consultations and negotiating at both the regional and the enterprise level.

A common feature of most of the strikes that have occurred in South Africa is that their causes are seldom identified beforehand. Employers usually have to ferret out the causes during or after the strike, and invariably the major causes are not strictly labor relations related, but are more ideologically inspired by the differing objectives of management and labor: management aims at profits while workers demand a greater share of the wealth.

This delay in identifying the reasons for a strike could, of course, also reflect the failure of the employer's particular system of communication to permit effective articulation of the mounting resentment. Under these circumstances it is seldom possible for management to take specific preventive action.

If the assumption that political and social frustrations affect in-plant labor relations is correct, then we must anticipate that labor unrest will continue to occur until meaningful political change for blacks occurs. Given the South African record on political change, we can expect continued turbulance on the labor front as unions and blacks ever more frequently flex their muscles. Conflict will continue, but because conflict is an essential means of initiating the process of change, this is not strictly a disadvantage but is also a strength of the system.

Let us examine the question whether the American labor experience prepares U.S. management for the politicized South African situation. The American experience is characterized by an industrial relations system that is generally accepted by both management and workers. In the United States, the social revolution took place—or is taking place—within that system.

Fundamentally, however, American industries are accommodating minority groups whereas South African industries are—or should be—endeavoring to accommodate a majority group. The South African majority was always excluded from the system, and therefore the system itself has become the symbol of oppression. Although this majority has no alternative to offer, in large part because it has been denied the opportunity to develop an alternative, it feels morally obliged to destroy the existing system. In the process it is groping for fixed points, the common denominator being solidarity, which in the workplace translates into shop floor negotiations. From there the situation is fluid and dynamic; no textbooks or imported systems can offer resolution.

In this setting, there is no room for armchair specialists or idealists, unless the idealist is sufficiently realistic to know that pragmatism will ultimately prevail. Emerging unions do not need parameters, and in South Africa today they have no common rules, order, constraints, or discipline.

Fundamentally, labor relations in South Africa are influenced by factors so different from those operating in the United States that the U.S. experience cannot provide guidelines for most South African labor issues.

It is, therefore, not reasonable to expect American management to be prepared for this situation. What we South Africans need is patience, endurance, confidence, and the will to succeed. Solutions can only evolve in South Africa, they should not be imposed from outside.

This is the sociopolitical background against which management will have to perform their tasks in South Africa in the 1980s. How should they respond to this situation and can they influence it?

Deracializing Business

In broad terms the objective of management should be to deracialize the business environment in South Africa. Actions must be taken which are external to the corporation as well as internal. Externally, management should continue to lobby government to provide blacks with forums to air political grievances, thereby circumventing the infusion of political issues into the industrial relations system. Internally management should continue to deracialize management at the fastest possible pace.

More specifically, we should strive to implement the Sullivan Principles with vigor, not only in letter but also in spirit. The Rev. Leon Sullivan stated his intentions for the principles thus: "To promote programs which can have a significant impact on improving the living conditions and quality of life of the non-white population, and to be a major contributing factor towards the end of apartheid."[1]

But critics have observed that the principles fail to call for the elimination of pass laws, the migrant labor system, and influx control; they do nothing to promote black property rights, the right to live with one's family, equality of opportunity in education and technical training, or equal access to housing and health care.[2]

Translating the view of the critics into practice will assist business in South Africa in implementing both the spirit and the letter of these principles.

Changes can occur in three areas: the workplace, local communities, and the country in general. Prerequisites for successful social change are, first, a strong and articulated commitment from U.S. management on the subject, and second, an imaginative and determined implementation at the local level.

In the workplace and the community, the most urgent needs of the majority population exist in the fields of housing, education, and training. The problems in these and other areas arise from laws, from attitudes and from resource scarcities.

A major first step for companies has to be that of facing up to and doing something about white employee attitudes, especially among supervisors. Several companies have already initiated and made considerable headway with training programs to improve interpersonal communication with emphasis on company-oriented interracial issues. This is a tough area to deal with, because historical tensions are increased by the threat whites perceive in the increasing number of skilled blacks in the workplace. However, if people can learn to treat one another with dignity and respect within the workplace, they may recognize that it is possible to do so outside the workplace as well. Employers should also address the issues of minimum wage levels, union recognition, training, and the other grievances that give rise to unrest on the shop floor. Furthermore, workers should be involved in decisions on these and other issues that affect them at their level of operation.

Housing. Companies can put pressure on administrative boards and the central government to make more land available for housing and supporting facilities for black people. On the question of infrastructure, the companies can commit themselves to providing some part of the roads, electricity, sewage, and other services if the government makes the land available. In the financing area, companies can provide guarantees to individual employees to secure mortgage bonds from building societies (the recognized funding institutions in South Africa) and provide low-interest loans to their employees to help them build or improve their homes.

Education. Companies can, either individually or jointly, fund the building or expansion of schools through organizations such as Teach and Read (school-building and library projects funded privately) or the Adopt-a-School programs. They can provide scholarships to black student teachers, especially in the very critical math and science areas, in addition to assisting with programs to upgrade the skills of all existing teachers in black schools. Firms can contribute to those universities, both black and white, which have black teacher and entrepreneurial training programs. Moreover, they can provide scholarships to black students to attend white schools, colleges, and universities in South Africa, which is legally permitted, as well as scholarships to study in the United States. Firms can also support the South African Institute of Race Relations, which offers scholarships, bursaries, and bridging programs and also administers these on behalf of donors.

On a more general level, companies can use their funding leverage in these areas to encourage white educational institutions, universities and others, to lower the racial barriers to blacks. This is not easy, but it has been done.

Training. To train people for jobs, companies can hire black high school graduates as trainees and provide the best of them with scholarships to technical schools or universities after a certian employment period. Firms can commit to hiring a high ratio of black apprentices in our apprentice programs and work toward rapid improvement of the black-white journeyman ratios in plants. They can hire black college students during summer vacations as temporary employees to expose them to the industry and business life.

More important, perhaps, from the industrial relations viewpoint, is the urgent need to assist with the training of trade union leadership. This training should not only focus on the running of unions, but should specifically include and emphasize basic business principles, economics, accounting systems, human relations and the principles of the free enterprise system, because the free enterprise system appears to be at risk in South Africa.

Entrepreneurship. Finally, depending on the nature of the corporation, we can commit resources to the development of black suppliers to our manufacturing operations. To stimulate the development of black entrepreneurs, such as automobile dealers or parts dealers, we can contribute resources, deposit resources in the African Bank, cooperate with the National African Federated Chamber of Commerce (NAFCOC) to help develop small black businesses and support the NAFCOC's industrial training seminars.

At the national level, in the areas of housing and education, companies can do more than they have done to press the government for amendments to the Group Areas Act, in order to ease restrictions on where blacks can live or conduct a business. We can also press the government to introduce a uniform education system, administered by a single authority, which would do more than most other things to improve the quality of black education.

Black South Africans distrust the law. Infringement is easy, and most black South Africans only come in contact with the law when they have allegedly violated it. In their judgment, therefore, the law is something that is used to punish them.

There has begun in South Africa, a public interest law firm known as the Legal Resources Center, whose purpose is to provide legal assistance to black South Africans. Despite all the inequities of South African law, black people do have some rights under those laws, which can be attained for them if they have proper legal representation. It is the function of this public interest group, and one hopes there will be many more in various cities in South Africa, to ensure that blacks who are charged with offenses receive adequate legal representation.

What companies can do, particularly American companies, is to give all the financial support possible to organizations such as this, so that in the long run black South Africans will develop the respect for law which will be necessary when the time comes for them to play a significant role in the politics of South Africa.

On the question of apartheid, we are often faced with a very complicated choice: deciding whether to work in—or outside—an existing segregated structure. Take housing, for example. Are we harming or helping if we build better houses in segregated black communities? I think we are probably helping, but wherever there is a choice, and there are areas of choice in training, education, and sports facilities, companies should use their limited resources to choose and press for an option that is multiracial rather than segregated.

In determining our own labor relations practices, it is important that we consider the government stance on this issue. In doing so, we may well remove one of our crutches, namely, the tendency among management to blame government for our own inability to innovate change.

Government is on record that it is committed to the principle of freedom of association and voluntarism, that there should be a minimum of state interference in the private employer-employee relationship. On a practical level, government is encouraging training and manpower development, especially during the current economic downturn.

Government maintains, however, that employers have been slow to implement official labor reforms and to utilize the opportunities created in the areas of industrial relations, training, productivity, and social security. Government believes it has to prod, pull, and coerce employers into taking action in these areas.

With regard to labor relations, the employer can choose to implement the most liberal and integrative options for change. Black South Africans have practically no political rights, yet they have, as of today, some trade union rights, which did not exist a couple of years ago.

Conclusion

As trade unions grow in numbers and in strength in South Africa, black workers will exercise their rights with increasing determination and to broader purpose. Continued turbulence can therefore be expected on the labor front. But labor peace will not come simply by improving wages and working conditions, on the one hand, or by hard-fisted strike-breaking action, on the other. Industrial relations must become an integrated part of a comprehensive social policy through which employers demonstrate their commitment to addressing the urgent needs of black South Africans both inside and outside the workplace.

Notes

1. *South African Outlook*, May 1979, p. 67.
2. *Ibid.*, p. 74.

4
Industry and Labor: A Trade Union Perspective

Halton Cheadle

T rade unions that have recruited and represented African workers have had a long and bitter struggle for recognition with both the state and capital. For well over fifty years since the formation of the great Industrial and Commercial Union in the early 1920s, the organization of African workers has been repeatedly and ruthlessly suppressed by both government and capital. The great surges of union activity among African workers in the 1930s, 1940s, and 1950s ended in increasingly repressive rounds of suppression. The South African Congress of Trade Unions, for twenty years the largest and most representative trade union federation of African workers, was hounded into exile in the mid-1960s by capital and the State. The open organization of African workers had become all but impossible.

The next surge of trade union activity began in the early 1970s and came of age in the Durban strikes of 1973, the largest general strike in the history of South Africa. Over 100,000 African workers over a period of two months struck for higher wages. The first of the "new" or "emergent" trade unions were formed in the wake of the strike. In May 1973 the Metal and Allied Workers Union was inaugurated, and by October 1973 the National Union of Textile Workers and the Chemical Workers Industrial Union had been formed. These three unions formed the core of the Trade Union Advisory Co-ordinating Council (TUACC), which in 1979 was the major group of unions to form the Federation of South African Trade Unions (FOSATU).

Similar developments took place in Johannesburg, with the founding of Sweet Food and Allied Workers Union; the Paper, Wood and Allied Workers Union; Engineering and Allied Workers Union; and the Building and Construction Workers Union. These unions formed the Council of Trade Unions, a loose federation that was the forerunner of the Council of Unions of South Africa (CUSA). In Port Elizabeth the

The author wishes to acknowledge Modise Khoza for his research on certain aspects of this chapter.

African United Automobile Workers was formed, and in Cape Town the all but defunct African Food and Canning Workers Union was revived.

The State's response followed the traditional pattern. By February 1974 the leadership of the recent Durban unions was placed under house arrest and banned from further trade union and other activities. The next round of leadership was banned from trade union activities two years later. From the beginning of the new cycle of unionization, the state has detained union leaders,[1] banned trade union leaders,[2] sought to persuade employers not to recognize or have dealings with the new unions, arrested and convicted thousands of workers for striking, prohibited union meetings from taking place,[3] arrested union members and officials for addressing workers in open air gatherings,[4] prohibited trade unions from receiving practical assistance from foreign trade union sources,[5] used its complex web of racial legislation to harass African members and officials, and denied African unions offices in the central business districts.[6]

The state harassment of African trade unions was matched by the hostility of capital. Workers were dismissed for trade union activities.[7] Employers installed alternate representative structures to communicate with their African workers in order to exclude or forestall African trade unions. Capital cooperated with the state in employing security police informers, passing on information on union representatives to the security police and calling in police to disperse peaceful strikes.[8] That the trade unions not only survived but extended their influence under such repression is testimony to the deep-rooted belief in trade unions among African workers and to the success of the unions' defensive strategies.

The extent and nature of the repression was one of the more important formative influences on the structure of the African unions. In order to counter the periodic removal of trade union leadership by detention and banning, these nascent unions emphasized leadership at the workplace. The disruptive effect of temporary or permanent removal of trade union leadership from head or branch offices was thereby minimized. Throughout the early years, the actual outlawing of the unions was considered to be a real possibility and the survival of the union movement in such an eventuality was premised on an organized retraction into the workplace. The accent on workplace organization also gave concrete expression to the strong democratic tradition within the African working class. The structure of the unions reflects the employee election of workplace leadership (shop stewards) and the crucial role of the shop steward in the leadership structures of the union.

Capital's hostility to the resurgence of African trade unions also contributed to the consolidation of trade union organization within the workplace. The victimization of union organizers and sympathizers made open organizing efforts all but impossible. Recruitment accordingly tended to be conducted in secret in the township and in the workplace. In most cases the presence of the union was only brought to the attention of the employer once a majority of workers had been organized and individual victimization by the employer was often frustrated thereby. In more hostile employer environments, the unions seized control of the works committees, specifically established by the state in order to preempt the formation of trade unions for African workers. Ironically, the state's promotion of a system of plant-based worker committees for African workers and employers' enthusiastic implementation thereof contributed to the tradition of plant-based bargaining from which both the State and certain employers are now endeavoring to extricate themselves.

Forged as they are in such different circumstances, these new unions have sought to structure their unions differently from the unions in the United Kingdom, Europe, and the United States. In certain instances the union structures formally incorporate shop steward leadership. For instance in the FOSATU unions, the constitutional structure ensures that the supreme executive body of the Union comprises workers' representatives only, the officials of the union attend *ex officio*, without voting rights. This executive is drawn from representatives of the different branch executives of the union which include a number of shop stewards from each workplace in the branch. The branch representatives are in turn appointed by the shop stewards committee in the workplace, and members of the shop stewards committee are elected by the general body of workers.

This emphasis on workplace organization and democratic unionism was a major influence in the collective bargaining practices of the new unions. African workers had, since the inception of the statutory collective bargaining system with the passage of the Industrial Conciliation Act in 1924, been excluded from participation in the industrial councils, statutory collective bargaining forums, comprising an equal number of registered union representatives and employer representatives for a particular bargaining unit, which was usually industrial or occupational in nature. Trade unions that organized African workers were not permitted to register until 1979, because registration was denied to unions that recruited persons other than "employees," and "employee" was defined under successive Industrial Conciliation Acts so as to exclude Africans. Such unions were accordingly excluded from participation in industrial councils and the other machinery for settlement of disputes provided by the Act. The exclusion from the statutory collective bargaining system, the accent on workplace organization, the relatively few factories organized all combined to shape an alternative tradition of collective bargaining. The new unions sought to arrange their collective bargaining relations primarily at the level of the workplace, explicitly incorporating the shop steward as the central actor in such arrangements.

The first demand for a formal recognition agreement was made by the three-month-old National Union of Textile Workers and the Textile Workers Industrial Union at Smith and Nephew, an English multinational firm located outside of Durban. In 1974 the unions and the company negotiated and entered into the first recognition agreement. The draft proposal submitted by the unions was drawn from the existing contract between the United Auto Workers and the Ford Motor Company in the United States and a contract between the United Steelworkers and an American steel company. The agreement included formal recognition of the unions, the election of union shop stewards, a grievance procedure, a dismissal procedure, a negotiation procedure for wages and other conditions of employment, an arbitration procedure, a peace obligation, and various trade union facilities.

Much of what was negotiated in the Smith and Nephew agreement has come to be standard in recognition agreements today, such as formal recognition and grievance procedures, dismissal procedures, and peace obligations. The first major development therefore was to separate the recognition and procedural agreement from agreements on terms and conditions of employment such as wages and hours of work. Without the support of a statutory duty to recognize a representative union in an appropriate bargaining unit, as is found in the U.S. National Labor Relations Act, bargaining arises solely from the employer's agreement to do so.[9] To give effect and content to that duty, the tradition has developed in South Africa whereby the long-term constitutional arrangements for collective bargaining between an employer and the union are negotiated separately from and in most cases prior to the negotiation of substantive agreements on terms and conditions of employment. The recognition agreement is generally concluded for an indefinite duration, terminable on good cause for a breach of the agreement or upon loss of representativeness.[10]

It is estimated that there are some 500 recognition agreements now in existence covering over 150,000 workers. So much has this new system of collective bargaining taken root that the director general of the Department of Manpower has gone on record as saying that this form of collective bargaining has become an integral part of industrial relations in South Africa.[11] The industrial court has given its imprimatur for this development by ordering employers to enter into recognition agreements,[12] albeit with their consent, and in a number of cases ordering employers to negotiate or at least consult representative trade unions before engaging in a retrenchment exercise.[13] The amendments proposed to the Labor Relations Act in 1984 specifically address themselves to such agreements by requiring copies to be lodged with the Department of Manpower and by endeavoring to get unregistered trade unions to comply with the constitutional and administrative provisions of the Act by making the enforceability of such agreements dependent upon compliance with those provisions.

Many employers, as is evident from the number of agreements concluded, have responded positively to the development of a collective bargaining system that is responsive to the needs and aspirations of African unions. Many employers, however, have resisted and tried to obstruct not only this form of collective bargaining but also unionization of the work force itself. Among them rank several prominent U.S. multinationals, all highly rated Sullivan Code signatories.

The traditional, although decreasingly common, response is to refuse recognition. There are several variants on this refusal. The first is premised on an explicitly antiunion policy such as is evident in corporations such as IBM and Motorola. Motorola, for instance, refused to recognize the Metal and Allied Workers Union after it had acquired a majority representation at one of its establishments, on the grounds that it did not recognize trade unions anywhere in the world, including the United States. The implications of resisting trade unions in South Africa are different from those that might be applicable elsewhere. First, a company's refusal to recognize African unions, even if it does not affect the company's own investment, will certainly lead to stepped-up calls for the withdrawal of all U.S. companies. Second, trade unions are one of the few legal and legitimate organizations open to African workers and—with the ballot box denied—represent one of the only direct levers to the machinery of government. The refusal to recognize a trade union is therefore a political act. It is viewed by African workers and the African community as an act of political oppression. Third, because of the political dimensions of the struggle for recognition, large-scale community and international support, whether in the form of boycotts or public outcry, is real and ready to be translated into concrete action within a very short time.

Another variant of the refusal to recognize a representative trade union is the practice of setting conditions to recognition such as prior registration of the union or prior membership of an industrial council. Registration of trade unions is still a controversial issue. Until 1979, when the state began to introduce its labor reforms, registration was open only to trade unions that did not have African workers as members. When the state permitted the registration of unions that recruited

African workers, almost all the African unions refused to register, on the grounds that the labor reforms excluded migrant workers (that is, workers, who because of the state's policy of influx control, are not permitted by the reforms to reside permanently in the urban areas). When this restriction on migrant workers was lifted, many unions registered on condition that the terms of registration would not be accorded on a racial basis. It was only after lengthy litigation in the Supreme Court that the right to nonracial registration was won.[14] Throughout this period of uncertainty and controversy, the U.S. multinational Colgate-Palmolive refused to recognize the then unregistered Chemical Workers Industrial Union (CWIU) until it had complied with the law governing the registration of trade unions. Registration is and was voluntary. There was no statutory obligation to register. Colgate's insistence on registration was—in the context of the larger controversy over registration—seen as an endorsement of government policy in general and racial registration in particular. This celebrated recognition dispute was finally resolved after the institution of a countrywide boycott of Colgate products, the support of the international trade secretariate, the International Chemical Union Federation, the threat of an international boycott, and the institution of a legal strike that would have had widespread community and trade union support had the company not agreed to recognize the CWIU at the last moment.

This particular line of resistance is no longer pervasive, since the major South African corporations, such as Barlow-Rand and Anglo-American, have agreed to recognize and negotiate with representative trade unions irrespective of whether the union is registered or not.

The employers' participation in the industrial council system is often used as a basis for rejecting the advances by a union for recognition at the level of the establishment. The industrial council system is a system of statutory collective bargaining institutions for different industries or parts of industries in different areas. The industrial council includes an equal number of representatives from the trade union party and the employer party. The council, whose funds are levied from employers and employees in the industry, normally employs staff to administer the council and its funds and inspectors to monitor the agreements entered into between the trade unions and the employer representatives on the council. The agreement is made binding not only upon the parties to the agreement but to all nonparties as well. This is effected by the promulgation of the agreement as a regulation to the Labor Relations Act.

The industrial council system excluded the participation of the African workers since its inception. Restricted to white, "colored," and Indian workers, these collective bargaining institutions became over time unrepresentative of the work force. For instance, in the Industrial Council for the Iron, Steel, Engineering and Metallurgical Industry, trade union parties represented less than 20 percent of the workers in the industry immediately prior to the labor reforms introduced in 1979. In the Industrial Council for the Transvaal Knitting Industry, the trade union party represented less than 1 percent of the workers in that industry in 1979. Their sectional and unrepresentative nature has led African workers to view these councils with considerable suspicion, although some of this suspicion appears to be abating as more and more the African unions are now entering industrial councils and transforming them into more representative and credible forums for collective bargaining.

The industrial council is invariably a multiemployee bargaining unit, and employer insistence that collective bargaining take place only at the industrial council overlooks the different nature of bargaining at the level of the establishment and bargaining at the level of the industry. Bargaining at the level of the industry is primarily the regulation of minimum terms and conditions of employment, thus setting a statutory floor to competition among employers and workers in the same industry. One of the peculiarities of labor law in South Africa has been the use of collective bargaining agreements as the basis of minimum wage regulation. Industrial council agreements are extended by ministerial notice to employers and workers not party to that agreement but within the industrial scope of the council. Bargaining at the level of the establishment, while it may not set terms and conditions of service less favorable to employees than the minimum set down by the industrial council agreement, seeks to establish the *actual* as opposed to the *minimum* wages and working conditions applicable to that establishment. Wage bargaining at the level of the industrial council will seek to redress the loss of income caused by inflation and in some cases to seek to improve the standard of living. On the other hand, wage bargaining at the level of the establishment will concern itself with arguments specific to the productivity and profitability of the establishment itself. This argument is all the more compelling at those establishments where there is a history of the employer paying more than the minimum wages prescribed by the industrial council agreement. This is the nub of the present dispute between the Metal and Allied Workers Union, and the U.S. multinational McKinnon Chain. While the company is prepared to recognize the union and grant it facilities, it refuses to bargain with the union in respect of wages and working conditions because wages and working conditions are determined by the Industrial Council for the Iron, Steel, Engineering, and Metallurgical Industry, notwithstanding the fact that the company has historically paid over and above the minimum level set by industrial council agreement.[15]

This refusal to countenance dual bargaining is at odds with the growing realization that the new tradition of bargaining at the level of the establishment can be complementary to bargaining at the level of the industry through the institution of the industrial council. Piet van der Merwe, the Director-General of the Department of Manpower, has recognized these developments and stated:

> Collective bargaining is, furthermore, going to grow as a result of the voluntary recognition of trade unions by employers in terms of bipartite agreements, as opposed to "compulsory recognition" where statutory provisions oblige employers to recognize a registered union under certain conditions.
>
> I believe that there is going to be a particularly fast growth of collective bargaining at the level of the enterprise whether we like it or not, and this is going to give rise to a number of new problems, particularly problems of union multiplicity, inter-union conflict and coordination.
>
> Levels of collective bargaining are, in future, going to be determined very largely by the objectives of emergent trade unions, and by internal and external pressures on individual employers to recognize, for bargaining purposes, any organization which is representative of all or a particular group of workers employed by them. At the present moment, there are clear indications that a number of trade unions favor enterprise-level bargaining above industry-level bargaining through the Industrial Council system, and that a growing number of employers are entering into recognition agreements. In this regard, I need to emphasize that the Government has committed itself to a policy of nonintervention in the regulation of labor relations including reciprocal recognition agreements between employers and employees...
>
> It may be necessary for us, therefore, to closely examine our hitherto strong preference for industry-level bargaining, to come to grips with reality and to recognize the need for and the advantages of bargaining at the level of the undertaking in certain circumstances. At the same time, we should examine in what ways enterprise-level bargaining may be structured to complement industry-level bargaining instead of replacing it, and in what way the disadvantages of enterprise-level bargaining can be minimized.[16]

There is a prevailing assumption among multinational companies that their collective bargaining experiences elsewhere can be imported and applied in South Africa, without recognizing some of the peculiarities of the South African industrial relations environment. The U.S. multinational, Dresser South Africa, called upon its industrial relations director in the United States to assist in the negotiations with the Metal and Allied Workers Union over recognition. The company's draft agreement reflected Dresser's own experience and bargaining structures in the United States. The language was technical, the procedures long and complex. It excluded what it termed "sensitive personnel" such as staff, security personnel, time-keepers, and foremen. This exclusion is, in the South African context, often counterproductive. Very often it is from this strata of employees that many trade unions draw their leadership. In the context of the widespread illiteracy among workers, this leadership often plays a crucial role in the initial stages.

Sophisticated agreements with exact delineations of bargaining units, like the agreements common in the United States, are the product of a long history of collective bargaining, which over time has broadly established the accepted contours of bargaining and bargaining units. What Alec Erwin, the former general secretary of the Federation of South African Trade Unions, has said about wage bargaining is generally applicable: "In contrast to the highly sophisticated bargaining in the advanced industrial countries, based on productivity measures, manning levels and a host of other factors, bargaining in South Africa is stark, brutal and concerned with a living wage."[17] It is not possible to suppress wage bargaining for decades and then in a matter of a few short years expect the new unions to join companies in a sophisticated wage bargaining that ignores the very specific environment of South Africa.

It is a common occurrence to find an absolute prohibition on industrial action in company recognition proposals. Such a proposal ignores the fact that having been excluded from collective bargaining until recently, the tradition of self-help in the form of sporadic and wildcat strikes will die hard. The proper response is to recognize that strikes will occur and to develop credible procedures, which will, in time, provide a more consistent and effective method of resolving disputes.

While there might be a large measure of consensus in Europe and the United States as to what is negotiable and what is not, in South Africa there is no such consensus. Attempts to predetermine the contours of collective bargaining will simply produce a collective bargaining arrangement that is not responsive to the industrial relations environment within which it is to function. There are dimensions to collective bargaining in South Africa which are not reproducible elsewhere. Africans do not have the franchise. The alternative of changing the conditions of employment through the ballot box is denied them. Accordingly African trade unions cannot do what their U.S. and U.K. counterparts do when they fail to achieve their goals through collective bargaining, namely use their political power to effect their goals through legislation.

More matters must be dealt with by collective bargaining in South Africa, not fewer. Safety, housing, benefits, pensions, and social welfare all fall within the ambit of what is negotiable in South Africa. To insist that the managerial prerogative to hire should not be subject to the scrutiny of the trade union overlooks the fact that there is no legislation prohibiting racial discrimination in employment (and it is unlikely that such legislation will be considered while Africans are denied the franchise). Moreover, there is, in South Africa, a well-established tradition in management to use the racist social structure as a means of managing the firm. Foremen and managers are often appointed not because they are skilled but because they are white, and thus the organization on the shop floor and in the enterprise as a whole reproduces the social structure of domination in society. It is legitimate for the African workers to combat this form of racial discriminiation by compelling employees not to adopt discriminatory policies.

The balance struck between the employers' prerogative to dismiss and the workers' interest in job security in other jurisdictions does not take into account the fact that for African migrant workers, the loss of a job also means a loss of his right to reside in the urban area, the loss of the ability to find other employment in the area, the immediate uprooting of himself and his belongings and the abrupt departure from the urban area within seventy-two hours of his dismissal. The catastrophic consequences of dismissal starkly reveal why job security is at a premium in the South African context. Not to take this into account and not to realize that the balance between the respective interests elsewhere will be different from the balance struck in South Africa is myopic.

Because of the state's failure to provide sufficient proper housing and the pressure on multinationals to engage in social responsibility programs, many multinationals have started to provide limited housing for their employees. While the managers of these companies may decide to engage in such programs for diverse reasons, workers in the companies, the beneficiaries, wish to have a say in such policies. They wish to have a say in how much of the company's resources should be allocated for such programs, the type of assistance, the kind of housing. One company, in line with its commitment to the Sullivan Code, decided to build a few quality houses, which would have been too expensive and out of reach of the ordinary workers, the beneficiaries who need such housing most. The workers argued for assistance to improve their existing homes and the purchase or construction of low-cost houses for those that did not have homes.

African trade unions have grown spectacularly since 1973 and have recruited an estimated 100,000 workers. There is no evidence that this growth will decline, indeed everything points to their increasing size, influence and power. These unions will be a significant force for change in South Africa. Already they have forced the state to retract from the initial qualified admission of Africans to the statutory industrial relations system. They have forced it to remove every reference to race in the Labor Relations Act. They have forced the government through widespread strikes to withdraw a pensions statute. While the exercise of trade union power, where the membership does not have the vote, tends to be reactive, these trade unions promise to be a major force in the dismantling of apartheid and the creation of a democratic society in South Africa.

Notes

1. *Survey of Race Relations in South Africa 1982* (Johannesburg: South African Institute of Race Relations, 1983). (Twenty-three trade unionists were detained in South Africa by the South African government in 1981, plus 266 more in Ciskei; 15 in South Africa, plus 5 in Ciskei in 1982; and by September 1983, 9 in South Africa and 22 in Ciskei.)

2. See, e.g., *South African Labour Bulletin* 5, no. 2 (1979):77 (an estimated 30 trade unionists were banned between the years 1973 and 1977); *Survey of Race Relations 1980* (Johannesburg: South African Institute of Race Relations, 1981), p. 91 (ten senior journalist members of the Media Workers Association of South Africa were banned in 1981); *Survey of Race Relations 1981* (Johannesburg: South African Institute of Race Relations, 1982), p. 259 (four trade unionists, office bearers, and officials of the Motor Assembly and Component Workers Union of South Africa were banned in 1982).

3. See magistrates' powers under the Riotous Assemblies Act, Act 17 of 1956, and the Internal Security Act, Act 74 of 1982.

4. See *Survey of Race Relations in South Africa 1981* (Johannesburg: South African Institute of Race Relations, 1982), p. 187 (1982 arrest of Taffy Adler, official of the National Automobile and Allied Workers Union, for recruiting workers at a bus stop); *Rand Daily Mail*, February 24, 1984 (February 1984 arrest of "Skakes" Sikhakhane, general secretary of Food Beverages Workers Union, for attending a gathering of workers on strike in order to get information from the workers for the purpose of making representations to the company).

5. See Fund Raising Act 107 of 1978.

6. See the (Johannesburg) *Star*, December 14, 1981 (the General Workers Union, the African Food and Canning Workers Union, and the South African and Allied Workers Union were evicted from office premises on the grounds that as African unions they were not permitted to take offices without a permit in the central business district that is zoned for white occupation only).

7. There are innumerable allegations to this effect, but the victimization cases in the South African Supreme Court stand as testimony to this practice. *Kubhekha v. Imextra (Pty) Ltd* 1975 (4) SA 484(T); *Piet Bosman Transport Committee v. P E Bosman Transport Company* 1979 (1) SA 389(T); *Maponya v. A Mauchle t/a Precision Tools (Pty) Ltd* (unreported); *Metal & Allied Workers Union and Another v. A Mauchle t/a Precision Tools (Pty) Ltd., International Law Journal* 1, part 3 (1980):227; *Makhanya v. Bailey* No. 1980(4) SA 713.

8. From the figures drawn from the *Survey of Race Relations* for the years 1973 to 1982, the police have intervened in strikes approximately 1,386 times.

9. There are indications that the industrial court is moving toward imposing such a duty where no other collective bargaining structure (such as an industrial council) exists. See *United African Automobile and Allied Workers v. Fodens (Pty) Ltd., International Law Journal* 4 (1983):212.

10. In *Bleazard v Argus Publishing Company and Others, ILJ* 4, part 1 (1983):60, the industrial court held that unless there was good cause an employer could not withdraw from a collective bargaining agreement.

11. *Supplement to Weekly Bulletin*, no. 48, December 3, 1981, pp. 2–3.

12. *National Union of Textile Workers v. Braitex* (unreported, 1983); *Foden's case* (above).

13. *Foden's case* (above); *Metal and Allied Workers Union v. Stobar Reinforcing (Pty) Ltd and Another, International Law Journal* 4, part 1 (1983):84.

14. *Metal and Allied Workers Union and others v. Minister of Manpower Utilization and others* 1983 SA 238 NPD.

15. *Rand Daily Mail*, April 2, 1984.

16. Quoted from a speech to Anglo-American.

17. Author's notes.

5
Corporations and Urban Community Development

Griffiths Zabala

E ffective community development programs are urgently needed to address the problems facing black communities in the urban areas of South Africa. Because vast numbers of both private and public organizations involved in community development already exist within the urban areas of South Africa, a critical question is the extent to which these organizations achieve their goals. This chapter examines the constraints within which such organizations operate and the conditions that affect their success or failure. From the depressing array of difficulties facing black urban communities in South Africa, the key areas of education, housing, and employment are chosen as the primary focus.

When we consider the possibility of involvement by U.S. firms in community development, we must be aware of the current attitude of these communities toward American firms, for this attitude will crucially affect the reception and ultimately the effectiveness of any program that is undertaken. There is a growing consensus among urban blacks in South Africa that community development is a palliative rather than a problem-solving strategy. The United States in general and U.S. corporations in particular are more and more regarded as the enemy by the majority of urban blacks. At a time when blacks, as consumers and workers, are gaining increasing influence in the South African economy—and demonstrating increasing militance—this is a problem that firms can ill afford to ignore.

Community Development Defined

Community development, in the best sense, consists of indigenous groups working collectively and individually to improve their quality of life. Thus, effective community development in the urban areas of South Africa involves the following:

1. Community change through participation by a wide spectrum of people at the local level
2. Economic and social progress for the whole community
3. Mobilization of people directly affected by a problem
4. Leadership development and community education

Examining these four criteria reveals that effective community development means building a solid foundation for democracy.

Urban blacks face myriad problems that could be addressed through community development programs. The initial problem in providing such assistance is that the current South African government will not permit effective community development programs except through the so-called national states or homelands. First, the government fears change which it cannot control. Second, the government has stifled black efforts that conflicted with their own initiatives. Black initiatives are seen only as subversive and never as promoting social and economic progress in the community. The only acceptable type of community development is "separate development" with emphasis on *separate* and not on development.

Of course, the community problems facing urban blacks in South Africa are so varied and complex that a single strategy of community development can be only part of an overall solution. A broader approach encompassing social action and social planning is ultimately necessary for sustained progress. But the foundations for such an approach can be laid now through the development of specific, well-focused programs of community assistance.

Constraints on Community Development in South Africa

The major agents for community development in both urban and rural areas of South Africa are associated either with the government or with churches. Government activities, through the Department of Cooperation and Development, lack both the credibility and the resources to facilitate changes and encourage community participation. Churches lack the resources to build the structures that would facilitate community development and are unable to get government support to do so. Neither of these existing channels adequately serves the needs of American firms that wish to contribute to community development.

A second difficulty stems from the uncertain status of blacks in urban areas of South Africa. Any community worker or sponsor of any project wants to know the impact of his or her input to a situation. This impact surely depends on a number of things, including: the manner in which it will affect existing social structures, the permanency of the achieved results, and the extent of improvement that will be achieved in measurable terms.

The success of any community development project will therefore depend crucially on the stability of the community being assisted. Current South African government policy undermines community stability. Under the guiding policy of "separate development," urban areas are reserved exclusively for the white population. In the last several years the government has pursued an aggressive and merciless policy of resettlement. This policy is aimed at eliminating the so-called black spots—black communities located in what has been declared white territory—by forced removals of black families to the barren reservations called "homelands."

The structure of the South African economy limits the effectiveness of community development. South Africa is often described as a "dual economy," representing the characteristics of both developed and underdeveloped countries. The line between developed and underdeveloped parts of South Africa is a racial one. The benefits of industrialization have accrued exclusively to the white metropolitan areas of Pretoria-Johannesburg, Cape Town, Port Elizabeth, and Durban-Pinetown. The abundant cheap labor of black workers has clearly been crucial to the rapid industrialization, but influx control and the use of migrant labor have sharply restricted the benefits received by black workers. Given that the availability of cheap labor is undeniably an attractive feature (at least in the short run) of operating in South Africa, the question is whether such firms will undertake community development projects that promote structural changes or simply those that add window dressing to the status quo.

Urban Needs and Problems for Community Development

Community development is an attempt by the people themselves to eradicate the social ills of society. For this to happen, the people must identify their problems, work out solutions to the problems, and implement those solutions.

The urban communities have made numerous attempts at organizing themselves and have in the process of identifying their problems come up with different interpretations of the causes of these problems. These differing interpretations are often the product of ideological differences. There do exist, however, commonly identified needs arising from the root causes of the difficulties that plague the urban people and indeed South African blacks in general. Any meaningful progress in South Africa will require a greater degree of self-awareness and self-reliance among blacks. This can come only through investment in education, housing, and employment.

Education

Effective community development requires that people be able to understand their own situation, identify problems, and work out solutions to these problems. Education is therefore central to any such effort. Yet, it is common knowledge that South Africa's education system is "racially and culturally" biased and that blacks receive inferior education designed to make them servants for the whites and not to become self-assertive. The system of education for blacks allows them only differential access to the economy. Since the 1976 riots, black education has been superficially improved. The salaries of black teachers have increased slightly and more beautiful school buildings have been built in Soweto, but the quality of education has not changed.

Education therefore remains one of the most serious needs in black communities within South Africa. Estimated per capita expenditure including capital expenditure for 1983 was R1385 for whites, R872 for Indians, R593 for "coloreds" and R192 for blacks. The pupil/teacher ratios for the same year were whites 1:18, Indians 1:24, coloreds 1:27, blacks, 1:43.[1] It is still common within Soweto to find a class with 60 to 70 black pupils taught by one teacher. Illiteracy, which is not uncommon among blacks in urban areas, is even worse in rural areas (see appendix A). This state of affairs inhibits the process of community development by which people solve their own problems.

The extent to which the education system designed for blacks affects their roles and assertiveness in work situations, as well as their job opportunities is ghastly. J. Butler, training manager for the Barlow-Rand Group, has stated that because of lack of literacy, "many workers could not understand negotiating skills, nor represent other workers on committees or works councils."[2] Industrial organization in South Africa is still highly bureaucratic. Because they are better educated, whites are in supervisory and management positions. Blacks, however, occupy more routinized jobs since they lack the education necessary to be managers. It is not a surprise therefore that the number of blacks in managerial positions remained at 3 percent in 1981.[3]

Housing

The single worst problem facing the South African urban black is housing. Various factors account for this problem, including:

Population increase;

Rapid inflow of people from outside areas to the urban centers seeking jobs irrespective of government policy;

Lack of finances for self-built housing;

Lack of infrastructure for housing in urban areas;

Lack of land;

Legal constraints.

These factors together have increased the cost of housing for blacks and have also lessened the quality of life for the people in urban areas. Squatter settlements have sprung up around every major metropolitan area in South Africa, but as the incidents of Crossroads, Inyanga, Inanda, and other such areas point out, such areas cannot provide a long-term solution to the housing needs that exist within the urban areas. Effective community development must therefore address itself to this problem.

Employment and Unemployment

The urban areas of South Africa carry the hope and promise of jobs and an end to unemployment. Since 1977 unemployment has been repeatedly estimated at about two million blacks, or between 16 and 20 percent. The problem is made worse by the increasing flow of blacks from the homelands to the urban areas.

Each of the problems creates others. The enormous caseloads that confront the social worker, be they marriage disputes, juvenile delinquency, crime (often reported so widely and in bold letters in South African newspapers), point to nothing else except the absence of jobs, poor housing conditions, and lack of education that should enable people to evolve their own means of survival.

Legislation preventing the development of black entrepreneurs, specifically the Group Areas Act, adds to this mess. Even where black effort has been started, the infrastructures for developing black business did not exist (until recently through the National African Chamber of Commerce and the African Bank). This state of affairs has significantly increased black unemployment. Programs to redress this situation through community development are urgently needed.

Support from U.S. Firms

Programs to address the three major problems of education, housing, and employment urgently need the active support of U.S. corporations.

Education

Education unlocks the capacities of people. For this reason, support of education should be a high priority for U.S. firms. Since a large number of people drop out of schools, both formal and informal education must be supported in order to increase the literacy of the black population in the urban areas of South Africa and indeed the rest of South Africa. Although increasing literacy and numeracy through adult education centers needs attention, education for survival—skills and technical training among the adults—needs very special attention.

The shortage of skilled labor is one of the most pressing problems facing the South African economy. The support for university training and technical college training for blacks must be increased. The fact that only 2 to 4 percent of blacks occupy professional and skilled jobs while over two thousand vacancies exist in these categories demonstrates the extent of the problem. Priority in education and training should emphasize human development rather than simply the erection of new buildings. Scarce resources can reach more people if they are spent upgrading existing buildings and using them to their fullest potential.

Housing

Having discussed the enormous housing backlog in urban areas and the related causes and consequences, namely, population size, income distribution, scale of urbanization, and skill distribution, what remains to be discussed is how this need could be met.

Businesses have undertaken significant efforts to redress this situation. Despite these efforts, increasing numbers of blacks cannot afford even minimal housing. In general, U.S. firms should not only set aside funds to assist their own employees with housing but should also assist in the development of sites and services, especially for the disadvantaged members of our community.

At present the loans allocated, whether for ninety-nine-year lease or thirty-year lease, are like a step ladder dangling in the air with no one able to reach the lowest rung. Only a very small percentage of the population that needs housing is reached. Providing better housing for the upper income level so as to create openings in the lower levels has not succeeded, and the housing problem continues to worsen.

U.S. firms interested in redressing these ills can do two things. First, they can encourage cooperative self-help housing. Second, they can pay salaries that will enable people, irrespective of their position in the firm, to afford decent housing.

Unemployment and the Informal Sector

Since industry cannot generate enough jobs and since the cost per job created in industry is so high, alternative means to create jobs must be found. The outcry of support for the informal sector and the development of black entrepreneurs has received little hearing so far. Attempts to promote black entrepreneurship have been made by various firms through their social service programs and public relations programs. Most of these efforts, however, seem to have been done for public relations purposes only, and not from genuine concern for uplifting the community. But if unemployment is to be reduced, home industries must develop, markets for the informal sector must be strengthened, and the skills of people must be upgraded.

Through involvement with informal sector self-help groups over the past six years I have observed that great potential exists within the informal sector for self-reliance, but this potential is greatly curbed by the fact that people lack sufficient skills to carry out their objectives. Where people have those skills, lack of financial resources to carry out their work remains an obstacle. Management expertise is wanting because of the lack of literacy, which led, in the first place, to the people being unskilled workers. The informal sector needs better markets as well as a better understanding of marketing. Finally, the continued harassment by the local authorities of people active in the informal sector poses a serious threat to its existence.

If this situation is to be redressed, U.S. firms must help support activities that will encourage the existence and growth of the informal sector. These activities could include:

Lobbying for legislation granting legal recognition to the informal sector;

Supporting and building up skills training programs for people in the informal sector and actively participating in the upgrading of these skills consistent with market demands;

Developing and setting up financial houses solely to support activities of the informal sector;

Developing and creating within South Africa's own industry possible markets for the informal sector;

Encouraging the development of new small businesses by setting up skills training programs that meet specific industry needs and encouraging groups of trainees to form their own firms with which corporations can then contract for particular jobs;

Accrediting workers in the informal sector as a way to increase both their self-image and their productivity. (This requires that firms recognize the skills and inputs that the informal sector can provide by creating markets as well as opportunities within their own industries.);

Supporting training within labor movements and encouraging such labor movements and their recognition by U.S. companies irrespective of whether they are "registered" or "unregistered" as a necessary step to facilitate better industrial relations.

If U.S. firms are seriously committed to addressing the problem of urban black unemployment, they should seriously consider these activities.

Conclusion

Although the policies of the South African government present imposing obstacles, U.S. corporations can play a meaningful role in promoting community development of urban blacks in South Africa. The choice facing U.S. firms and the U.S. government, however, may seem like a choice between the devil and the deep blue sea. The types of projects that will most easily impress shareholders in America or please the South African government will not, in general, be those most helpful to the black urban community.

True community development involves the participation of community members and promotes structural change leading to self-sufficiency. For this reason, firms that act in the best interests of black South Africans may find it difficult to demonstrate to outsiders that they have made important contributions: true community development does not produce impressive buildings or other tangible signs of progress. Instead, it produces intangible progress: a populace that is educated, employed, and self-governing.

If U.S. firms wish to promote genuine community development in South Africa, they must be willing to identify themselves with black interests. Corporations can best do this by working through the informal sector to improve the educational, housing, and employment opportunities of blacks. By proceeding in this way, U.S. corporations will become partners of blacks in the process of community development rather than merely charitable donors. For the true spirit of community development lies not only in the advancement of blacks, but also in the participation of blacks in the advancement process itself.

Notes

1. *Survey of Race Relations in South Africa 1983* (Johannesburg: South African Institute of Race Relations, 1984), p. 420.

2. *The Star* (Johannesburg), May 15, 1981.

3. *Survey of Race Relations in South Africa 1981* (Johannesburg: South African Institute of Race Relations, 1982), p. 214.

6
Corporations and Rural Development

Oscar Dhlomo

Multinational Corporations and the Third World

One of the things that makes our world so complicated—albeit interesting at times—is the fact that almost every human activity can be judged at different levels. War is a tragic phenomenon, wasteful of human resources and brutalizing of man's spirit. But at another level, a just war is a powerful solidifying agent that binds populations together and produces patriotic fervor and great motivation for self-sacrifice.

One has to look at international trade and multinational corporations in the same way: at different levels. Multinational investment in a Third World country brings expertise to that country and usually introduces new training methods and skills. Depending on the type of activity one is considering, multinational corporations spread the effects of powerful modern technology and machines, allowing new resources to be tapped in developing countries. They also help to bind Third World countries into the international community.

Yet, at another level, multinational corporations have some very unfortunate effects. A powerful multinational corporation usually brings to a Third World country management skills that are superior to those of existing operations in that society. Multinationals have greater reserves of capital and can weather slack periods with greater ease. Quite often they bring highly efficient labor-saving technology that allows them to pay high wages to relatively few employees. They are often less prone to labor unrest than less well-established local companies. For these reasons they are better able to compete in the marketplace than local companies. In fact, if their policy so inclines, they can buy out local companies, thereby leading to monopoly or near-monopoly formations. Furthermore, they often bring in expatriate management, closing off avenues for advancement for local managers.

At still another level, that of international trade, multinational operations can create large and profitable markets for certain local Third

World products. Local producers will concentrate on these products. The local governments, anxious for foreign exchange, will encourage such concentration. As a consequence, local production becomes less and less diversified, making the Third World country more and more vulnerable to international market fluctuations. Some local economies have in this way become less and less able to feed the local populations.

Hence the ultimate effects of some multinational operations is to distort local economies, to increase the dependency of the societies on the international economy, and to raise unrealistic expectations among the local labor force.

Thus, in terms of the benefits they have bestowed on Third World countries, the balance sheet of multinational operations presents a very mixed picture indeed. Depending on the level at which one chooses to consider multinational corporations and trade, one can reach very different conclusions about the desirability of their presence in Third World countries. Bearing this in mind, one should avoid hasty judgments of multinationals, and consider all the levels of effect. A Third World leadership must try to sort the good from the bad. It must try to encourage the benefits and reduce or limit the distorting effects. Often this is very difficult, because some effects are long-term and indirect and therefore difficult to predict. Nevertheless, a Third World leader, in the light of the accumulated experience, must take a strong stand on the issue of multinationals, however difficult that may be.

The theme of this chapter is that multinational corporations must operate in close collaboration with local planning for development. They may extract their benefits but in return must assist the local societies in countering at least some of the ill-effects of their operations in that society. In this way a real partnership for development is possible—an interplay between national and multinational endeavors.

The Situation in South Africa

In South Africa the role of multinationals in the local economy is much more complicated than the one I have described for the Third World generally. In South Africa the less-developed regions of the country are the equivalent of the less-developed societies of the Third World. These less-developed regions are the rural areas of the so-called homelands, or "national states" as they are referred to in the policy of "separate development."

These so-called homelands are in fact the depressed regions in our common economy. As numerous studies, including the Buthelezi Commission, have noted, rural areas have been excluded from the growth of industrial infrastructure and physical plant in the so-called white or common areas of the country. The lack of infrastructure makes the task of rural development a painfully slow and expensive process.

Furthermore, the developed areas of the country act like a suction, drawing away most of the trained manpower and able-bodied labor to work as migrants in major industrial cities like Durban and the Witwatersrand. Typically, we find in our rural areas that only women, children, and the least productive men remain behind.

Therefore, the rural areas of South Africa, within which the "homelands" are situated, are subject to many of the same economic distortions that Third World territories experience. To make matters worse, some rural areas of South Africa are in immediate juxtaposition to thriving industrial and commercial regions, which lure away skilled manpower and consumer spending. For example, research has revealed that most of the money earned by people who live in KwaZulu, where I come from, is spent outside its boundaries.

This is one major reason why we in KwaZulu resist the idea of independence from the Republic of South Africa. The goals of separate development imply that the black regions must all eventually become sovereign states. The major purpose behind this policy is to remove our right to South African citizenship and end our rightful claims to participation in the political and economic life of the country as a whole. Through independence, the South African government wishes to deflect our claims to citizenship and voting rights in the common society.

We, however, know that the most basic concern of the people we lead is to maintain and strengthen their rights and opportunities in the rich economy and developed society of South Africa as a whole. We dare not sell out the citizenship of our people. Furthermore, we do not wish to become yet another Third World economy, struggling vainly to counteract the distorting effects of complete dependence on the major developed centers. We are part of South Africa and we are determined to share fully in its growth.

Notwithstanding the fact that we are and will remain an integral part of South Africa, the reality is that we live in a depressed region of the country. Even if a majority government were to come to power in South Africa tomorrow, the leaders of that government would still have to grapple with the problems of rural underdevelopment. Our regional KwaZulu government and administration therefore have a particular responsibility to make sure that a region in which we have some administrative say contributes fully to the overall growth of the South African economy. This is a responsibility we dare not escape, but it is not the only one.

In South Africa today the rural areas, including the so-called homelands, are the only places in which blacks can own land and farm. Hence, the future of black farming and agriculture in South Africa, for the time being, depends entirely on the successes these regions can achieve through rural development. Our responsibility to promote black agriculture goes hand in hand with our responsibility to encourage black entrepreneurship. There is no doubt that rural areas in South Africa provide the most fundamental problems and challenges of black development. It is in these areas where most of the problems of South African blacks are concentrated.

The Role of Multinational Corporations

The black people of South Africa need help in their task of developing the rural areas. Help is needed in educational development, in industrial development, in community development, and in rural development.

Educational Development

The bulk of the school-going population among blacks in South Africa lives in the rural areas. In KwaZulu alone we have over one million pupils in school. This represents roughly one-third of South African children of school age. Yet schools in the rural areas of South Africa are overcrowded, poorly equipped, and are manned by unqualified and underqualified teachers. In most schools in the rural areas some children are taught under trees because of the scarcity of classroom accommodations, while others sit on cold cement floors during lessons because of the lack of classroom furniture. Children are forced to learn without the aid of properly equipped school libraries and science laboratories.

Advances in rural education have been painfully slow because black parents in the rural areas shoulder the burden of paying for the building of schools and in some cases even pay teachers' salaries. If industries in South Africa, be they national or multinational, expect rural areas to supply them with skilled manpower, then these industries must contribute toward the improvement of the quality of education and training in these areas. In KwaZulu, for example, we need to build more academic high schools, technical colleges, and teacher training colleges. At today's prices, a well-equipped high school of sixteen classrooms costs about R400,000 to build and a well-equipped technical college costs about R3 million. Without the close cooperation and financial support of multinational corporations, such vitally important investments in the future of black South Africa will never be made.

Earlier I indicated that the future of black farming and agriculture in South Africa depends on the development of rural areas. Yet peasant farmers in the rural areas are not trained in the modern methods of tilling the soil. We do have one agricultural college in KwaZulu which trains extension workers who assist peasant farmers in the rural areas. For agriculture in the rural areas to develop into a viable commercial activity, however, there is need for the training of hundreds of potential farmers at high school level. Only from the ranks of these students can we then produce well-qualified teachers of agriculture for the schools. Assistance from multinational corporations, ranging in scope from the sponsorship of individual students to help in the construction of new educational facilities, could stimulate dramatic advances in rural education and agricultural production.

Rural Development

Nearly one-half of black labor in South African industry is migrant or commuter labor. This means that the mass of South Africa's labor force is drawn on a daily or weekly basis from black rural areas.

The regional black governments have the responsibility of providing all social services and amenities for the home communities of these migrants. In fact these regional governments bear the costs of the "production" and "reproduction" of a huge component of South Africa's labor force.

Industrialists are rightfully concerned that the governments of the countries in which they operate or invest ensure a reasonable quality of community life for the people they employ. Most industrialists know that the quality of home life and community life of their labor affects productivity and stability in their work forces. They willingly pay taxes on company profits in order to contribute to the fiscal revenue out of which the government will provide benefits, amenities, and services for their workers.

In South Africa, however, industrialists should realize that a large and growing part of their own labor forces do not receive services provided by the central administration. It is the regional governments in the rural areas which have to look after the quality of community life of the black migrant and commuter sectors.

Let us take Durban, for example. Of the entire black labor force in the Durban industrial region, less than 20 percent by rough calculation, are eligible for community benefits and services of the central government departments. All others are the responsibility of KwaZulu. KwaZulu not only administers the large urban townships around Durban but also the rural and periurban communities from which migrant labor is drawn.

The business community in South Africa has recognized the need for the private sector to become involved in improving the quality of life of blacks living in urban areas. The Urban Foundation, established by major industrialists in South Africa, is now seven years old. Thus far no equivalent "Rural Foundation" has been established to improve the quality of life in the communities from which migrant workers are drawn. We have heard of certain possibilities in this direction. Various groups have certainly studied the problems and explored possibilities, but nothing concrete has emerged thus far. This is another area where multinational corporations can significantly contribute to the improvement of the quality of life in the rural areas. Multinational corporations should establish a Rural Foundation in South Africa similar to the Urban Foundation because of the importance of the rural areas in maintaining industrial and labor peace in South Africa. In the massive Durban strikes of 1973, when as much as two-thirds of the region's productive plant was paralyzed, the prime movers were migrant contract workers from KwaZulu. Recently, we have seen massive militant labor activity in the eastern Cape. Most of the black labor involved resides in, or in theory is due to be based in, black areas of the Ciskei.

The most significant challenge to the rise of economic opportunities for blacks lies in rural development. Population densities are mounting rapidly under the impact of government-forced resettlement programs and the high black birth rate. In KwaZulu, well over one-third of the rural citizens do not have land of their own—they are mainly tenants and subtenants on other people's land. The same problem exists in other rural areas all over South Africa. It is therefore in the rural areas that the most basic challenges to the social responsibility of industry lie.

Generally speaking, rural areas are characterized by an almost complete absence of the services and facilities that could combat problems such as disease, unemployment, and the destruction of the resource base through overgrazing, soil erosion, and the cutting down of trees to provide firewood.

What we need are Rural Service Centers, each with a small staff of well-trained coordinators. The Rural Service Centers should function as a focus for all the various government services provided in the areas like health and welfare services, adult education, and teacher-upgrading services and agricultural extension. These should as far as possible be drawn together under one roof. To these services should be added a market and a marketing organization to take the local produce of more successful farmers; a rural credit bank or some other form of credit organization; a seed and fertilizer store; a craft-training and marketing outlet; a small technical training center for the development of rudimentary mechanical skills associated with rural industry; a tractor co-operative or a form of assistance to assist tractor ownership by small-scale ploughing contractors; a center offering advice on small livestock production, for raising poultry, and animals like rabbits, hamsters or pigeons; and a general advice bureau. The coordinator's role would be to mobilize the communities to form various committees and associations to steer the various activities and to undertake self-surveys of needs in the areas. The coordinators would also encourage the various government services to function on an integrated basis in the rural areas. Additionally, they could efficiently channel outside voluntary aid and assistance into the activities of the service center.

Regional governments in the rural areas like KwaZulu do not have the financial resources to establish such centers, although we have a clear policy of trying to coordinate our normal services to provide an integrated package in rural areas. We need outside assistance.

What we would like to see is private companies or multinational companies "adopting" one or more rural areas, assigning staff members with good organizing ability to assist our own service personnel both in establishing viable service centers and in training local coordinators.

If private companies aided those areas from which they draw many migrant workers, the benefits to themselves would be obvious, even in the short run. We would, however, like to encourage companies to avoid piecemeal operations and to join together as groups of firms to tackle particular areas. We would also like to see such companies entering into partnership with regional administrative bodies such as the KwaZulu Development Corporation in establishing such programs in rural areas.

This request is not merely a request for multinational companies to exercise a social or moral responsibility. We in the region of KwaZulu have tended to become cynical about claims of moral responsibility from whatever quarter. It seems to us to be a poor basis for cooperation, since it inevitably involves the expectation of gratitude. We do not see the need for favors or charity.

We see the need for assistance as arising out of two very hard and objective realities. The one I have already mentioned. We are "servicing" the community support systems of employees in the common economy. We are rendering a developmental service to industry. This is a reality that the South African government chooses to overlook in its anxiety to cut us out of the framework of political competition. Industrialists, however, would be unwise to ignore this reality because it affects their labor.

Second, social "stress" in the black rural areas of South Africa is increasing: Population densities are mounting, and more and more younger migrant workers do not have land they can call their own. In the past the stability of migrant labor in South Africa depended in large measure on the fact that the migrant worker had a sheet anchor of security in the form of his land back home in the rural area. He could endure the privations of living in single quarters in compounds and hostels secure in the knowledge that the *real* quality of his life was somewhere else.

Today, a young migrant worker does not have this safety valve. He is denied full access to life in the city by influx control (or pass laws) and he may not bring his family to town with him. And yet he also is more and more likely not to have a secure family base with land and cattle in a rural area. He does not have a world of his own. This is the kind of worker who is most prone to discontent and demoralization. This is the kind of worker who may feel he has nothing to lose.

Large multinational corporations may believe that they are immune to these stresses. They, after all, are the capital-intensive companies who are least likely to depend on poorly skilled migrant workers. Yet even they are dependent on migrant labor, if only indirectly. They sell their products to other companies that use migrant labor. They buy raw materials from companies that use migrant labor. And a breakdown of stability in the labor force will affect the economic climate to everybody's detriment.

Therefore, my appeal is not for charity but for self-interest. The black rural areas are the soft underbelly of South Africa's stability. If there will be an armed insurrection in South Africa, it will most probably start in the rural areas and not in the urban centers. We as black regional governments and the private sector have a shared responsibility to countervail the effects of ideological policies that undermine stability.

Conclusion

Perhaps understandably, multinational corporations in South Africa have concentrated their community development efforts near their operations—that is, in the urban areas. But this overlooks the social and economic realities of the South African government's policy of "separate development." In particular, the migrant labor system, upon which industry depends, places severe strains on rural areas. Only if educational and economic opportunities in these areas improve will industry be able to count on a stable and productive work force.

These difficulties are magnified by the absence of central government support in the so-called homelands. The refusal of the South African government to recognize these areas as part of our common nation highlights the importance of coordinating the efforts of multinationals through a Rural Foundation. By coordinating assistance in this way, corporations can best aid the regional governments in bringing about the fundamental changes in education and agriculture necessary for rural self-sufficiency.

South Africa is a country of very great promise in the Third World. It can be an example of balanced and sustained development. It can also hold out a very profitable future for most large multinational corporations. It could, however, disintegrate before our eyes as the old Rhodesia did. We as black leaders have a difficult political task ahead of us. We cannot deal with the task of rural development alone. Private corporations can provide crucial assistance. It is in their interest to help us, and I believe that we can count on that help.

Part III
Four South African
Perspectives

7

Strategies in the Struggle for Liberation in South Africa and the Shape of Political Events to Come

Gatsha Buthelezi

I have taken it upon myself here to discuss the broader aspects of political developments currently taking place in South Africa, and to isolate the factors that I regard as being pertinent and determinant of the future political scene. I make my remarks within the context of the factors surrounding the role of American firms in South Africa.

I regard it as my responsibility to pose a South African black point of view and to do so as a black strategist. In all my reading and throughout all my traveling and in the numerous discussions I have had about politics in South Africa, I find debate on whether to invest or disinvest in South Africa an activity unparalleled in futility. Nowhere else in the world do I find an example of the impossible being discussed so earnestly as a real option.

The people who call for disinvestment fall into a number of categories. First, there are those bad South African strategists who have abandoned active work in the country and have fled abroad to mount a struggle against apartheid from other countries. They are like fish who leave the water to go swimming, or farmers who leave the land to go farming, or bankers who leave their vaults to go banking. As a strategist, I believe that if a course of action has failed for twenty-five years, it does not represent a viable option. No sound business or financial strategist would persist in an operation that had run at a loss for twenty-five years if it was only blind faith that encouraged him to continue.

When we boil things down to their essentials, South Africans who leave their country to take the struggle for liberation abroad can have only three avenues of attack. One is to formulate subversive concepts and to disseminate them in South Africa; another is to prepare themselves for an armed struggle; and the third is to mobilize international opinion against apartheid and against the South African government. I understand the kind of sentiments that drive people to seek these options. The horrors of apartheid and the degradation that blacks are forced to endure, I must admit, may be too much for some. I can understand human beings fleeing from the sheer horror of it all. I can understand human beings being blinded by their anger, and I can understand human beings seeking to escape the dungeons of South African jails. Understanding why South Africans flee our borders and seek refuge elsewhere does not lead me to accept that they have viable alternatives to the kind of constructive engagement that is possible inside the country. After twenty-five years of futile activity by South Africans abroad, supported as they are by millions upon millions of dollars, and applauded as they are by nation after nation, they have achieved nothing and yet there is no end in sight to the support they receive.

This, then, is one group calling for disinvestment, and we note in passing that the call for disinvestment is associated with support for the armed struggle. I must pause here to reinforce what I am saying. In this discussion, I am not talking as a strategist who is concerned with any one ideology or any one theory of man and society. As a pragmatist with my feet on the ground inside the country, with an organized following of 350,000 people, and as a representative of people in every walk of life, I say simply that these disinvestment and violent options do not work. They have not worked for twenty-five years and they will not work for as far as we can see forward. Whatever our persuasions are, whatever stand we take, and with whomever we associate, the acceptance of failure should be common cause among us. Violent options are not real options for us, and economic sanctions against South Africa will not cripple the country. As a politician involved in practical politics I must decline to support a program that has failed for twenty-five years and will in all likelihood fail for another twenty-five years. Simply put, we cannot afford to back a losing strategy.

For the last twenty-five years we have had foreign investment in South Africa. Firms in South Africa that are foreign-owned play an important role in the field of labor relations and job creation, and they will continue to do so. The hard facts of the matter are that South Africa is not tottering in the face of military threats, and the South African economy is not reeling from the consequences of withdrawing capital or withholding investments. However we clothe the strategies in idealism and moral injunctions, they remain failing strategies, and they will remain failing strategies as far as we can see ahead.

It is not difficult to explain why these failing strategies have been adopted by those who have fled the country's borders: There are few other options open to them. When we look beyond the South Africans involved in the lobby for disinvestment, we are faced with a more complex scene. There are many people who support the call for disinvestment, or support the call for an armed struggle, because there is something noble in their makeup. This element of human nobleness rallies them behind those who are outcasts and who are refugees from the land of their birth. This nobleness seeks to support these outcasts and refugees in whatever they are doing. The support for black South Africans in exile at its noble best is support for the exiled and the homeless and is support for the options they elect to serve. This support is not given on the merits of the options, it is given on the grounds of being the elected options of exiles. A great many who support South African exiles seek to avoid imposing their wishes on them. It is support for those who are regarded as freedom fighters, and it is support for the options they elect to serve.

I understand the burning indignation of European or North American people and the anger flowing from that indignation, which would virtually support the devil himself to eradicate the scourge of apartheid from the face of the earth. I can understand moral pressure groups supporting indignation and supporting those with refugee status in exile proclaiming themselves to be South African freedom fighters and the custodians of South Africa's future. I can even understand this feeling of the morally indignant going beyond support for economic boycott to manifest itself in refusals to associate with South Africans in sports or cultural activities. In the same way, I can understand a sense of futility, a sense of anger, a sense of fear, a need to keep out of jail, which drives South Africans into self-exile. This, however, does not lead me to agree with their choices as correct strategic options available to us. In the same way I also understand the indignation in Western support groups for these options, but again understanding does not imply agreement. For me, the pertinent observation is that there are over twenty-two million blacks in South Africa who have alternative options that are viable.

For me the pertinent observation is that it is those inside the country who have a pivotal role. If any indignation rises to support our exiles, it should be an indignation which seeks to clothe and to feed and which perhaps goes further than this to support those staggering along the borders of human hell from which the refugees fled. The refugees have removed themselves from the suffering of the people. They have sought options that are in fact easy options and not available to us in the country. If they arouse emotions, it should be the emotions which seek to sustain them in their sojourn in foreign lands, but which at the same time direct support to viable options that are found in the actual battlefields against apartheid in the country.

Support for economic sanctions and boycotts against South Africa are, however, rooted in altogether different sentiments. There is a reformist element in every Western democracy which seeks to gather momentum in its own country by espousing the problems of Third World representatives in their midst. A black refugee from South Africa is a market-able product in the domestic scene for those who are campaigning against capitalism in a Western society. For those who believe that churches should have a social conscience, black South Africans in exile who have fled from white political, economic, and social domination, are also marketable products. Black South Africans in exile are grist for many a European and North American mill. To speak like this is one of the personal burdens I have to bear. In having to do so I find myself estranged from some of my brothers and sisters in the struggle. I also find myself estranged from many good and sensitive people who have rallied around black South Africans in exile and supported their options simply because they are their options.

Having evinced this understanding, I must reveal how deeply disappointed I am by those who know what I am saying is true, but feel under no obligation to become relevant to the process of change in South Africa because their vested interests are secured. Self-interest for them is narrow in scope and related to immediate gratification. Much of the suffering in South Africa can be traced to irresponsible capitalism and white economic greed in commercial and industrial undertakings impervious to pleas from the suffering and the dying. When I talk about the armed struggle and economic boycotts as strategies that are not viable for us in our prevailing circumstances, I am saying no more than just this. I say "in our prevailing circumstances" because we cannot accept or reject the armed struggle simplistically. We are all convinced that it is true to say that Mozambique or Zimbabwe would not have been liberated had a section of the population not resorted to violence.

The South African government's ultimate sanction is violence, but it has used violent tactics long before any ultimate position had been reached. In the final analysis, it may well be the threat of violence which brings people to the point of making real changes. As yet we cannot make a final analysis of whether change in South Africa will necessitate the employment of violence. My own conviction is that the burden of our responsibility should lead us to use nonviolent tactics. It is in nonviolent democratic strategies that I see most hope, because at this point in time they are the only viable strategies open to us.

Political apartheid is a massive, defensive wall built around white economic interests. Early white settlers who moved into the country regarded themselves as having a God-given right to occupy whatever territory lay before them and to annex it in the name of whatever crown they represented. The whites established themselves by acts of war. Their violent options were in fact viable and they exercised them with great effect. The sheer weight of their technical innovations in the machinery of war enabled them to subjugate blacks. They had a vast expertise in killing people, and they employed that expertise with great effect. I myself come from a warrior stock who faced the full might of the British army's firepower with clubs and spears, and even with bare hands. My great-grandfather Chief Mnyamana Buthelezi was the commander in chief of the king's army at the time of the Zulu annihilation by the British in 1879, and the king who ruled then was my maternal great-grandfather.

Thus, when I speak about violence, I speak about it as one with a heritage of violence, and I speak as a leader of a people who were subjugated by violence. We understand the business of violence. I have in the very marrow of my bones a deep insight into the nature of violence which makes me aware of its repugnance as a means of regulating human behavior. Apartheid is the outcome of the employment of violence. It is the worst form of human subjugation which has ever been used by man against man. It shows how dangerous it is to use violence for political purposes and reminds us that the use of violence must remain only as an ultimate option.

For me as a black South African, those who grow fat under the umbrella of apartheid are perhaps even worse than those who maintain apartheid by the use of violence. There are many industrial undertakings, including foreign undertakings, led by those who agree in private with everything I say and who know in the heart of their hearts that I am right, but who only have visions of extending this year's balance sheet and next year's business. There is a kind of credo among those in free enterprise which leads many to scream beneath their breath that it is good to make a buck under any circumstances, but that to make two bucks under difficult circumstances is better. They see some kind of challenge in making their buck in the midst of our misery. They get some kind of precarious sense of satisfaction by walking along the knife edge between government displeasure and black labor displeasure. There are those who profit from apartheid, who sit under the violent umbrella that nurtures apartheid. I understand these things just as well as I understand that violent options and economic boycott options will fail.

We need the Sullivan Principles as the beginnings of corporate responsibility in South Africa. We need the Sullivan Principles as a beginning because the constraints that are not provided by threats of violence and economic sanctions must be provided through other means. Much has been said about the principles and strategies that are needed to get more firms to observe the Sullivan Code. I will therefore confine my discussion to broader political issues within which the Sullivan Code must be considered.

If we turn aside from the unrealism of those who opt to mount an attack on South Africa from without, we must look at the options that are available to those inside the country. Many felt that there were no longer internal options when the South African government banned the African National Congress and the Pan Africanist Congress in 1960. People became dismayed and were radicalized when their political organizations were smashed and their leadership were jailed and dispersed. But beyond this they were also intimidated by the awesomeness of Afrikaner political determination, and the monolithic nature of the National Party's ideological approach. They saw Afrikanerdom moving from excess to excess. They saw it advancing on every black bastion of freedom and they were overwhelmed by the awesomeness of the scene. The years 1948–1960 were truly impressive from the point of view of the growth of sheer naked power and brutality in the country. I grew up during those years; I cut my political teeth at that time, and I shared in the vibrant black tremors as one after another black initiative was defeated by white brutality. Growing white brutality, and particularly Afrikaner brutality in the National Party, gave rise to despair, which led many to justify the move to violence and to abandon democratic opposition.

It was only in the latter part of the 1970s and now in the 1980s that it has become patently clear that apartheid itself is a nonviable option and that it cannot be made to stand forever. The National Party and Afrikaner *baaskap* dreams of 1948 had to be abandoned. They fought economic integration, and now the whole of the government's strategy is based on the acceptance of economic integration. In 1948 they envisaged working toward a situation in which there would be residential separation, and so-called white areas would become whiter and black areas would become blacker. This philosophy of separate black and white areas was based on the principle that blacks had no rights other than the right to sell their labor in white areas. Every statistic shows that each year since 1948 all "white areas" have become increasingly multiracial, with most of them numerically dominated by blacks. The present policy of recognizing the permanence of so-called urban blacks, and of providing economic facilities and local government for them would have been a 1948 National Party heresy. Job reservation was a cornerstone of 1948 National Party thinking; skilled jobs for whites and unskilled jobs for blacks was the rule. Job reservation played a very important part in the edifice of ideological apartheid. Since 1948 economic expansion has obliterated job reservation as a viable option for whites in South Africa. There is no such thing as job reservation for whites any longer in South Africa. The hard logistics of reality have dismantled it.

In 1984 the notion of black trade unions was unthinkable. Black trade unionism is now an accomplished fact in the country, and another cornerstone of 1948 National Party thinking has crumbled. By no stretch of anybody's imagination is he or she entitled to say that I believe that the liberation of blacks in South Africa is an accomplished fact. All I am doing is pointing to the fact that in the late 1950s and early 1960s, we did not have the perspective that we now have; and it is only now with hindsight that we can say that those who fled because they were overawed by white brutality and the monolithic nature of Afrikaner nationalism, should have remained. The victory for the black struggle is not in the balance. It will come. Victory is ours. Our concerns are to hasten it and to be victorious with the minimum amount of suffering and the least loss of life.

I would like us to look at the promises and the dangers in the current situation. The promise is there because whites are in fact totally dependent on blacks in our country, and blacks are totally dependent on whites. The interdependence of blacks and whites demands political reconciliation. Every rational policy must favor one South Africa with an integrated economic and political system. The black population of South Africa now stands at twenty-two-odd million souls and the white population numbers a little above five million people. The white population is virtually static but the black population is growing at the average rate of 3 percent per annum. The sheer weight of numbers is a vital political dimension in South Africa.

The logistics of a high population growth must be very frightening to white South Africans. Population growth is exponential in nature, and the problems of white political ideologists are compounded by the birth rate in black society. In the particular part of South Africa where I live, KwaZulu, we also have a rapidly expanding black population which must make white supremacists feel very insecure. If I were a white supremacist and faced the current Zulu demographic facts, I would be terrified out of my wits. More than half of all the over five million Zulus are fifteen years of age or younger. Over the next twenty years when this population marries and begets children, we will have a situation that will break the seams of every bit of apartheid that we now know. It may well be that apartheid strategists will find more reinforcing cords to strengthen the fabric of suppression, and they will discover more devious means of subjugating a people. That remains a possibility. The fact is, however, that current apartheid cannot contain the kind of expanding black population we have in our country.

I am not using the birth rate as a secret weapon against apartheid. As every social scientist knows, birth rates throughout the world are inversely proportional to economic prosperity. The poorer people are, the higher the birth rate is. All I am indicating is that we are about to witness a process by which apartheid will be put under stresses and strains by demographic factors, and that it will have to make adjustments in an attempt to maintain its domination. This is a political process in itself. All I am stating is that we are not facing a static situation. Politics is not in an apartheid straitjacket. There is urgent political work to be done as Afrikaner nationalism attempts to redesign its apartheid shackles to meet the new circumstances. I for one do not believe they will be able to do so. They will not be able to do so because there will be a growth in viable opposition with the acceleration of dependency of whites on blacks.

The economic consequences for apartheid are too grave for white South Africa for it to continue forever in its present form. I do not believe that the whole Afrikaner nation will be prepared to become poorer each year to enforce apartheid. I believe that the Afrikaner, as is the case with every other nation, will rebel against increasing poverty in its own midst. Black consumer power in South Africa now exceeds white consumer power; and here again, I am pointing to the fact that circumstances are creating viable political options and that we do not have to espouse the failing options of violence and boycott actions.

The economic integration of southern Africa deepens the set of circumstances that will ultimately favor a struggle against apartheid, and it is in these circumstances that we must understand the present prime minister's desperate drives to plaster the cracks of his apartheid edifice. Again, I want to state that by no stretch of anybody's imagination must he or she see what I am saying as the basis for complacency. All I am saying is that there is an unlocking of circumstances which gives political and democratic opposition to apartheid options. As we exercise these options, we will have room for maneuvering, and, through the exercising of these options, we will be strengthening the moral fiber of the people of South Africa, which is good for the struggle even if the worse comes to the worst.

The involvement of South Africans in these options is going to come about as a consequence of black initiatives such as we have seen in the Buthelezi Commission. For black options to be relevant they will have to move away from racist politics, and each step that moves us away from racism will be a major element in the restructuring of the moral fiber of the country. I am under no illusions that black South Africans can solve the country's problems. They cannot. They can only display the initiatives that can lead to solutions. By the very nature of our society and its problems, the solutions will have to be multiracial, or perhaps more strongly put, they will have to be race-free. There is perhaps a subtle point to be made here which will only be substantiated by future events. This is the point that we may well have black options and black action, but unless they are race-free, they will not survive. This implies that we can have white action which is race-free which will survive.

Inkatha, for example, is a black organization in which membership is available only to blacks. It has a valuable contribution to make as a black initiative, but of all the organizations to have been founded in the country, Inkatha is, from a racist point of view, one of the most liberated. It is possible to pursue black obligations without being racist.

If there are vulnerable areas in the edifices of apartheid, if there are soft spots in the underbelly of Afrikaner racism and in the National Party's political program, if blacks are in a position of having power advantages as the consumers in society, and if the whole of apartheid ultimately rests on economic factors in which blacks play a dominant labor role, then there will be a vast range of opportunities for political action within the country. The present South African government's whole intention is in fact focused on limiting such opportunities. We are facing perhaps what will turn out to be a last ditch stand by apartheid supremacists to rig the political future in their favor. Prime Minister P.W. Botha's political brashness and his whole political style reflect the degree of political panic that is beginning to pervade the corridors of power in South Africa.

While I thus hold out hope for the prospect of black politicial involvement in democratic and nonviolent options, I do so in the awareness of how easily the scales can in fact be tipped. Quite emphatically the 1976 South African scene was not a planned strategy. It was an eruption of frustration and anger which was spontaneous and which in many respects was inevitably indiscriminate. We face a situation in the country where such eruptions may occur with greater frequency. I repeat, they are not political options. I repeat, they cannot be planned and will not be planned. But they have a hard political reality about them, and there is a threshold we could pass in which their frequency and intensity would be such that we would face a runaway scene.

I return to the demographic fact that over half of the people in Kwa-Zulu are fifteen years of age or younger. There are thus over 2.5 million young people soon to enter the labor market, soon to require housing, hospitals, social services, and so on. As things now stand, we have got no prospect whatsoever of meeting the demand for jobs or houses or hospitals or classrooms. Huge squatter settlements are developing around every major city where people occupy shanties that are little more than shelters made out of corrugated cardboard. These are the kindling sticks of black anger. The jobless, the homeless, and the people uncared for by the institutions of the country are not freedom fighters who can employ violence scientifically as a viable option. If we mismanage our politics at this crucial point, they could become cannon fodder for frightened whites who could begin shooting blindly at anything black that threatens. It is in fact with some difficulty that one perceives a future in which spontaneous outbursts of violence will not become politically problematic for those of us who struggle for freedom and for social, economic, and political sanity.

It is in these circumstances that the present prime minister is girding his South African loins and preparing for the worst. He is a great one to talk about a total onslaught. He talks about South Africa as being threatened by communism and subversion. He talks about the total onslaught against white South Africa on the military, the political, the cultural, and the economic fronts. But what he is in fact really doing is pulling all the National Party's bogeymen out of the dark cupboard simultaneously to frighten white South Africa into becoming more efficient at killing. If there is any threat to South Africa it is constituted by this preparation for killing, and we face the paradox that the very preparations for killing, the very preparations for war on our borders, prejudice peace within the country. The machinery of war being prepared for our borders is a machinery that will be turned loose to wreak great havoc on internal dissension if that dissension boils over as it is bound to do.

Prime Minister Botha is preparing for a horrible future. Whether he is doing so wittingly or unwittingly is irrelevant to the fact that he is doing it. Not only is he preparing for the worst in this way, not only is he introducing more stringent demands on whites to participate in army call-ups, not only is he extending the age limit for such call-ups, and not only has the length of such call-ups been systematically increased, but those who are called up do not experience the peacetime military training Western industrial countries regard as necessary. Young men trained by the South African Defence Force have in fact to employ their military skills in military operations in which people are maimed and killed. The prime minister's mobilization of white South Africa and their employment in shooting wars will shut off all hope of political solutions in the future.

When Botha first assumed power, he cried out: "Adapt or die." There was at that point in time the prospect of adaptation, and many of us with a deep sense of South African responsibility gave him the benefit of the doubt and appealed to the world to give him an opportunity to show us what kind of mettle he was made of. It has become increasingly clear that either we were wrong in our first perceptions or internal political dissent within Afrikanerdom has inhibited the forces of change operating within its body politic.

From a strategist's point of view, it does not particularly matter which is true. The net result of Botha's premiership to date has been the movement toward hardline politics. In his term of office we are now facing an apartheid attack on human dignity unparalleled in the annals of South Africa's political history. The proposal to enlarge Swaziland and in so doing to coldbloodedly rob over a million black South Africans of their South African citizenship and their rights to oppose apartheid, is apartheid at its brutal worst; it is classical apartheid; it is a hideous dropping of iron curtains between one South African and another South African. It is a brutal divide and rule step and it has the ugliness of deeply implicating a member of the Organization of African Unity and the United Nations.

Prime Minister Botha's drive toward a confederal state, in which white South Africa will form the dominant party, is a systematic attack on black constitutional rights, and it aims to remove black opposition from white political domains. His evolution of the political machinery of the President's Council leading to the kind of recommendations it is making is another body blow to democratic prospects. To divide brother against brother by giving the Indians and "coloreds" of South Africa different vested interests to those of Africans is politically provocative to the extreme. Furthermore, to involve so-called urban blacks in a political dispensation that is different from that of so-called rural blacks is once more to divide and to rule. What I am now saying underscores the point that I am not politically complacent. It also underscores the point that I make when I say my rejection of violent options and many boycott options does not stem from a complacency which is blind to the urgency of the present situation and which does not recognize the dire perils we face.

It is in this total set of circumstances of escalating political problems and expanding political options that foreign firms must play a role in South Africa. Enlightened self-interest must surely now demand a very much more penetrating attack on resistance to change in the country than that promoted by the Sullivan Principles. If we cannot do the little required in order to implement the Sullivan Principles, we will fail in the task before us. For many black South Africans, or perhaps even for most black South Africans, the Sullivan Principles represent the bare minimum in corporate responsibility. South Africa will in the 1980s witness a real political battle between the forces of apartheid and the forces of democracy. In a very real sense, history is shaping the whole country up for a final political showdown.

When I talk about a final showdown, I do not imply that there will be a quick end to apartheid. The struggle in South Africa could yet be long and bitter, and the length and the bitterness of the struggle will be intimately influenced, or even determined, by institutionalized responses to the human dilemma. If industrial and commercial undertakings are not innovative, and if the benefits the people derive from them are not more comprehensive, we will face a severe crisis. If the various associations and groupings that have been formed among business and professional bodies do not attack the problems facing South Africa effectively and realistically, we will be facing a crisis. If the trade unions in the country and the churches in the country each in its own way and in its own circumstances do not contribute a great deal more to the process of change than they have done in the past, we will face a crisis. At this moment we have to escalate constructive involvement in the internal processes of change as rapidly as we can. The need to do so is urgent.

We have , unfortunately, to face another set of problems in our overview of the present political circumstances and the direction of future trends. This is the problem which is created by the dangerous illusion that protest politics gives rise to real political action in the country. Protest politics rallies people who are angry and articulates their position to gain applause. Protest politics produces celebrity leaders who come and go one after the other, each in turn soliciting the support of protest from outsiders, particularly from the Western world. While black South Africans posture and prance politically to court white liberal support in the West, the forces of apartheid smile. Changes in South Africa must be revolutionary changes, even if they are not brought about by a classical revolt. All things are not brought about by a classical revolt. All things revolutionary begin with the hard work of organization. Protest politics alone saps our will to organize. The welding of people into viable groups at the local level, to form constituencies in which disciplined leadership can act, is an essential part of the struggle for liberation. The evolution of a form of politics in the country which is compelling not only for the liberal West, but also for the socialist bloc and all the members of the Organization of African Unity, is essential. We must have a groundswell political movement with mass support which brings people together at the local, regional, provincial, and national levels. It must be an organization of people within the realities of the marketplace, and while the element of protest will forever remain valuable wherever there is social injustice, the reliance on protest alone must cease.

I speak not as Gatsha Buthelezi trumpeting his own cause and articulating his own feelings. I speak from the midst of a people who have rallied behind the things I am saying. I speak with their voice. It is for them that I am making the points I have made, and it is on their behalf that I appeal to U.S. firms to resolve to become more effective. We have to take a far greater step forward than persuading more people to subscribe to the Sullivan Principles.

Inkatha is a black organization with vast implications for the country. It is preeminently the most important political organization in the country. It has the support of the masses and it enjoys support in every walk of life. When we hold a Youth Conference, six or seven thousand youngsters who come from every part of the country congregate. No other political organization can even hold mass meetings which draw that number of the general public to them. When Inkatha rallies the people for a mass meeting in Soweto, thirty or forty thousand people flock there to share their political drive with one another. Inkatha's mass support is structured and it is the beginning of constituency politics that will eventually drive apartheid into a political chamber of horrors that will make future South Africans shudder.

8

White Power Politics: Economic and Political Choices Facing South Africa

Leonard Mosala

> It is a feature of modern South African history that the large-scale migration of black South Africans from their historical territories to "White South Africa's" rapidly developing urban-industrial areas brought about a complex array of economic, social, administrative and political problems. The Government is endeavoring to resolve these problems within the framework of *its* policy of "Multi-national Development," also known as Separate Development, which is an attempt to find a "Democratic" solution for South Africa's plural problems.
> ... In terms of Government policy, the concept "non-homeland Black" in no way implies the existence in "White South Africa" of either an ethnically homogeneous or conversely, a denationalized mass of black persons who have no political, social kinship or cultural ties with their states. The social and political future of these blacks is not interlocked with that of the white nation of the Republic of South Africa. [Writer's emphasis]
> *South African Official Yearbook,* 1978

This statement expresses in a nutshell the political mind and philosophy of the majority of white South Africans today. It is rooted in the political history, custom, and tradition of South Africa. But, it is also an indication of the future political and economic course of the country.

Made only two years after one of the most traumatic experiences in the history of the struggle of black people for democratic freedom, it demonstrates the determination of the white political power elite to maintain white supremacy in South Africa at all costs.

Historical Perspective

To understand the dynamics of South Africa's racial politics and the structuring of its society, it is important to look at the history and traditions of the South African society. Racial discrimination in South Africa has its roots in the social, political, and economic development of the English and Afrikaner communities comprising "white South Africa." But, above all else, it is rooted in the Afrikaner's fear of equality with the numerically superior black people. Allied to this fear of equality is the almost pathological desire to maintain his ethnic identity even at the cost of others' rights. Ironically, this very desire to maintain ethnic identity contains the seeds of its own destruction.

Evidence of this fear of equality and the desire to maintain the Afrikaner identity can be traced back to the time of the Great Trek. Before leaving the Cape Colony and British rule in 1839, Afrikaner leader Piet Retief wrote: "We are resolved that we will uphold the just principles of *Liberty*, but while we will take care that no one will be held in a state of slavery, *it is our intention to maintain such regulation as may suppress crime and preserve proper relations between master and servant.*" The servants were, and were ever to be, those who were not white.

Anna Steenkamp, another of the more educated Voortrekkers wrote: "We withdrew so that we would have none of that ungodly equality between white and black." The fear of equality was the primary reason for the Great Trek. It is still the fundamental factor in the shaping of South Africa's political and economic order today.

The National party in South Africa has been the custodian of Afrikanerdom and, as such, has inherited the Afrikaners' aspirations and fears. It was swept into power in 1948 on the platform of *Swart Gevaar* ("the black danger") and has never been able to break out of the limited horizons of Afrikanerdom and see South Africa's society in a broader perspective.

Clinging to the view of South Africa as an exclusively white nation, the party has been unable to "satisfactorily" unscramble the stark reality of the presence of South Africans of non-European stock, who press for the right to be recognized. This failure has led to many contradictions in the defining of the racial South Africa the party envisages.

Political and Economic Inequality

Right from the start white South Africans have ensured that the locus of political and economic power would reside in the white community. They used this monopoly of power to exclude black South Africans from meaningful participation in the national political and economic decision-making organs of the country.

While whites have enjoyed universal franchise, this has been denied black people on the ground that it would lead to black majority rule and thus to the end of Western civilization in South Africa. White South Africa has sought and gained much support in the West as the custodians of Western civilization in a continent that is otherwise still in the Dark Ages. Also important in gaining the support of Western governments has been South Africa's strategic value to the continued security of the West as well as its continued supply of strategic minerals. Businessmen have supported white South Africa because South Africa represented a safe and secure place to invest with an abundant, cheap, and easily available supply of black labor.

Western involvement in South Africa stems, therefore, from self-interest. It is encouraged by the appearance of long-term political stability and by the perceived ability of the South African government to maintain the status quo. For as long as conditions exist for the safe and profitable business activity, both the governments of the West and businessmen with interests in South Africa will maintain their involvement. This will continue whether the political system of that country is seen to be unjust or fair and whether this association perpetuates the injustice or not. The evil of apartheid has been evident from the start. It has increased with the passing of time, but the international associations with that system have not decreased, even though this system has been loudly condemned by these self-same people.

What then is the explanation for the lack of realistic action to correct a situation that is so patently in conflict with some of the most cherished values of Western democracy? Is it that the interests of the West are best served by the status quo? Or do businessmen have too much respect for the government? Or is it simply the lack of leadership on the part of the business—both foreign and local—which could mobilize the forces of industry to act in concert in matters that, at time, conflict with their own economic interests? I believe that the answer lies somewhere in the honest answering of these questions.

Apartheid's Manifest Injustices

To understand the brutality inherent in the ideology of apartheid, one needs to see the system in operation. Far too many people speak authoritatively about conditions in South Africa when they have hardly seen the backyard of the society.

When we speak about South African society, we in fact are speaking about two distinctly different societies in terms of wealth and opportunity. We are speaking about that affluent, highly developed industrialized society: white South Africa. But we are also speaking about that highly controlled, poverty-stricken, Third World society: black South Africa.

If you walk the streets of Johannesburg, Pretoria, or Cape Town at night, you see no sign of black South Africa. For at nightfall it slips out of sight into its ghettoes in the backyards of white South Africa.

By 1981 South Africa had divested itself of nearly eight million of its former citizens. This was achieved through the passage of the so-called status acts, which gave homelands "independent" status. No country in the world has a constitution that permits the government coercively to expel its own citizens. But South Africa, in its relentless pursuit to translate the ideology of apartheid into reality, had done it. In the process, some of the sacred principles of democratic government had been transgressed. The concept of freedom had been destroyed in the South African political system. Basic human freedoms for which men have given their lives, freedoms for which nations have gone to war, suddenly did not apply to millions of people. Their freedoms, their rights had been wiped out with contemptuous impunity, and the world did not appreciate the magnitude of this crime, the enormity of the human suffering this act would cause. These people had no choice. They were not to say whether they wished to be citizens of "homelands" they had never seen and many others would never see. They were simply disowned and allocated out of South Africa to nowhere!

No one knows the fate that awaits the other fifteen million black people who "belong" to the other, not yet "independent" homelands. They face an uncertain future. They can only wait.

No one who from the sidelines observes this tragic drama unfold can ever appreciate the intense bitterness, the unbounded hatred that the implementation of this callous policy is engendering in the black community. If there is anything in South Africa that is likely to cause a racial holocaust, it is the brutal implementation of this abhorrent policy.

The "separate development" policy is the greatest political swindle in history. Not only has this policy deprived millions of black people of their inalienable birthrights, not only has it condemned three-quarters of the South African black population to perpetual poverty and economic deprivation and servitude, but it is also the most divisive ploy of the white government, one that has caused unmendable divisions in the ranks of black people. These divisions will seriously affect the capacity of black people to achieve their political and economic objectives.

Whether they are formally independent or not, black homelands will remain on the periphery of the white-controlled economically viable metropolises. They will never become fully self-supporting economically. They are, therefore, and will be for the foreseeable future, reservoirs of cheap, easily available labor to be used as required by the white economy.

The Problem of Inequality

Despite the great numerical preponderance of the black population in South Africa, its share of the gross domestic product and the allocation of resources remains disproportionately lower than that of the whites. In 1973, the average per capita share of those who are not white of the gross national product was only 11.4 percent of that of the whites. A study by an economist at the University of Cape Town showed that in 1978 South Africa had the most inequitable distribution of income of ninety countries surveyed by the World Bank.

The educational deficit was even worse. In 1976 there were 1.25 million people in South Africa who had passed matriculation, 89% of whom were white, 5% African, 3.3% Asian, and 2.2% colored. There were 167,000 university graduates, of whom 93% were white, 2.2% African, 2.2% Asian, and 1.8% colored. Expenditures on the black child are about 14% that of the white child. (See appendix A.)

The Group Areas Act, Removals, and
Administration of Pass Laws

From the passage of the Group Areas Act to the end of 1980, over 132,000 colored and Indian families have been forcibly removed from the residential and business districts that they have inhabited for decades, and some for generations. Twenty-four hundred white families were similarly removed. The following land allocations were made to the communities that had been moved: 137,000 hectares were allocated to the colored and Indian families while 761,800 hectares were allocated to the white families, an allocation of 0.97 hectares per colored or Indian family and 310 hectares per white family.

But these numbers are dwarfed by the government's massive and relentless removal of Africans. To date, over two million people have been removed from "white" and urban areas and resettled in the homelands.

The Role of Business

The foregoing figures sketch the outlines of the situation facing business in South Africa. We all know that the ownership of the major portion of the South African economy is in the hands of people, many of whom have publicly professed their stand for enlightened political policies and proclaimed themselves ready for change toward a fair and just society: a society where all people will have equality of opportunity. But how few are those who are prepared to stand up and be counted when the occasion demands!

I believe that the economic sector is the one area where structural changes could be made immediately if the owners and leaders of this sector would back their talk with action. The question is, how many of them really want to bring about change that may mean reduced profits and lowered standards of living and reduced social privileges for the white community? But, on the other hand, who can afford the drastic, perhaps total, losses in the event of a racial confrontation occurring as a result of the continued suppression of black aspirations?

The challenges that face South Africa today offer very few alternatives, and the options shrink with the passing of every day without positive action. Employers must be prepared to take the lead at least in the dismantling of apartheid in the economic sector. There are enormous opportunities for well-planned and well-directed action in this area, not least among which are those offered by the emergent black unions. The successful management of industrial relations in the coming days will have a profound effect on the present economic and political structure in South Africa.

Businesses must be careful to avoid the official rhetoric about change. Even those sincere in their efforts will have little credibility if they use the same governmental language in which blacks no longer have faith.

A great deal of talk about change is taking place both in South Africa and outside. All this talk is in terms of the future and after many years of listening to it we still have to hear those engaged in it say we have brought down these structures of apartheid and tomorrow that one is coming down. We must distinguish between desired change, in which those affected have a say, and allowed change, ordered without regard for those who are affected. Prime Minister P.W. Botha has made it clear that no change will take place outside the framework of government policy. This change will take place through the "homelands" structure as the major vehicle for the realization of political aspirations for blacks, and the new tricameral Parliament for "coloreds" and Indians. We know that the envisaged change in the administration of the pass laws will in fact tighten the screws further on the rights of blacks to sell their labor at the highest available market price, and on their rights of residence.

But is this what black people want? Is this what Sharpeville and Soweto were about? Is this what the so-called consolidation of the homelands, which we all know has caused the uprooting of more than two million blacks, aims to achieve?

South Africa is moving along a road that must ultimately bring about a violent clash of the two races in that land. If Sharpeville and Langa did not get the message home to the white community and their leaders in 1960, Soweto put that country firmly across the Rubicon in 1976. Soweto demonstrated clearly that the new generation of black people is no longer prepared to occupy a position of perpetual subservience to the white man in the country of their forefathers, that they were no longer prepared to be excluded forever from the political life of their country and from meaningful and gainful participation in the economic activity of the country, and that they would not stand as spectators while the white Parliament makes laws for them which reduce them to stateless and homeless persons in their own country.

A new spirit of defiance is sweeping the black masses, a defiance that has heightened their awareness of the political and economic forces at their disposal. No longer is the government's repressive action against community leaders a restraining force against black political expression, as was the case in 1960. No longer are white liberal organizations accepted as spokesmen in the definition of black problems and the prescription of solutions thereto.

As was the case in 1976, the signs of deepening racial polarization, increasing potential for confrontation, are clearly visible, and only fools will fail to see them. Of course, in every situation of revolution there are always those who sleep peacefully through a raging fire of human anger and action. South Africa will be no exception to this rule.

After 1960 it took more than ten years for blacks to recover from the shock they received from the guns of apartheid at Sharpeville and Langa and from the ruthless assault the government mounted against their political leaders and organizations.

It took them another five years to collect the pieces and start building a semblance of political organization. In 1976, while the shock shook the adult population, it also aroused in them a determination to resist those same guns and the same police shock treatment and to stand with their children.

The destruction of their leadership did not deter a new leadership from emerging almost immediately. This has been the case with every wave of arrests, detentions, and bannings of every new generation of leadership. True, the black struggle has felt the serious blows dealt it by the government, but the spirit and the determination to resist have remained.

The boycotts of classes by colored, Indian, and black students, the increased labor unrest throughout the country, and the quick revival of political organization at the grass roots level are but a few of the signs of what can be expected in the future.

In taking on the might of white South Africa, blacks are fully aware that they will have to reckon with increased help to the South African regime from the Western countries with massive economic interests in South Africa. This has been the case in other countries where people were struggling to change the status quo. Angola, Mozambique, and later Zimbabwe had to face this same situation, but even this intervention did not change the course of events in those countries.

South Africa cannot be an exception to the process of change that has swept southern Africa. If things are left the way they are, it is reasonable to expect that the course of events will follow the pattern of other countries. The only questions that may differ are the *how* and the *when*.

Western countries cannot go on backing a losing horse. Soon the stark reality of the changing alternatives for trade will hit them. They will have to choose between the short-term benefits of supporting the white regime and the long-term gains of taking action now that will enable them to retain the major markets of the continent.

For even the best forecasts will show that time is not on the side of the status quo. Whites cannot succeed much longer in forcibly suppressing black aspirations. They cannot win in the long term.

White South Africa must be made to see sense before it is too late. We know it will be hard, very hard indeed, for white South Africa, but there is no longer any alternative if that country is to be saved from the certain disaster that apartheid is pushing it to. South Africa must talk to those leaders of black people it has jailed, forced into exile, or banned—to those leaders in whose wisdom and leadership the mass of black people have faith. Only in this way can an acceptable formula for real change be worked out.

Nothing will be gained from talking to those leaders the government has created for black people unless their mandate has been tested and confirmed by the majority of black people through an acceptable test. Critics may say that the South African situation is a no-win situation and that it is wise to take what the government gives now and ask for more, if possible, later. Others may take the view that white South Africa is too strong to be pushed into a political formula they do not want. But until black people are afforded a stake in the political and economic life of the country, the struggle for liberation from racial injustice will continue, and, in the long run, black people cannot lose this contest.

9
The Imperative of Enlightened Self-Interest in South Africa

Tony Bloom

As a South African businessman, I am uncomfortable about my country's emergence as a major business risk and profile analysis area for many American corporations. For many years under generally favorable economic conditions and with them friendly governments on our borders, attention was directed to other troubled areas in the world. South Africa was allowed to to pursue its internal policies free from the attentions of the international community. All this has changed immensely in a time frame that is very short indeed when viewed from an historical perspective.

We are now talking at a time when South Africa is confronted with uneasy internal calm, at a time of increased terrorist activities along the borders of the country, at a time of economic recession and growing unemployment in South Africa. We are talking at a time of widespread international pressure, not only from countries of the Third World and the Eastern power bloc (which is to be expected given their interest in destabilizing the entire area) but indeed pressure from all the member states which make up the Western, capitalist-based world, and which until not so long ago were viewed by South Africans as allies in their perceived stand against communism.

Of course, the penny in this respect has finally dropped: Protestations of anticommunism are no longer a ticket to respectability in the Western world, and as has been realized even by the South African government and its supporters, racism has become the supreme and ultimate sin of the second half of the twentieth century.

The diplomatic response of the United States (and indeed other Western countries) to South Africa's position and its government's intransigence was counterproductive until very recently, when the doctrine of "constructive engagement" was enunciated by the present administration. The previous Carter-Mondale-Young approach of official estrangement prompted by "human rights" violations was viewed by many South Africans, opponents of the government as well as their supporters, as an ill-defined and counterproductive exercise that tended to harden rather than change attitudes. This approach was supported by the woolly policies of the previous Labour government in England, who were not to be outdone and who rushed into endorsing the popular parrot-cry of "One man, one vote." More thoughtful students of the South African scene (including arch-opponents of apartheid such as Harry Oppenheimer) have characterized this approach as a premature recipe for disaster in the South African context. No one who has any in-depth knowledge of South Africa really believes that universal suffrage on the Westminster pattern is the short-term solution to our problems, or even if it were, that the present South African government would have the remotest intention of allowing it, except over their dead bodies. But it is one thing for a foreign power to press South Africa into ridding itself of an unjust system of government based on racial discrimination, and quite another thing to seek to impose simplistic solutions based on the concept of one man, one vote as the only permissible solution.

Of course, no amount of diplomatic ineptitude or lack of imagination can excuse the odiousness of apartheid or the tendency of the South African government to stifle dissent by reaching for the handcuffs and attempting to govern by fear and repression whenever confronted by organized political opposition among or on behalf of blacks. Let me make my own stand perfectly clear: I believe that the South African system—where racial segregation is not only socially condoned but also meticulously endorsed and institutionalized in a carefully constructed statutory network of discriminatory legislation—is totally unacceptable to any civilized person or nation in the world today. Discrimination, particularly institutionalized racial discrimination, is an evil, and I use the word "evil" advisedly. It is, in my view as a devoted and committed South African, politically suicidal, economically unjustifiable, and morally repugnant.

Discrimination that is embodied in statutes is also in stark contrast to the firmly held beliefs of the U.S. government. This has meant that for the American companies doing business in South Africa, their business has become an issue of more than simple economics. In an article in *Fortune* magazine some years ago, Herman Nickel (later U.S. Ambassador to South Africa) drew attention to the fact that hardly any U.S. corporation with interests in South Africa had escaped shareholders' meetings at which the chairman was subjected to cross-examination and criticism pressing him to explain why they still chose to do business in South Africa.

Most of the criticism came from church groups and universities. But it would be foolish to pretend that these are irrelevant protest groups—at least in the case of the universities, which include the greatest names in the United States—or that they are without influence far beyond their own particular investment policies. These critics argue that *anything* that is done in South Africa that makes a contribution to its economy also helps to prop up the repressive system of apartheid; and that the South African government is so immune to rational persuasion that it would only react to the stark reality of an American economic withdrawal. This is an approach that is negative and destructive—harmful to the very interests it purports to assist.

One might well ask—Why should the American companies bother? Why should they need to face this barrage of repetitive, hostile criticism? After all, for many of them, their South African interests represent only a fraction of their total interests, an infinitesimal part of their international operations.

The answer is simply that the issue is too important for U.S. corporations to adopt that attitude—too important from the point of view of their long-term strategic interests, and too important as a fundamental question of principles, too important from the point of view of the lives and hopes of their employees in South Africa.

In this scenario, what role is there for the business community? The business community in South Africa, and the international business community with interests in South Africa, have a unique opportunity and an important and constructive role to play. Indeed they shoulder a heavy responsibility. They have the ability to become a major force for change and a source of constant pressure on some of the main and most intolerable aspects of discrimination, which, when they are broken down in the work environment, spill over into many other aspects of society. This involves the adoption of a philosophy of corporate social responsibility and corporate leadership in South Africa.

We all know that evolution and acceptance of a doctrine of social responsibility is relatively new and still controversial. The idea that business has one and only one objective—to maximize profits—was the consensus for the better part of business history and this view is still currently held by some eminent and notable business thinkers.

Our active involvement can be justified on the basis that it is patently obvious that it is in our interests to operate in a stable and healthy society, a society that is not jeopardized by the deterioration of conditions in its environment. Let us be clear—there can be no profits for business and no future for people in a disintegrating community, a community characterized by unemployment, civil disorder, or crime.

In South Africa, formal acceptance of a doctrine of social responsibility was slow, but there are now many examples of companies, my own included, which involve themselves in the broader issues of society as part of their formal corporate objectives, and whose annual reports specifically refer to their actions in this area. And in South Africa this is doubly important because generally speaking (and unlike most other Western countries) business finds itself to the "left" of the government and an important force for change and social reform.

But the trend is a painfully slow adjustment. It involves the process of having to change attitudes that have been formed over many years, and perhaps we should not expect utopia overnight.

Those who do business in South Africa are familiar with the so-called Sullivan Principles, promulgated in 1977; six principles endorsed by the U.S. State Department and subsequently by many of the U.S. corporations doing business in South Africa. Broadly speaking, they involved the basic philosophies of nondiscrimination in employment, equal opportunity, and upward job mobility. At the time of their promulgation they were, strangely, even favorably commented upon by Connie Mulder (the then minister of information in South Africa and now one of the leaders of the ultra-right-wing breakaway Conservative party), although somewhat unwillingly and obliquely. Codes became fashionable at the time and the European Economic Community (not to be outdone) also jumped onto the bandwagon—issuing their own set of rules, a somewhat hasty and not terribly well-conceived document that attracted a spate of criticism, both in South Africa and abroad.

Finally, a Code of Employment Practices was issued by the Urban Foundation, a body formed by the South African business community after the 1976 riots in Soweto which seeks to promote and enhance the quality of life of urban black communities in South Africa. Recognizing the importance both of providing material benefits to employees and of changing the attitudes of blacks and whites at their most frequent point of contact—the workplace—the foundation felt it necessary to jolt South Africa's employers out of their then comfortable lethargy. Hence they issued guidelines intended to result in significant, meaningful, and most importantly *immediate* changes in the South African environment. This code was an important document because it embodied the elimination of discrimination in all aspects of employment practice as its overriding and basic premise. Remember that this was a code made in South Africa by South Africans for South Africans and thus more acceptable as being free from the taint of foreign interference or imposed solutions. Interestingly, it was endorsed by employer bodies representing something like 90 percent of South African employers. Regrettably, it has not succeeded as well as was originally hoped, mainly due to its voluntary nature and the absence of any monitoring mechanism.

The Sullivan Principles, on the other hand, have in my opinion achieved a great deal—perhaps not as much as its more radical groups would have liked, but perhaps more than some of its skeptical critics expected. In a broad sense they clearly focused attention on injustices in employment practices generally. By setting out certain standards (albeit in some cases somewhat ambiguously—but standards nevertheless), they attempted to measure progress (sometimes in an imperfect and often irritating fashion); however, few can deny that very significant progress has been achieved in many areas. American companies can take pride in the achievements that have been made and in the fact that they are in the forefront of promoting change for the better in South Africa. Clearly, U.S. companies are not alone in this respect; many European communities have done equally important pioneering work and there are, happily, a number of South African companies (some of them the largest employers in the land) who can also take a great deal of credit. A look at the corporate and social objectives of South Africa's largest industrial company, Barlow-Rand, and its achievements amply illustrate this point. And I would like to believe that my own company has made a contribution in this area as well—we certainly spend enough time and effort on it, although we are far from perfect and have much yet to accomplish.

But most U.S. companies need in no way be ashamed of their record. Discrimination has been dismantled on a wide scale; jobs created; hundreds of thousands of people of all colors trained; upward job mobility increased; families positively affected through pension funds, bursary schemes, and home loans; and trade unions assisted and recognized in their formative years. These points, by no means exhaustive, represent a very considerable catalogue of progress and achievement. Much remains to be done, but the trends are clear. Training and education are especially important. For many blacks, company training courses represent a major and significant part of their entire education. These courses enable them to upgrade themselves and make inroads into many skilled and supervisory positions that were formerly the domain of whites only.

Despite the fact that one can expect the codes to diminish in importance over the years, a major opportunity still exists for U.S. (and other foreign) companies to play a constructive role—to act in terms of and expand the principles and philosophies underlying these codes and to conduct their affairs in South Africa according to them.

I say that I expect the codes to diminish in importance not only because of the significant progress already made, but also because of the growth and strength of the trade union movement among blacks over the past few years. This was not so at the time of the promulgation of the Sullivan Principles and the Urban Foundation Code, when black trade unions were unable by law to obtain statutory recognition. The legislative framework has changed completely for the better, and trade unions are a major factor today. The black trade union movement, incidentally, although still in a formative stage has played a generally constructive and responsible part to date in the field of industrial relations. At the end of 1981 there were 200 registered trade unions, white, black and mixed, representing 1.1 million workers. A total of 260,000 black workers was represented by sixty-one of these unions compared with 100,000 at the end of 1980. Generous legislative incentives have also been provided for training, and in this field substantial progress has been made since 1980, resulting in the training of almost 350,000 workers in 1981, compared with roughly 100,000 in 1979; the figure for 1982 is expected to total close to 500,000.

Over 360 American firms operate in South Africa. The total American investment in South Africa amounts to over $2.6 billion, and American firms employ over 150,000 people of all races. If one assumes an average family unit of four persons (a not unreasonable assumption for South Africa), then there are over 600,000 people whose lives, ambitions, and aspirations can be affected by the policies of American companies. There is an enormous potential for influencing an even larger circle if these corporations continue to set the pace in the dismantling of the apparatus of discrimination in employment, to set the pace in the civilized treatment of their employees, in their training and promotion programs, and in the granting of socioeconomic benefits that substantially benefit those employees and their families.

I argue strongly and persistently for the extension rather than the diminution of American interests in South Africa. I argue for the extension of diplomatic, cultural, athletic, and economic ties with South Africa. I argue for increased investment, not boycotts—for U.S. corporations to lead by example, not to isolate by withdrawal. To demonstrate in an effective and practical manner that enterprises can be run on a nondiscriminatory basis and yet remain viable. To maintain moral integrity and at the same time to achieve constructive gains. To use the carrot instead of always the stick. And to lead, as the world expects them to. There is no need to become a part of the system.

Every time that an international colored sportsman plays in South Africa, racial barriers tumble and changes in attitudes occur for the better. And every time that a black visitor to South Africa is refused admission to a restaurant, other restaurants clamor to admit blacks on an integrated basis. Every time an American corporation desegregates a canteen, promotes a black manager, or increases the skills and job opportunities for black staff members, other corporations gain the courage to do so. Payment of a fair rate for the job, training programs, promotion opportunities, pension benefits, medical aid assistance, housing subsidies, educational bursaries for employees' children, and legal counseling are but a few of the constructive and positive programs in which U.S. business can continue to involve itself, and not only from philanthropic motives—in most cases it makes good economic sense as well.

Anything that promotes and influences the material well-being of workers in South Africa is worth doing. I go further: in the nonbusiness field I would like to see a flood of academics, artists, and athletes of all races coming to South Africa—by all means firm in their intention to perform before desegregated audiences only. And I believe it would be difficult and extremely embarrassing for the government to do anything but go along with the situation in the face of their often expressed, but seldom carried out, intention to move away from discrimination.

There are often heard objections to cooperation in the sporting and cultural fields, based on the premise that South Africa's isolation has been responsible for much of the removal of petty apartheid. This is undoubtedly true to an extent, but I believe a great deal more can be accomplished by active and constructive leadership.

All of us involved in the free enterprise system must reexamine our role in society and question to what extent the scope of our activity should be extended in order to protect the values which we have built up over the years and which we cherish. All of us must ask ourselves, more than ever before, to what extent our particular areas of expertise and knowledge can be put to use in effectively improving the environment and opportunities for all in South Africa, and correcting patent injustices.

I have stated in South Africa that I am sorry to say that too many South Africans, who have the qualification and the capabilities to make a contribution, have been guilty of sitting on the sidelines for far too long. For a South African, it is a basic duty to involve himself or herself in every aspect of South African life whether political, economic, or social. Indeed, in a highly complex country like ours, many issues tend to be all three.

I have urged business leaders (and the leaders of professions such as the legal profession, the accounting profession, the medical profession, and so on) to be honest and outspoken in their beliefs and to have the courage of their convictions to state those beliefs, whatever they are, openly and in public. To do this we need the support of like-minded friends and allies—friends and allies who have strategic, moral, and business interests in the promotion of a stable and democratic region in Africa.

South Africa is very much at the crossroads—the government now has to summon its courage and choose its road. If it chooses the road that will carry its bold statements about adaptation and the removal of discrimination into practice, then one can proceed with some confidence that the potential of our great country can be realized. If on the other hand, South Africa were to choose the other road, cling to the obstinacies of the past, retreat into its heavily armed white stockade, and embark upon another disgraceful wave of arrests, bannings, and detentions without trial, then, although I have no doubt that we will survive, the period that lies ahead is not going to be a pleasant one.

The responsibility for the choice is heavy and it is here that the United States and its political and commercial interests can make a positive and lasting contribution. Economic and political isolation is a negative and retrogressive step. It will not persuade South Africans to accept otherwise unacceptable formulas and would undoubtedly intensify the paranoid siege mentality that ripples below the national psyche of South Africa. The stifling of U.S. interests would merely remove a positive and constructive influence, and would cause hardship and suffering among those who need help most. No problem was ever solved by walking away or quitting on it.

As Herman Nickel pointed out in the *Fortune* magazine article mentioned earlier, the prospect of a lower level of U.S. involvement worries blacks deeply. He quotes Freddy Sauls, described as a battle-hardened union organizer for blacks and coloreds in the auto industry, as saying, "It is all very well for people to urge disinvestment who sit in a safe country in some nice office 8,000 miles away. But if the American auto plants here closed down, I fear for thousands of men looking for work and literally wondering where the next meal would come from." Nickel found that the vast majority of blacks firmly rejected any notion of foreign economic boycotts of their country.

Ask Chief Gatsha Buthelezi; or Lucy Mvubelo, a dedicated black trade unionist; or Percy Quoboza—formerly one of South Africa's leading black journalists, an implacable foe of apartheid and yet a dedicated believer in nonviolence—who is also strong in his view that U.S. companies have the potential of becoming one of our most vital links of bringing about peaceful change and liberating blacks from what he describes as "pride-killing paternalistic charity." In the United States, ask someone like Vernon Jordan, who after "searching his soul, cannot join those who call for disinvestment."

In the words of President Banda of Malawi, "You cannot convert anyone if you isolate him because you then deny yourself the opportunity of preaching to him, of persuading him to change his attitude." But there will be other views. The vocal minority of radicals and revolutionaries who profit from anarchy, destruction, and chaos, and who are resolved to destroy any structure that strives to harmonize with Western, democratic, capitalist values.

It only remains, therefore, for those companies who are operating in South Africa to ask themselves these questions:

Are wages for nonwhites in their companies advancing fast enough?

Have they moved toward equal pay for equal work and do they provide equal employment opportunity?

Are they spending sufficient time, money, and effort on training their workers?

Are they promoting on merit alone and actively seeking out blacks with the requisite qualifications for managerial positions?

Can they do more in South Africa to improve the living standards and job opportunities for workers?

Are they making a significant and constructive contribution toward quality of workers' lives outside the work environment?

Are they providing sufficient support for general charitable and philanthropic projects which will benefit all sections of the community?

Are they (and their management in South Africa) speaking out on matters of national importance such as removals, detentions, insidious applications of the Group Areas Act, and so on?

There are immense opportunities for the practice of enlightened self-interest in South Africa. In deciding on your policies, I urge those of you who have not visited South Africa to do so, and those of you who have visited us to do so again because much change has taken place. South Africa's problems and challenges are quite unlike those in any other country of the world—South Africa is unique in its history, its achievements, its ratio of black to white, and yes, even in the material benefits of income, housing, education, welfare, and health of its black population. It is also sadly unique in its disregard for human dignity.

A reasonable future for all the people of South Africa cannot possibly be linked to a lessening of economic ties between the United States and South Africa. Disinvestment, partial or total, will achieve little other than its value as a moral salve and perhaps the applause of the Third World and the Eastern bloc. It will certainly not achieve what black South Africans need for themselves. Let us ask ourselves the question—Would a lessening of economic ties give them freedom from hunger, unemployment, or fear? Will it contribute toward the goal of equal opportunity? Or will it bring with it the chaos of a Congo, the civil strife and misery of a Ghana, the grinding hunger of a Burundi, or the despotic cruelty of a Uganda?

The answer to a diminution of ties must be an unequivocal *no*. I am convinced that there is a much more important role for American companies to play—to join with the enlightened South African and other companies in being the cutting edge of the movement for acceptable change in South Africa.

I take strong issue with the conclusions of the report issued by the Rockefeller Foundation insofar as it suggests "nonexpansion" of U.S. interests in South Africa—economic growth in South Africa can only be beneficial to the process of dismantling apartheid generally, and the faster the growth, the faster that process will be. Six to eight million jobs for new black work seekers alone will have to be found in the next 20 years. It is obvious that this cannot be done without the aid of foreign investment. Inevitably this process and the growth in the economy will bring with it improved political rights.

American corporations can and must assist in this process. It is to their own commercial and economic, political and moral advantage, and in their country's strategic interest. It also accords with their humanitarian ideals and proud record on human rights.

As George Ball wisely pointed out some years ago, U.S. policy should be directed not toward isolating South Africa further, but to bringing it into harmony with the twentieth century and providing social values that are espoused by other noncommunistic democratic nations. Diplomacy, he argues, is "like politics—the art of the possible; if the U.S. uses its leverage towards the unachievable ends it will merely create a mess. This is no time for flamboyancy or moral blustering, but for that quiet, carefully conceived, consistently articulated, arm's length diplomacy which is the essence of statesmanship." I quite agree.

10
The Challenge Facing Business in South Africa

Hermann Giliomee

T hree recent statements have profound bearing upon the future of business in South Africa. The first statement I take from an interview I once conducted with the previous prime minister of South Africa, John Vorster. I had the great fortune to interview him on the very day Prime Minister Mugabe took office in what is now Harare, Zimbabwe. We both listened to a radio broadcast of the event, and then I asked him this question: "What is your judgment of Ian Smith at this moment? Was he doomed by history to hand over power to a radical government or did he have alternatives which he squandered?" Mr. Vorster was frank in his reply. "He had a thousand chances, but he always shopped around for a better one than the one on the table."

And then Mr. Vorster recounted the wonderful story of how he told Mr. Smith in 1973 (or 1974) that he had just negotiated with Zambia and Britain a new deal for Rhodesia. In terms of this deal, sanctions against Rhodesia would be lifted and the bridge over the Zambezi opened, provided Mr. Smith would accept a black government in fifteen years' time. "Take it," Vorster urged Smith. "No," said Mr. Smith, "I don't accept it. I shall only accept a black government in thirty years' time." Vorster countered by asking Smith whether he did not know the story of the sultan's horse. A sultan had sentenced two men to death but just as they were being dragged out to be executed the sultan said: "I shall commute the sentence of any of you who could make my horse talk." The next day one of the men was being dragged through the streets to be beheaded. As he came to the executioner's block he saw the other man standing free. "Wait," he cried, "I must talk to this man." And when he was led to the free man the prisoner shouted: "What did you tell the Sultan? *I* said it was impossible to make a horse talk, so he sent me to my death." "Too bad," replied the other man. "I said to the Sultan I can make a horse

---

This chapter was originally delivered as a paper in November 1982 to a senior management seminar of Mobil Southern Africa held in Cape Town.

talk, but I need a year. And you know, a lot can happen in a year. The horse can die, the Sultan can die, and a lot of other things can happen."

The second story concerns a prominent foreign academic with an interest in South Africa who at a rather heavy drinking session asked one of the leading Soviet experts on Africa how the USSR would react if a black government came to power in South Africa within the next five years. The Russian replied simply: "We shall be very sorry. If a black government comes to power in five years' time it will be a dreadful bourgeois, capitalist stooge of the West. We want the conflict to drag out at least fifteen to twenty years, becoming sharper and messier, and then we shall get a nice radical, socialist pro-Soviet black government in South Africa."

The third statement encapsulates the conclusion of Stanley Greenberg's book, *Race and State in Capitalist Development*, which examines the role of business in divided societies like Alabama, Ireland, and South Africa. In all these societies business clung to the comforting belief that it did not have to worry about political crises because economic growth would steadily make the political problems more tractable. Economic growth, so the theory goes, will dissolve the bitter racial and ethnic divisions between whites and blacks, or Protestants and Catholics; if given free rein, business would generate wealth and new relationships between divided peoples.

As we know, this theory did not work out in Alabama and Ireland. While business waited either to be given free rein or for the economic forces to take effect, racial violence began to engulf society. While there was still a measure of political stability, big business was the one force in society that had the potential political leverage to induce government to abandon statutory discrimination. But big business invariably lacked the will or the courage to confront government and exert concerted pressure. When violence finally became endemic, as in Alabama in the early 1960s or Ireland after 1969, it was too late for big business to do anything meaningful to contain violence, restore stability, promote reform, or even go on "doing business as usual." Business became one of the chief targets of the feuding parties. Within two years after violence erupted, Northern Ireland was losing exports, orders were dropping, there was a lack of business confidence, new industries would not locate in Ulster, capital was not forthcoming, productivity was dropping, and businesses were regularly disrupted. Between August and December 1971, eighty industrial companies had suffered bomb damage; nine had not resumed production, and seven had gone out of business entirely. Northern Ireland's Chamber of Commerce and Industry despaired that industry and commerce had become the chief targets of the bombers. Business was reeling: It never thought that things would come to this.

Northern Ireland was fairly peaceful for the preceding forty years, business was good, and economic growth was supposed to sweep away all the ancient barriers that set people apart. If anything, things have steadily deteriorated since 1971 and recently Northern Ireland has entered a new spiral of killings and brutalities.

These three statements are directly relevant to the challenge facing business in South Africa in the 1980s. Business must make a horse talk—to get blacks, or rather an important section of blacks, to accept the capitalist system and to promote those political reforms that will forestall the fate of Northern Ireland descending upon South Africa. But business has, figuratively speaking, only a year to do so. If they wait fifteen to twenty years, the dream of the Soviet expert on southern Africa will become true and South Africa will have not only a black government, but a nice radical Trotskyite government completely beholden to the USSR. And so we are stuck with the unhappy dictum of Greenberg: that business usually wakes up too late to their real challenges, including their political challenges; that it is always reacting to crises rather than trying to preempt them.

Key Political Trends

What will be the political and economic environment in which business will have to operate in the next ten to fifteen years? Predicting the future is a risky business, particularly in South Africa. I would rather restrict myself to history, but for the purpose of this chapter I shall take the liberty of extending into the future some of the basic trends in our current political situation. There are three important trends, described in the following pages.

A Political Vacuum at the Top

The political editor of a leading international business journal recently remarked to me that however unpleasant apartheid might be, the truth is that South Africa has discovered the brutal secret of ruling a racially divided society and ensuring stability and growth. This is the formula of a united ethnic group seizing the state and governing the other ethnic groups through the old strategem of divide and rule. This ethnic dictatorship must push through just enough reforms to keep business—and the State—prosperous. But it must do nothing that will weaken its grip on the levers of power and must brutally repress any challenges to its system of rule. In his view this is how South Africa has been ruled for the last thirty years.

As we all know, the one essential element in that formula is steadily disappearing, the ruling ethnic group is no longer united. Over the short term the danger of a growing assault by the far right wing has receded somewhat. But over the medium term the National party has little reason to be complacent. The white electorate's interests diverge too much, while their tax rate is made ever heavier by a government wasting money on ideological schemes and having to spend an increasing proportion of the budget on security and black social services. The potential of support for parties of the far right from the white working and lower middle class squeezed by taxes and inflation should not be underestimated.

The time will soon come when only a coalition can pass those reforms that would give both the black groups and the West the essential modicum of hope for peaceful change. But of course coalitions do not come about simply because reasonable men think that it is a sensible idea. An ethnic government, which Prime Minister Botha's government still is, will pay a very high price for the restoration of ethnic unity. It may even sacrifice reforms essential for economic growth and political stability in order to prevent the ethnic split from widening. This is not particularly reprehensible: It is simply the way politics, particularly ethnic politics, works in a political system like ours.

This entails a high price for business. Stability, economic growth, and industrial peace in South Africa will become ever more directly related to the measure of geographic growth and job mobility blacks will enjoy. Until fairly recently, stability and a high rate of growth were possible despite the existence of influx control and the Group Areas Act. But as I shall argue later, it is these barriers to the free movement of people that pose the greatest threat to future growth and stability. Until a few months ago business could still hope that the Wiehahn-Riekert dispensation, when fully implemented, would lift the barriers sufficiently to begin seriously the urgent task of bringing blacks into the mainstream of the economy and dismantling social and economic apartheid. In the present political climate one can only foresee an intensification of influx control and of most of the Group Areas regulations. It will be one of the greatest challenges of business to get these issues back on the agenda of reform and embark on serious negotiations about them with the government.

Growing Radicalization of Blacks

Ever since the end of the Second World War, blacks have felt intensely aggrieved by the segregation enforced by apartheid. The political turmoil of 1960 and 1976 was directly related to black frustrations arising from these policies and in particular to the labor system resting on the pass laws and influx control. To its credit business recognized in 1960 that this labor system was incompatible with economic stability. In July 1960 the Associated Chambers of Commerce (ASSOCOM), the Federated Chambers of Industries (FCI), the Steel and Engineering Federation of South Africa (SEIFSA), the Chamber of Mines, and the Handelsinstituut issued a memorandum on the pass laws and influx control stating that they created a feeling of insecurity among blacks, undue restrictions on freedom of movement of blacks, unnecessary interference with black family life, and considerable friction between the police and blacks.

Unfortunately, however, business unanimity on this issue soon evaporated, as did any desire to flex business muscles in pursuit of reform. FCI counseled against organized commerce and industry, making their collective weight felt in the political field and stated that it had to "work within the compass of what Parliament determines." In the end only ASSOCOM stuck to its guns.

Following the upheavals in Soweto and elsewhere in 1976 many business leaders met in Johannesburg. They opted for supporting self-help programs and housing for blacks, and they established the Urban Foundation to achieve these ends. However, they avoided the major flash points such as voting rights, influx control, pass laws, and "separate development." Certainly some very commendable work has been done over the last five years both by the Urban Foundation and by individual companies in the field of black housing. Yet in the meantime, despite insistent lobbying by the Urban Foundation, a draft bill on the "orderly movement of people" has been drawn up that will make influx control more rigorous than ever.

This bill is a major threat to political and economic stability in South Africa and should be of immediate concern to any company that has even a relatively small black labor force. Let me digress briefly on the system on influx control and why it constitutes a challenge to business.

I recently worked full-time for five months on a special project called "The Implications of Rural Poverty" for the Unit for Future Research at the University of Stellenbosch. My main conclusions about the effects of the system of migrant labor and influx control on the political and economic environment of South Africa include the following:

1. *Over the long run the system of migrant labor destroys any hope of the population of the black "homelands" feeding themselves.* In the homelands a steady deterioration of subsistence agriculture is occurring. It is likely that subsistence agricultural production is now only one-quarter of what it was in 1948. That is the case because farming in the homelands has been increasingly replaced by migrant labor trans-

mittances as the chief source of income of families. What happens is that the returns on agriculture have become so poor in comparison with migrant labor earnings that most able-bodied men choose to leave the land. Consequently families invest in education for their children to prepare them for a migrant's career rather than a career in agriculture. At the same time migrant earnings are too low to permit investment and capital accumulation in homeland agriculture. This combination of the best-educated men being absent for eleven months a year, the lack of capital, and tribal limitations upon women, who have to do most of the farming, makes it almost impossible to introduce meaningful reform in subsistence agriculture. Migrant labor makes it extremely difficult for the homelands to industrialize. The fact that thousands of the men work for much higher wages in the modern sector tends to push the internal wage rate up to uneconomic levels. Consequently, in 1980, the homelands were able to absorb only 15 percent of the new work-seekers that their own population growth generated between 1972 and 1975. And this will become worse because the low level of economic development militates against a decline of the birth rate—fertility rates usually do not decline until development has reached a reasonably high level.

2. *Influx control together with the trend toward capital intensification makes it impossible for the modern sector of South Africa to soak up labor surplus.* Between 1945 and 1980 South Africa moved from being a labor-absorbing economy to a labor-extruding economy. There are several reasons why the high economic growth rate did not cause a proportional increase in employment. Part of the answer is to be found by comparing what happened in the 1960s and in the 1970s. In the economic boom of the 1960s there was only a small rise in real wages and a decline in the relative labor surplus. In the 1970s, however, the expansion of urban employment of Africans was much slower, with a considerably greater rise in real wages.

The slower growth of the economy to a large extent explains the slower growth of employment, but low economic growth cannot explain the greater rise in wages. We must look at the great worries the mines experienced in the early 1970s about the breakdown of migrant labor supplies from the neighboring countries, particularly Malawi and Mozambique, the considerable international pressure that was exerted on South African companies and multinationals to improve the working conditions of their workers; and the black trade union movement which could bargain for higher wages. Add to these factors the permissive, and perhaps even encouraging, attitude of the state to real wage increases as a way to ensure the smallest possible urban black presence.

The South African economy in the 1970s behaved as though it faced a labor shortage at a time when a huge surplus was still available in the homelands and the white rural areas.[1] In 1977 it was estimated that at any given moment about half the potential migrant labor force was not employed. Given the declining ability of subsistence agriculture in the homelands to provide work, one must assume that this half is increasingly unemployed rather than underemployed.

One of the major facts of our recent economic history is that real wages have been prematurely bid up, fueling black unemployment. South Africa faces a growing unemployment problem with homeland work-seekers increasingly unable (because of inferior education and influx control) to bid effectively on the urban labor market. In the homelands people are facing an ever more desperate struggle to survive. A recent survey has found that about one-third of the migrants have no land, that about two-thirds of the migrant workers in the cities have to send money home for food, and that about two-thirds of the migrant labor force worry about whether they have sent enough money home to feed their families.

All this leads me to the conclusion that the entire overseas movement to pressure South African subsidiaries of U.S. companies to increase the wages of their black labor force has been fundamentally misguided. While paying higher wages to blacks may be in itself enlightened, it simply adds to the forces increasing the rate of black unemployment. It tends to make companies trade higher wages for blacks off against the reduction of the African work force. It helps to create a privileged group of black insiders at the price of the increasing marginalization of the outsiders. I believe external pressure on South Africa can be beneficial but that it should be directed at helping all South African blacks, outsiders as well as insiders. I believe that if the overseas antiapartheid lobby had kept this goal in mind it would not have pushed for higher black wages but simply for the free movement of labor, and by that I mean unrestricted mobility for everyone living within the boundaries of South Africa as they were in 1961. Had they worked toward this goal, the overseas lobbies would have done far more for South African blacks as a whole than they have achieved through all their efforts over the last ten years. And multinational companies would have done much more to protect their assets and the system of free enterprise if they had insisted on hiring labor wherever they could find it rather than dealing with a protected insider black work force.

For business in general the facts about the extreme insecurity of the migrant workers might be cause for considerable concern. After all, migrant African men together with commuters constitute more than half of all economically active black men in the white areas. Yet a hard-nosed businessman could still argue that this poses no immediate threat to his business, that migrant work insecurity will not necessarily lead to migrant worker strikes (perhaps even the converse), and that the challenge to business is still to keep unit labor costs as low as possible. And managers of companies with few migrant laborers in their service may feel compassion for the suffering of blacks in the homelands but still argue that this does not affect the short- to medium-term profit calculations of their company as long as their own black employees are well paid. This brings me to my third point about migrant labor.

3. *The migrant labor system will lead to ever greater cleavages and tensions between whites and urban insider blacks and between insider blacks and migrant labor blacks. This will fatally undermine any strategy to win the hearts and minds of the so-called black middle class for the capitalist system.* A complex development can be expected in the 1980s. Starving and unemployed blacks will not stay in the homelands but will come to the cities, legally or illegally. Already 500,000 of the blacks in metropolitan Durban are there illegally. The overwhelming majority of the 600,000 people of Winterveld, the squatter camp in Bophuthatswana just outside Pretoria, live there illegally. And they will come in ever greater numbers. The state will try to build higher walls around our cities to keep them out—the government is now considering a fine of R5,000 for blacks found illegally in "white areas."

We will all suffer for this, for the free development of each is the condition for the free development of all. Influx control and the need to have a strong state to impose it will inevitably erode our few remaining civil liberties as the state resorts to ever greater powers to keep blacks out of the white areas and crush resistance. It also means greater harassment of the black insiders, for how can you avoid harassing the urban insider if you want to keep ten or twenty of his rural cousins out? Already existing conflicts between the black insiders and the migrant workers will increase because of sharpened competition among the working population for employment opportunities in the intermediate levels of the economy. In such circumstances I cannot see how the South African government can hope to coopt a meaningful number of urban blacks for our political order and the capitalist system.

Soon we shall get more effective black community councils in the cities. Given the present state of black politics, it will be most surprising if these councils are not taken over by a homeland-based political movement whose migrant labor element will dominate the permanent black element. It should come as no surprise if the movements taking control of the community councils will increasingly articulate the outsiders' claims—radicalized, desperate outsiders—and that the interests of black white-collar workers, the most favored employees of the multinationals, will take a back seat. What I wish to convey is the picture of a destabilized workforce of urban black workers acquiring not more security, as the Wiehahn-Riekert dispensation promised, but less security, not identifying more with the capitalist system but less. For stability can be achieved only if jobs are allocated not through the white man's law but through the operation of a free market for labor. Only then will the "haves" among the blacks form an effective political organization to protect their objective class interests against the "have-nots."

The Growing Ideological Challenge to the Capitalist System in South Africa

I have identified two trends so far, a growing political vacuum in government as the Afrikaner split deepens, and the radicalization of blacks—both of outsiders and insiders. Business leaders may still say that this is above all a problem for the National party politicians on the one hand and the army or security police on the other hand. The reforms that business desires may not be forthcoming, but nonetheless political and economic stability look assured for at least five to seven years. Here I would like to draw attention to a quiet revolution that has been going on for the last ten years that transforms the first two trends into serious concerns for business over the longer run. This is the revolution in South African historiography.

During the past fifteen years a new school of South African history has sprung up which is sometimes called "revisionist" or "radical" or "neo-Marxist", for it draws heavily on Karl Marx's emphasis on the class struggle and class exploitation. I am not a member of this school, but I know their work and as a historian I can assess their standing. I must frankly state that it dominates South African historiography at the moment and will continue to do so in the future. For obvious reasons, this school's history will be very attractive to the new generation of well-educated blacks.

Up to ten years ago, South African history writing was dominated by the idea that the capitalist economy was inherently rational, efficient, and beneficial to all in South Africa. It was, of course, thwarted by irrational and archaic race policies, but the capitalist economy was gradually winning out, gradually making nonsense of the racial system, gradually bringing progress and justice to South Africa. This was the dominant orthodoxy.

The new revisionist school sees everything in a radically different way. For them the central fact in South African history is "the super-exploitation of black labor by a racially structured capitalism."[2] They see apartheid and white supremacy as an integral and functional component of South African capitalism and economic growth. For them our present labor system, of which migrant labor forms such an important part, was instituted for the interest of business. The state and business combined to keep black labor as cheap and weak as possible. These historians see the pass laws, migrant labor, and segregation first of all in terms of a powerful capitalist principle: "We want the most possible work from blacks at the lowest possible cost and with the least possible responsibility for blacks." In the view of this school, apartheid is not inimical to the capitalist system—it is essentially designed to facilitate and increase capitalist exploitation. What is really the problem of South Africa is not the prejudices of the whites, but the subordination of blacks in order to exploit their labor more efficiently.

This interpretation simply skirts many important facts, but it will be folly to underestimate the great and growing influence of this school. Indeed it would be hard to deny the claim of one of the exponents of this interpretation that "the new, more radical and class-oriented way of looking at South African history and society, which emerged (in the early 1970s) definitely influenced the shape and thrust of political opposition to, and pressures upon, white domination in South Africa during the 1970s and into the present."[3] Moreover, the recent recession, which threw a large number of well-educated blacks into the streets, must certainly have increased the attractiveness of this radical class interpretation.

Very few migrants have probably read this new interpretation, but their daily experiences have led them to very much the same conclusions. A survey conducted in early 1982 by Schlemmer and Moller shows that migrants display the following attitudes toward business leaders: 91 percent thought they try to get as much work out of blacks for the smallest amount of pay; 94 percent thought they run to the police whenever there is a dispute; 84 percent thought they always try to replace black workers with machines; 85 percent believed they do not give black employees a chance to show their ability; 86 percent thought business leaders work with and support the government; 72 percent thought they do not care about blacks. There was not much evidence of positive attitudes. Only 40 percent thought that business helps black people by providing work and only 14 percent thought that business helps blacks by appealing to the government.

How can business answer these charges of superexploitation? Not by refusing to employ migrant laborers: this will be drawing exactly the wrong conclusions. It can shout "not guilty" and there will be some measure of truth in their reply. Many big businesses in South Africa have over the last ten years moved on to what one can call liberal capitalism, which demands a well-paid and secure labor force rather than badly paid and repressed workers. But this does not get these big businesses out of the dock. A vast underclass of migrant laborers—men turned into atomized strangers in their own land—will always be a living indictment of the exploitative nature of capitalism, very much like the dark satanic mills of the nineteenth-century Industrial Revolution in England that spurred not only Karl Marx but a whole array of liberal reformers to fight the excesses of capitalism. So long as South Africa has this underclass of migrant workers, business will be in the dock, accused of being an accomplice in oppressing a superexploitable black labor force. So long will migrant labor be presented as lying at the heart of both white supremacy and capitalism. And so long will there be no hope of genuine political and economic stability.

But what can big business do about migrant labor? First of all there must be an acceptance of its dangers which will also affect business. Second, it must accept that continued economic growth will not sweep away migrant labor: There must be political action. And political action will only come if business is prepared to make a very strong stand on this issue in the belief that migrant labor poses the greatest long-term threat to the survival of capitalism and stability in South Africa.

The Challenges Facing Business

Business faces three fundamental challenges. They are: (1) to formulate its own role in South Africa, (2) to renegotiate business's relations with government, and (3) to renegotiate business's relations with black South Africa.

Business's Proper Role in South Africa

Let me suggest an analogy. Business in South Africa is now rapidly moving toward the kind of position the large international oil companies found themselves in in the early 1970s. In *The Seven Sisters*, Anthony Sampson describes well how the international oil companies had to perform a delicate balancing act between the producing and consuming countries. The producing countries wanted a far greater price for their product and a greater share in the profits. The consuming countries wanted to preserve the way of life they were just becoming used to. It does not stretch the imagination much to see black South Africa in the place of the Arab or African producing countries and white South Africa in the place of the consuming countries.

The proper role of business in the 1980s will have to be very much that of the more enlightened international oil companies. It will have to become a buffer element between the producing and consuming countries, between black and white South Africa. It will have to be the thin lubricating oil between the two forces while doing business in between, detached from the special interests of either of the two forces.

Business cannot act as a buffer or a thin lubricating oil between black and white South Africa, however, if it does not first of all get consensus within its ranks about what the proper role of business within the political order of South Africa should be. Meetings of top and middle levels of management are needed to establish as broad a consensus as possible.

The discussion of three issues is central: (1) the principle of equality of opportunity for all; (2) the principle of freedom of association; (3) the political environment in which business wants to operate—and this involves a discussion of the political system in which blacks not only as customers but as proper citizens of South Africa could play a full role. And let's be frank: This will have to include a discussion of formulas for the real sharing of power between whites and blacks.

This leads us to a host of questions. Can American firms develop such a philosophy for doing business in our political order? Are they prepared to carry this philosophy out in the rough political world of South Africa, both on the national and regional level? Can they work together on an industry and perhaps interindustry basis and begin discussions on the way in which this philosophy should be implemented and on how negotiations with government could be conducted on these issues?

Renegotiating Business's Relationship with Government

We can isolate two different postures that business can take to government. It can get into bed with government and make hay while the sun shines, or it can assert itself as a force in its own right with its own clearly articulated views about what constitutes the true interests of South Africa.

As Shlemmer's opinion survey suggests, most blacks believe that business is getting into bed with government and is aligned with the cause of white supremacy. Business at this stage looks to be very much part of a team with the white political establishment in countering the total onslaught, breaking South Africa's isolation in world sport and discussing at the Carleton and Good Hope Conferences schemes that many interpret as intended to elaborate separate development. As a white sports lover I enjoy watching international teams brought to South Africa by whatever means, but if I were a business manager having to sell my wares to a growing black consumer market I would be worried about the kinds of signals sent out by my company's involvement in any kind of sports ventures of this kind.

Underlying efforts such as this is the view that a company is not a benevolent institution for world peace but that it is there to make as much money as quickly as possible. I would contend that this philosophy may work in other parts of the world but that it represents an extremely short-sighted view of the challenges facing business in South Africa. As a radical black government or, for that matter, a radical black opposition movement will certainly look with increasingly critical eyes at business in South Africa because capitalism in South Africa is linked so closely with both the present unequal distribution of wealth and white supremacy. And the oil companies will be particularly vulnerable if a radical black opposition movement starts gathering momentum: their role in the busting of oil sanctions against Rhodesia will certainly be remembered and exploited.

The challenge to business in South Africa is whether it will make use of its great resources to assert itself as a force in its own right, taking a long view of the future of South Africa and opting for long-term stability over short-term profits. This does not mean doing anything that is against business interests; it means in fact speaking up for capitalism or, rather, for what Jill Nattrass has called "reform capitalism." Perhaps the time has come to consider whether American firms, and large businesses generally, should become the spokesmen of a truly nonracial capitalism. Think about an advertisement in newspapers reading: "The survival of free enterprise in South Africa demands the free movement of labor" or "Desegregation of the factory floor makes no business sense without the desegregation of some residential areas."

Such actions may well involve costs. For businesses operating in a highly competitive and strategic field, confrontation with government can be uncomfortable. No one is suggesting that the Botha government will nationalize companies that start running advertisements in newspapers along the lines I suggested, but there is the risk of some lighter but quite unpleasant penalties that could be inflicted in the concessions and tax fields.

In its relations with the government, business seems at times to have become a prisoner of its own fears. Does business not still sometimes work with the stock image of a monolithic government based on a solid ethnic bloc guided by a rigid ideology of separate development and determined to squash all opposition, white or black? This government is on record in committing itself above all to the promotion of economic growth and the defense of the system of free enterprise. Skeptics may wonder if the preservation of Afrikaner rule is still not the highest consideration. All I can say as a student of this government is that one cannot be sure. As Harry Oppenheimer and many political scientists have observed, the rhetoric of today often becomes the policy of tomorrow.

The proviso is that there should be enough powerful forces in society to coax, cajole, and even coerce government to live up to its rhetoric.

A redefinition of business's relationship with the government must surely begin with business returning to some of the guiding principles of the system of free enterprise that have been almost fatally compromised in South Africa. Surely the system of free enterprise cannot be defended as long as influx control exists. Surely blacks cannot be won over to capitalism if business refrains from speaking up on the right of every man to sell his labor where he wants and for the fundamental principle of equality of opportunity. Here lies a unique opportunity for a company that wants to assume the role of an articulate defender of capitalism. No doubt the government will be irritated, but business can no longer postpone speaking out publicly about issues like Group Areas and influx control and the way in which these policies conflict with free enterprise. Until it does so, business will make no real headway against the suspicion, deeply seated in black South Africans, that business is simply hypocritical in its commitment to free enterprise.

A major challenge to business is quite simply to save the system of capitalism from being fatally undermined by cynicism among blacks that capitalism and white supremacy are in cahoots with each other. A redefinition of business's relationship with government must begin with business clearly spelling out its own philosophy, its own commitments, and exactly where it parts company with white supremacy.

Redefining the Relationship of Business with the Black Community

It takes no imagination to see the rise of black consumer pressure in the 1980s. Here I do not simply mean boycotts but what Jesse Jackson calls renegotiating black America's relations with corporate America. The challenge for firms is to preempt that consumer pressure.

Recently Jackson told the Chrysler Motor Corporation: "Obviously we will trade with people who will trade with us." He told Chrysler: "Last year blacks spent fourteen billion dollars in the auto industry. The black community is a substantial investor." Chrysler has immediately started negotiations with Mr. Jackson. In 1982 Jackson and his organization, Operation Push, started a campaign against Coca-Cola under the slogan "Don't Choke on Coke." He told the company that black Americans last year bought $300 million dollars worth of their soft drink and might not necessarily continue to do so unless certain benefits were returned to the black community.

The Coca-Cola Company was impressed enough to enter into negotiations with Mr. Jackson and at the end of the bargaining things went a lot better with Coke. They appointed a black to the board, doubled advertising in black newspapers, greatly stepped up involvement in their business system. After similar negotiations Kentucky Fried Chicken promised to double spending with black advertising agencies and to open one hundred black-owned outlets.

One does not know how long it will be before similar organizations as Jackson's Push spring up in South Africa with as much clout—but business in South Africa had better be prepared.

Conclusion

I would like to end with a quote taken from Anthony Sampson's *The Seven Sisters*:

> The big companies as they revealed when they shared out the oil during the oil embargo of the mid-seventies, had a unique machinery to enable them to be the world's oil controllers; but they were basically so predominantly American or British that other nations could never allow them that role over the long run. If they had lived up to their rhetoric they may have transformed their board and top management to reflect an awareness of both producing and consuming countries: thus they might have avoided the initial confrontation with OPEC.[4]

Let me translate that into South African terms. Big business in South Africa has the resources that given the will and the courage affords it a unique opportunity to push for faster change and mediate between black and white South Africa. However, business is so tied up with white supremacy that blacks are increasingly refusing to believe that business can or should play that role. If business wants to live up to its rhetoric it should now transform its role and relationship with both black South Africa and with the present government of South Africa. Only in this way can it avoid confrontation with South Africa's OPEC—the black community.

Notes

1. Charles Simkins, "Can black unemployment be solved?," unpublished paper presented to the Buthelezi Commission, 1981.
2. Frederick Johnstone, " 'Most painful to our hearts': South Africa through the eyes of the new school," *Canadian Journal of African Studies* 16, no. 5, (1982):5–26.
3. Ibid.
4. Anthony Sampson, *The Seven Sisters: The Great Oil Companies and the World They Shaped* (New York: Viking Press, 1975).

Appendix A
Statistical View
of South Africa

Population

Total: The official 1983 estimates of the population of South Africa (including the so-called independent homelands of the Transkei, Bophuthatswana, Venda, and Ciskei) are

Blacks	22,728,998	73.0%
Whites	4,748,000	15.3%
Coloreds (mixed race)	2,765,000	8.9%
Asian	870,000	2.8%
Total	31,111,998	100.0%

Homelands: The South African Institute of Race Relations has estimated the 1983 population of each of the ten homelands to be

Bophuthatswana	1,425,066
Ciskei	720,807
Gazankulu	554,602
KaNgwane	173,963
KwaNdebele	169,262
KwaZulu	3,691,785
Lebowa	1,884,194
QwaQwa	169,500
Transkei	2,502,317
Venda	339,808
Total	11,631,304

Population Growth

	Black	White	Colored	Asian
Birth rate per 1,000	39.1	17.0	31.0	20.0
Mortality rate per 1,000	11.0	8.2	10.3	6.1

Infant Deaths

	Black	White	Colored	Asian
1978	25,599	1,295	5,233	433
1979	27,990	1,325	5,856	538
1980	22,713	982	4,431	482
1981	21,605	1,067	4,839	494

Economy

Gross national product, 1981	$74.67 billion
GNP per capita, 1981	$2,770
Foreign trade, 1982 (Total of exports plus imports)	$27.44 billion
Major trading partners (exports plus imports)	
1. United States	$3.079 billion (10.6%)
2. United Kingdom	$2.779 billion (9.6%)
3. West Germany	$2.742 billion (9.5%)
4. Japan	$1.425 billion (4.9%)

Labor Statistics

Workforce

	1980	1990*	2000*	Increase 1980–2000*
Blacks	6,323,000	8,347,000	10,688,000	69.0%
Whites	1,938,000	2,248,000	2,435,000	25.6%
Colored	966,000	1,274,000	1,516,000	56.9%
Asian	263,000	344,000	413,000	57.0%
Total	9,490,000	12,213,000	15,051,000	58.6%

*Estimates

Unemployment

Reliable estimates of unemployment are unavailable for South Africa because of inadequacies in the government's method of collecting statistics. In 1980, official statistics showed an unemployment rate among whites of less than 1 percent while in the homelands unemployment was estimated at 27.5 percent.

Distribution of Workforce by Place of Work (1980)

	All Groups		Blacks	
"White" South Africa	8,064,000	93.1%	4,985,000	89.4%
Homelands*	602,000	6.9%	592,000	10.6%
Total	8,666,000	100.0%	5,577,000	100.0%

*Excludes the four "independent" homelands

Income (1980) (Average Monthly Earnings in Rands)

Sector	Blacks	Whites	Coloreds	Asians
Construction	173	898	276	454
Electricity	210	894	326	—
Finance and insurance	259	740	319	430
Government and services	168	634	229	420
Manufacturing	217	917	254	287
Mining	168	1,057	310	433
Trade and accommodation services	139	504	186	277
Transport and communi- cations	198	748	195	344

Education

Per Capita Expenditures (in Rands)

	1979–80	1982–83
Blacks	91.29	192.34
Whites	1,169.00	1,385.00
Coloreds	234.00	593.37
Asians	389.66	871.87

Pupil/Teacher Ratios

	1979	1983
Blacks	47.6:1	42.7:1
Whites	19.6:1	18.2:1
Coloreds	29.6:1	26.7:1
Asians	26.2:1	23.6:1

Functional Illiteracy (1979)

	Men	Women
Rural Blacks	65.4%	60.5%
Urban Blacks	39.9%	22.6%
Whites	0.0%	1.1%
Coloreds	24.7%	18.1%
Asians	6.7%	16.1%

Source: *Survey of Race Relations in South Africa 1983* (Johannesburg: South African Institute of Race Relations, 1984).

Appendix B
The U.S. Business Presence in South Africa

U.S. private direct investment in South Africa equalled $2.8 billion in 1982, an increase of 6.5 percent over 1981 and of 20.6 percent over 1980. The increase resulted primarily from a higher level of retained earnings by American companies in South Africa; capital inflows were believed to account for no more than $100 million of new investment over the two-year period. These investments are profitable: According to 1983 estimates, U.S. firms received an average 18 percent return on manufacturing investment in South Africa as opposed to 12.6 percent elsewhere; for mining investment, the return was 25 percent in South Africa and only 13.7 percent elsewhere. Indirect investments are more difficult to estimate. Approximately six thousand U.S. firms carried on an estimated $3.1 billion in trade in 1982. In 1983, Americans owned 25.6 percent of all South African gold shares, down from 30 percent in 1979. Total American portfolio investment in public sector stock was $1.7 billion for 1983. Loans by American banks to the South African public sector declined from $623 million in 1982 to $343 million in September 1984. New lending to the government by American banks appears to have stopped. Loans by American banks to the South African private sector, excluding banks, increased from $495 million in June 1981 to $1.1 billion in September 1984 and loans to South African banks increased from $1.08 billion in June 1981 to $3.5 billion in September 1984. In 1982, U.S. loans to South Africa totalled $623 million and U.S. purchases of krugerrands (South African gold coins) equalled $363 million.

The most conspicuous element of the U.S. business presence in South Africa is the more than three hundred U.S. firms that have operations there. There is no single, authoritative listing of such companies, but compilations have been made by the U.S. Consulate General in Johannesburg, by the Investor Responsibility Research Center (whose list is updated periodically in their publication, *The South African Review Service Reporter*), by the United Nations Center against Apartheid, by the American Chamber of Commerce in Johannesburg, and by the American Friends Service Committee.

The following is an unofficial list of U.S. subsidiaries and affiliates doing business in South Africa, compiled by the Commercial Section of the U.S. Consulate General, Johannesburg, in 1982. The Commerce Department warns that

> While extensive efforts have been made to ensure accuracy, it should not be assumed that the list includes every American firm in South Africa nor that every entry is correct. Companies are only included on the list when they provide the Consulate with information or when they come to its attention.
>
> The list includes only those firms in which American companies or individuals have a substantial direct capital investment in the form of stock, as the sole owner, or as a partner in the enterprise. No attempt has been made to include foreign firms operating under a contract, license, franchise or on a commission basis, where no actual American capital is involved. Noncommercial entities are not included.

Abbreviations and Symbols

(S) 50% or more American control

(A) 49% or less American control

(B) Branch or representative Office

*Not applicable or unavailable

Name, Address & Tel. No. of Local Firm	Product/Service Category	No. of Employees	American Parent or Associate
(S) AAF (Pty.) Ltd P.O. Box 10224 Johannesburg 2000 (726-5150)	Air pollution control	120	American Air Filter Co. 215 Central Ave. Louisville, KY 40277
(A) Abbott Laboratories SA (Pty.) Ltd. P.O. Box 1616 Johannesburg 2000 (942-3100)	Pharmaceuticals, hospital products, and infant nutritionals	147	Abbott Universal Ltd. 14th St. & Sheridan Rd. North Chicago, IL 60064
(B) ABC News P.O. Box 4516 Johannesburg 2000 (726-7280)	News	4	American Broadcasting Co. 1330 Ave. of the Americas New York, NY 10019
(S) ABS Worldwide Technical Services Inc. P.O. Box 4059 Durban 4000 (31-7517)	Engineering and marine technical services	15	ABS Worldwide Technical Services Inc. 65 Broadway New York, NY 10006
(A) AccuRay SA (Pty.) Ltd. P.O. Box 696 Springs 1560 (56-8826)	Servicing and spare parts for measurement control systems	21	AccuRay Corp. 650 Ackerman Rd. Columbus, OH 43202
(A) AFIA (see Monarch) P.O. Box 61115 Marshalltown 2107 (838-6711)	Claims settling agency	65	AFIA Worldwide Insurance 1700 Valley Rd. Wayne, NJ 07470
(S) AHSC SA (Pty.) Ltd. P.O. Box 2726 Johannesburg 2000 (39-6631)	Medical and surgical distributors	32	American Hospital Supply Corp. One American Plaza Evanston, IL 60201

Name, Address & Tel. No. of Local Firm	Product/Service Category	No. of Employees	American Parent or Associate
(A) Airco Engineering (Pty.) Ltd. P.O. Box 297 Bergvlei 2012 (786-7101)	Air conditioning and refrigeration equipment, turbines	220	Carrier Corp. P.O. Box 4806 Syracuse, NY 13221
(S) Air Express Int'l. Corp. P.O. Box 558 Kempton Park 1620 (970-1730)	Air freight forwarders	45	Air Express Int'l. Corp. 120 Tokemeta Rd. Darien, CT 06820
(A) Airshields of SA (Pty.) Ltd. P.O. Box 17664 Hillbrow 2038 (614-6245)	Medical equipment	14	Narco Air Shields Hatboro, PA 19040
(S) Alexander Howden Insurance Brokers P.O. Box 5919 Johannesburg 2000 (28-5420)	Insurance	370	Alexander and Alexander Int'l. Corp. 1211 Ave. of the Americas New York, NY 10036
(B) Allen, Louis A. Associates 132 Jan Smuts Ave. Parkwood 2193 (442-7366)	Management consultation, education, and research	6	Louis A. Allen Associates Inc. 3600 W. Bayshore Rd. Palo Alto, CA 94303
(S) Allenwest-GE Manufacturing (Pty.) Ltd. P.O. Box 5210 Benoni South 1502 (52-7211)	Industrial motor controls; components, flameproof gear, lighting, and lamps	330	General Electric Co. 1285 Boston Ave. Bridgeport, CT 06602
(S) Allis Chalmers Services Inc. P.O. Box 47038 Parklands 2121 (788-1487)	Servicing Allis Chalmers equipment	1	Allis Chalmers Corp. P.O. Box 512 Milwaukee, WI 53201

	U.S. Parent	Employees	Business	South African Affiliate
(S)	A.M. Int'l. Inc. 1834 Walden Office Sq. Schaumburg, IL 60196	370	Suppliers of business equipment	A.M. Int'l. (Pty.) Ltd. 295 Kent Ave. Ferndale Randburg 2194 (832-1961)
(S)	Amdahl International Corp. 1250 East Arques Ave. Sunnyvale, CA 94086	6	Computers	Amdahl International Corp. P.O. Box 39194 Booysens 2016 (683-6842)
(S)	American Airlines P.O. Box 61616 Dallas/Fort Worth Airport TX 75261	4	Airline sales	American Airlines P.O. Box 62131 Marshalltown 2017 (21-3409)
(B)	American Bureau of Shipping 65 Broadway New York, NY 10006	15	Ship classification	American Bureau of Shipping P.O. Box 4059 Durban 4000 (31-7517)
(B)	American Express Int'l. Banking Corp. American Express Plaza New York, NY 10004	4	Markets travelers checks	American Express International Inc. 600 Marbrook 123 Commissioner St. Johannesburg 2001 (23-5386)
(S)	American Int'l. Group 70 Pine St. New York, NY 10270	160	Insurance	American International Insurance Co. Ltd. P.O. Box 31983 Braamfontein 2017 (39-4111)
(A)	Arthur Andersen and Co. 69 West Washington St. Chicago, IL 60602	250	Accountants and auditors	Arthur Andersen & Company P.O. Box 3652 Johannesburg 2000 (21-4831)

Name, Address & Tel. No. of Local Firm	Product/Service Category	No. of Employees	American Parent or Associate
Branches at P.O. Box 2563 Cape Town 8000 (21-2350) P.O. Box 2050 Durban 4000 (31-5442)			
(S) Anikem (Pty.) Ltd. P.O. Box 84 Johannesburg 2000 (970-3911/20)	Industrial	93	Nalco Chemical 2901 Butterfield Rd. Oak Brook, IL 60521
(S) Applied Power SA (Pty.) Ltd. P.O. Box 39225 Bramley 2013 (786-4520)	Automotive service & industrial hydraulic equipment	32	Applied Power Inc. P.O. Box 325 Milwaukee, WI 53211
(S) Arlabs (Pty.) Ltd. P.O. Box 557 Kempton Park 1620 (975-0205)	Spectrographic instruments, sales and service	30	Bausch & Lomb Inc. 42 East Ave. Rochester, NY 14606
(S) Armco Autometrics P.O. Box 51940 Randburg 2125 (48-0530)	Suppliers of electronic equipment to mines	3	Armco Inc. P.O. Box 700 Middletown, OH 45042
(S) Armco Bronne (Pty.) Ltd. P.O. Box 61384 Marshalltown 2107 (838-3961)	Exploration	5	Armco Inc. P.O. Box 700 Middletown, OH 45042
(S) Armco Robson P.O. Box 63 Isando 1600 (36-8511)	Fabricated steel plates	88	Armco Inc. P.O. Box 700 Middletown, OH 45042

	South African Office	Business	Employees	U.S. Office
(A)	Arthur Young & Co. P.O. Box 4307 Cape Town 3000 (21-4520) P.O. Box 454 Johannesburg 2000 (836-7331/3)	Accounting and auditing	475	Arthur Young and Co. 277 Park Ave. New York, NY 10172
(S)	Asgrow SA (Pty.) Ltd. P.O. Box 653 Silverton 0127 (83-1165)	Plant breeding and seed marketing	60	Asgrow Seed Co. Kalamazoo, MI 49001
(S)	Asoma Africa (Pty.) Ltd. P.O. Box 32234 Bramfontein 2017 (725-2510)	Trading in metals and minerals	20	Associated Metals and Minerals Corp. 30 Rockefeller Plaza New York, NY 10020
(B)	Associated Press 7th Floor Union Centre West 52 Simmonds St. Johannesburg 2001 (838-7871)	News	4	The Associated Press 50 Rockefeller Plaza New York, NY 10020
(A)	Avis Rent-a-Car P.O. Box 221 Isando 1600 (36-2571)	Car rentals	500	Avis Rent-a-Car Inc. World Headquarters 900 Old Country Rd. Garden City, NY 10015
(S)	Ayerst Laboratories (Pty.) Ltd. P.O. Box 573 Halfway House 1635 (805-2081)	Pharmaceuticals	62	Ayerst Int'l. Inc. 685 Third Ave. New York, NY 10017

Name, Address & Tel. No. of Local Firm	Product/Service Category	No. of Employees	American Parent or Associate
(S) BBDO Advertising SA (Pty.) Ltd. P.O. Box 2983 Johannesburg 2000 (39-4071)	Advertising	340	BBDO Int'l. Inc. 383 Madison Ave. New York, NY 10017
(S) B-M Group (Pty.) Ltd. P.O. Box 9706 Johannesburg 2000 (39-5836)	Toiletries and pharmaceuticals	330	Bristol-Myers Co. International Div. 345 Park Ave. New York, NY 10022
(S) Badger SA (Pty.) Ltd. P.O. Box 78509 Sandton 2146 (783-4840)	Petroleum and petro-chemical engineers	7	The Badger Co. Inc. 1 Broadway Cambridge, MA 02142
— Balkinds Agencies (Pty.) Ltd. P.O. Box 10575 Johannesburg 2000 (29-9895)	Giftware	40	None—independent
(B) Baltimore Sun P.O. Box 2662 Johannesburg 2000 (29-6985)	Newspaper	1	The Sunpapers Baltimore Culvert & Centre Sts. Baltimore, MD 21203
(A) Bates Wells Kennedy P.O. Box 6547 Johannesburg 2000 (788-7350)	Advertising agency	400	Ted Bates Worldwide Inc. 1515 Broadway New York, NY 10036
(S) Beckman Instruments P.O. Box 963 Cape Town 8000 (46-1130) Branch offices in Durban and Johannesburg	Scientific and indus-trial instruments	57	Beckman Instruments Inc. 2500 Harbor Blvd. Fullerton, CA 92634

	Company (South Africa)	Description	Employees	U.S. Parent
(S)	Beech-Nut Life Savers Ltd. P.O. Box 78532 Sandton 2146 (783-7100)	Gums and sweets	656	Nabisco Brands Inc. 625 Madison Ave. New York, NY 10022
(S)	Bell & Howell SA (Pty.) Ltd. P.O. Box 31239 Braamfontein 2017 (724-9361)	Microfilm products and electronic instruments	100	Bell & Howell Co. 7100 McCormick Rd. Chicago, IL 60645
	Berkshire Int'l. P.O. Box 788 East London 5200 (000-0000)	Ladies hosiery and knitwear	960	Berkshire Int'l. Corp. P.O. Box 1022 Reading, PA 19603
	Big Dutchman SA (Pty.) Ltd. P.O. Box 276 Edenvale 1610	Livestock feeding systems	40	United States Industries 250 Park Ave. New York, NY 10017
	Black Clawson Ltd. P.O. Box 391527 Bramley 2018 (736-2785)	Paper-making machinery	6	Black Clawson Overseas 200 Park Ave. New York, NY 10017
	Black & Decker SA (Pty.) Ltd. P.O. Box 4934 Cape Town 8000	Power tools	63	The Black & Decker Mfg. Co. 701 East Joppa Rd. Towson, MD 21204
	Black Mountain Mineral Development Co. (Pty.) Ltd. P.O. Box 1167 Johannesburg 2000 (833-3811)	Base metal mine	1375	Phelps Dodge Corp. 300 Park Ave. New York, NY 10022
	Blue Bell Wrangler (Pty.) Ltd. P.O. Box 32200 Moberni 4060 (924224)	Casual clothing	600	Blue Bell Inc. P.O. Box 21483 Greensboro, NC 27420
	Boeing International Corp. P.O. Box 31393 Braamfontein 2017 (725-1840)	Co-ordinates Boeing functions in South Africa	1	The Boeing Co. P.O. Box 3707 Seattle, WA 98124

Name, Address & Tel. No. of Local Firm	Product/Service Category	No. of Employees	American Parent or Associate
(S) Bomag (Pty.) Ltd. P.O. Box 649 Kempton Park 1620 (975-9228)	Cranes; excavation and compaction equipment	50	Koehring Co. P.O. Box 422 Milwaukee, WI 53216
(S) Borden (Pty.) Ltd. P.O. Box 31633 Braamfontein 2017 (39-2865)	Milk and chemical products	300	Borden Inc. 420 Lexington Ave. New York, NY 10170
(S) Borg-Warner SA (Pty.) Ltd. P.O. Box 388 Uitenhage 6230 (2-9102)	Auto parts and service	800	Borg-Warner Corp. 200 South Michigan Ave. Chicago, IL 60604
(A) Bowring Barclays and Associates SA Ltd. P.O. Box 61787 Marshalltown 2137 (833-0011)	Insurance brokers	1050	Marsh and McLennan Co. Inc. 1221 Ave. of the Americas New York, NY 10020
(S) L.J. Buck Stripping (Pty.) Ltd. P.O. Box 1929 Durban 4000 (32-0502)	Ship charter operators	4	Leonard J. Buck, Inc. 95 Madison Ave. Morristown, NJ 07960
(S) Buckman Laboratories (Pty.) Ltd. P.O. Box 591 Hammersdale 3702 (6-1010)	Industrial process chemicals	28	Buckman Laboratories Inc. 1256 N. McClean Blvd. Memphis, TN 38108
(S) Bucyrus (Africa) (Pty.) Ltd. P.O. Box 482 Isando 1600 (36-2391)	Mining machinery	22	Bucyrus-Erie Co. 1100 Milwaukee Ave. South Milwaukee, WI 53172

Company (South Africa)	Employees	Business	U.S. Parent
(A) Bundy Tubing Co. SA (Pty.) Ltd. P.O. Box 506 King Williams Town 5600 (23442/3)	200	Tubing for automobile and refrigeration industries	Bundy Corp. 12345 E. Nine Mile Rd. Warren, MI 48090
(S) Burroughs Machines Ltd. P.O. Box 3996 Johannesburg 2000 (442-2111)	550	Business machines and computers	Burroughs Corp. Burroughs Place P.O. Box 330 A Detroit, MI 48232
(B) Business Week P.O. Box 31713 Braamfontein 2017 (37-8066)	1	News	McGraw-Hill Inc. 1221 Ave. of the Americas New York, NY 10020
(S) Butterick Fashions Marketing Co. (SA) P.O. Box 6269 Johannesburg 2000 (29-9117)	53	Importers and distributors of wholesale paper patterns	Butterick Fashion Marketing Co. 161 Sixth Ave. New York, NY 10013
(S) CBI Constructors Ltd. C.C. Box 99-005 Carlton Centre Johannesburg 2001 (21-7871)	500	Fabrication and construction of large metal plate structure	Chicago Bridge & Iron Co. 800 Jorie Blvd. Oak Brook, IL 60521
(B) CBS News Union Centre West 52 Simmonds St. Johannesburg 2001 (838-7545)	6	News	CBS News 545 W. 57th St. New York, NY 10019
(S) C-H Truck Components P.O. Box 14089 Wadeville 1422 (34-9124)	3	Truck components	Eaton Corp. Erieview Plaza Cleveland, OH 44114

Name, Address & Tel. No. of Local Firm	Product/Service Category	No. of Employees	American Parent or Associate
(S) CPC Int'l. SA (Pty.) Ltd. P.O. Box 1544 Durban 4000 (31-4461)	Manufacture of starches, branded grocery products	930	CPC International Inc. International Plaza Englewood Cliffs, NJ 07632
(A) Caltex Oil SA (Pty.) Ltd. P.O. Box 714 Cape Town 8000 (21-2550)	Petroleum products	2238	Caltex Petroleum Corp. 3020 Southland Center Dallas, TX 75201
(S) Carborundum-Universal SA (Pty.) Ltd. P.O. Box 1114 Port Elizabeth 6000 (4-6551)	Abrasives	819	Standard Oil Co. of Ohio (SOHIO) (through Kennecott Corp.) Midland Bldg. Cleveland, OH 44115
(B) Cardkey Systems of SA (Pty.) Ltd. P.O. Box 18304 Hillbrow 2038 (643-1426/643-8246)	Supply and installation of access control and security systems	11	Cardkey Systems 20660 Bahama St. Chatsworth, CA 91311
(A) The Carlton P.O. Box 7709 Johannesburg 2000 (21-8911)	Hotel	940	Westin Hotels Westin Bldg. Seattle, WA 98121
(A) Carlton Paper Corp. Ltd. P.O. Box 6473 Johannesburg 2000 (616-1890)	Tissue and nonwoven products	1850	Kimberly-Clark Corp. P.O. Box 2001 North Lake St. Neenah, WI 54956
(A) Carman Industries SA (Pty.) Ltd. P.O. Box 50876 Randburg (793-1186)	Vibrating feeders	40	Carman Industries Inc. 1005 Riverside Rd. Jeffersonville, IN

	Employees	Products	U.S. Parent
(S) Carnation Foods (Pty.) Ltd. P.O. Box 1274 Durban 4000 (32-8631) Direct subsidiary of Carnation Ltd.	1003	Food products and pet accessories	Carnation Co. 5045 Wilshire Blvd. Los Angeles, CA 90036
(S) Cascade Corp. (Africa) (Pty.) Ltd. P.O. Box 625 Isando 1600 (36-5611)	15	Forklift attachments	Cascade Corp. P.O. Box 25240 Portland, OR 37225
(S) Case, J.I. SA (Pty.) Ltd. P.O. Box 347 Isando 1600 (3-3461)	250	Construction and agricultural equipment	J.I. Case Int'l. 700 State St. Racine, WI 53406
(S) Caterpillar (Africa) (Pty.) Ltd. P.O. Box 197 (36-3381)	107	Tractor replacement parts	Caterpillar Tractor Co. 100 N.E. Adams St. Peoria, IL 61629
(A) Chamberlain's (Pty.) Ltd. Private Bag X6 Tokai 7966 (75-3150)	464	Pharmaceuticals and consumer products	Warner-Lambert Co. P.O. Box 377 Morris Plains, NJ 07950
(S) Champion Spark Plug Co. of SA (Pty.) Ltd. P.O. Box 33 Isando 1600 (975-5948)	92	Sparking plugs	Champion Spark Plug Co. P.O. Box 910 Toledo, OH 43661
(S) Chase Manhattan Overseas Corp. P.O. Box 9606 Johannesburg 2000 (834-7581)	15	Financial services; Southern Africa repre- sentative office of Chase Manhattan Bank NA	Chase Manhattan Bank NA 1 Chase Manhattan Plaza New York, NY 10031

Name, Address & Tel. No. of Local Firm	Product/Service Category	No. of Employees	American Parent or Associate
(B) Cheesebrough-Ponds International Ltd. P.O. Box 14001 Wadeville 1422 (34-9217)	Toiletries and cosmetics	550	Cheesebrough-Pond's Inc. 33 Benedict Place Greenwich, CT 06830
(B) Christian Science Monitor C/O Reuters P.O. Box 2662 Johannesburg 2000 (616-3539)	News	1	Christian Science Monitor Christian Science Center 1 Norway St. Boston, MA 02115
(S) Chrome Corp. SA (Pty.) Ltd. P.O. Box 8194 Johannesburg 2000 (21-7387)	Untreated chrome ore in bulk	9	Union Carbide Corp. Old Ridgebury Rd. Danbury, CT 06817
(S) Circle Freight Int'l. (SA) (Pty.) Ltd. P.O. Box 128 Kempton Park 1620 (826-4431)	Customs broking and freight forwarding	60	The Harper Group 545 Sansome St. San Francisco, CA 94111
(S) Citibank NA Ltd. P.O. Box 9773 Johannesburg 2000 (833-5736)	Commercial banking	220	Citibank NA 399 Park Ave. New York, NY 10043
(B) The Coca-Cola Export Corp. P.O. Box 9999 Johannesburg 2000 (39-4354)	Soft drinks	170	The Coca-Cola Export Corp. P.O. Box Drawer 1734 Atlanta, GA 30301

	South African company	Employees	Business	U.S. parent company
(S)	Colgate-Palmolive Ltd. P.O. Box 213 Boksburg 1460 (52.8236)	650	Detergents, toiletries, and household products	Colgate-Palmolive Co. 300 Park Ave. New York, NY 10022
(S)	Collier, P.F. Inc. P.O. Box 10513 Johannesburg 2000 (37.2462)	11	Publishing encyclopedias	Collier Inc. 866 Third Ave. New York, NY 10002
(A)	Computer Sciences (Pty.) Ltd. P.O. Box 31497 Braamfontein 2017 (39.5936)	550	Data processing and computer equipment	Computer Sciences Corp. 2100 East Grand Ave. El Segundo, CA 90245
(S)	Consolidated Pneumatic Tool Co. P.O. Box 105 Isando 1600 (36.6761)	200	Compressed air products	Chicago Pneumatic Tool Co. 6 E. 44th St. New York, NY 10017
(S)	Continental SA P.O. Box 51455 Randburg 2125 (789.3100)	5	Grain exporters	Continental Grain Co. 277 Park Ave. New York, NY 10172
(S)	Control Data (Pty.) Ltd. P.O. Box 78105 Sandton 2146 (783.5225)	330	Computers and related services	Control Data Corp. 8100 34th Ave. S. Minneapolis, MN 55420
(S)	Coty Div. of Pfizer (Pty.) Ltd. P.O. Box 782917 Sandton 2146 (802.4223)	87	Cosmetics	Pfizer Inc. 235 E. 42nd St. New York, NY 10017
(S)	Coulter Electronics P.O. Box 84 Halfway House 1685 (805.2056)	30	Medical and scientific equipment	Coulter Electronics Inc. 590 W. 20th St. Hialeah, FL 33010

Name, Address & Tel. No. of Local Firm	Product/Service Category	No. of Employees	American Parent or Associate
(A) Crane Packaging (Pty.) Ltd. P.O. Box 890 Springs 1560 (818.2031)	Engineering specialists	100	John Crane-Houdaille Co. Oakton St. Morton Grove Chicago, IL 60053
(S) Crown Cork Co. SA (Pty.) Ltd. P.O. Box 4 Isando 1600 (36.2244)	Crown corks, beer, and beverage cans, aerosol cans, bottling machinery	525	Crown Cork and Seal Co. Inc. 9300 Ashton Road Philadelphia, PA 19136
(S) Cummins Diesel Int'l. P.O. Box 78190 Sandton 2146 (783.4634)	Diesel engines	5	Cummins Engine Co. Inc. P.O. Box 3005 Columbus, IN 47201
(S) Cutler-Hammer SA Ltd. P.O. Box 14089 Wadeville 1422 (34.9124)	Industrial motor control equipment, components, and control systems	300	Eaton Corp. Operations and Technical Center 4201 North 27th St. Milwaukee, WI 53216
(S) Dames & Moore P.O. Box 78200 Sandton 2146 (783.7120)	Environmental and engineering consultants	15	Dames and Moore 445 S. Figueroa St. Los Angeles, CA 90071
(S) D'Arcy-MacManus and Masius (S.A.) (Pty.) Ltd. P.O. Box 4984 Johannesburg 2000 (788.7330)	Advertising and marketing	125	D'Arcy-MacManus and Masius Worldwide Inc. 360 Madison Ave. New York, NY 10017
(A) Defy Industries Ltd. P.O. Box 12004 Jacobs 4025 (45.1802)	Small and major appliances, cast iron baths	4000	General Electric Co. 1 River Rd. Schenectedy, NY 12345

South African Company	Employees	Products	U.S. Parent
(S) Derby Metals and Minerals (SA) (Pty.) Ltd. P.O. Box 4829 Johannesburg 2000 (833.5300)	62	Metals, minerals, chemicals, and fertilizers	Phibro Salomon Corp. McGraw-Hill Bldg. Rockefeller Center 1221 Ave. of the Americas New York, NY 10020
(S) DHJ Industries SA (Pty.) Ltd. P.O. Box 3672 Durban 4000 (25.6221)	160	Interlinings, shoulder pads, collar stays, and supports undercollar melton	DHJ Industries Inc. 1040 Ave. of the Americas New York, NY 10013
(A) Diners Club SA (Pty.) Ltd. P.O. Box 10727 Johannesburg 2000 (37.3244)	108	Executive charge card	Diners Club Inc. 18th Floor 575 Lexington Ave. New York, NY 10043
(S) Dow Chemical Africa P.O. Box 9170 Johannesburg 2000 (789.1909 & 789.2036)	110	Chemicals and pharmaceuticals	Dow Chemical Co. P.O. Box 1726 Midland, MI 48640
(S) Dow Corning Africa (Pty.) Ltd. P.O. Box 152 Bedfordview 2003 (53.6927)	8	Silicone products	Dow Corning Corp. P.O. Box 1767 Midland, MI 48640
(S) Dresser South Africa (Pty.) Ltd. P.O. Box 14043 Wadeville 1422 (34.1521)	955	Construction mining, drilling, conveying, crushing, dust collecting and fuel dispensing equipment	Dresser Industries Inc. 1505 Elm St. Dallas, TX 75221
(S) Drew Ameroid SA (Pty.) Ltd. P.O. Box 300 Paarden Eiland 7420 (51.0500)	23	Chemical and engineering supplies and services	Drew Chemical Corp. 1 Drew Chemical Plaza Boonton, NJ

Name, Address & Tel. No. of Local Firm	Product/Service Category	No. of Employees	American Parent or Associate
(S) Dun and Bradstreet (Pty.) Ltd. P.O. Box 4522 Johannesburg 2000 (28.3150)	Credit and marketing information, publications and collection services	620	Dun and Bradstreet Int'l. Ltd. One World Trade Center Suite 9060 New York, NY 10048
(S) Duracell SA (Pty.) Ltd. P.O. Box 672 Bergvlei 2012 (786.4353)	Primary cells and batteries	26	Dart and Kraft Ind. 2211 Sanders Rd. Northbrook, IL 60062
(S) Du Pont De Nemours Int'l. Societe Anonyme P.O. Box 783753 Sandton 2146 (783.4785)	Plastics, synthetics, and pharmaceuticals	21	E.I. Du Pont De Nemours and Co. 1007 Market St. Wilmington, DE 19898
(S) Echlin-Charger Mfg. Co. (Pty.) Ltd. P.O. Box 83033 South Hills 2136 (613.4421)	Automotive parts	320	Echlin Manufacturing Co. Box 451 Branford, CT 06405
(S) Ecolaire Africa (Pty.) Ltd. P.O. Box 32044 Braamfontein 2017 (39.1110)	Power stations	6	Ecolaire Inc. 2 Country View Rd. Malvern, PA 19355
(S) Eimco SA P.O. Box 921 Kempton Park 1620 (826.2444)	Underground mining machinery	247	Envirotech Corp. Box 1211 Salt Lake City, UT 84110
Electrode Co. SA Ltd. P.O. Box 43 Meyerton 1960 (2-1433)	Graphite electrodes	700	Union Carbide Corp. Old Ridgebury Rd. Danbury, CT 06817

Company	Employees	Products	U.S. Parent
Eli Lilly SA (Pty.) Ltd. P.O. Box 98 Isando 1600 (36.7254)	129	Pharmaceuticals and agricultural products	Eli Lilly and Co. 307 East McCarty St. Indianapolis, IN 46206
Elizabeth Arden SA (Pty.) Ltd. P.O. Box 8 Parow 7500 (59.1241)	80	Cosmetics	Eli Lilly and Co. 307 East McCarty St. Indianapolis, IN 46206
Embecon (SA) (Pty.) Ltd. P.O. Box 890 Germiston 1400 (51.8263)	91	Manufacturers and suppliers of products for improving cement	Master Builders Div. of Martin Marietta Corp. 23700 Chagrin Blvd. Cleveland, OH 44122
Emcon Communications SA (Pty.) Ltd. P.O. Box 3985 Durban 4000 (33.3595)	100	Two-way radios	J. Gerber & Co. 855 Ave. of the Americas New York, NY 10001
Engelhard Industries SA (Pty.) Ltd. P.O. Box 370 Bergvlei 2012 (786.5940)	14	Fabricated precious metals	Engelhard Corp. Menlo Park, CN 40 Edison, NJ 08818
(S) Envirotech (Pty.) Ltd. P.O. Box 70 Isando 1600 (36.5411)	370	Mining equipment	Baker Int'l. 500 City Parkway W. Orange, CA 92668
(S) Esachem SA (Pty.) Ltd. P.O. Box 43394 Industria 2042 (672.5436)	25	Chemicals	National Chemsearch Corp. Box 2170 Irving, TX 75602

Name, Address & Tel. No. of Local Firm	Product/Service Category	No. of Employees	American Parent or Associate
(S) Esso Standard SA (Pty.) Ltd. P.O. Box 78011 Sandton 2146 (783.5413)	Petroleum products	220	Exxon Corp. 1251 Ave. of the Americas New York, NY 10009
(S) Estee Lauder (Pty.) Ltd. P.O. Box 31233 Braamfontein 2017 (39.5851)	Cosmetics	100	Estee Lauder Int'l. Corp. 767 5th Ave. New York, NY 10022
(S) Ethnor (Pty.) Ltd. P.O. Box 273 Halfway House 1685 (805.2110)	Pharmaceuticals	391	Johnson and Johnson 501 George St. New Brunswick, NY 08903
(S) Euclid SA (Pty.) Ltd. P.O. Box 742 Johannesburg 2000 (29.1651)	Off-highway mining and construction trucks	3	Euclid Inc. 2221 St. Clair Ave. Cleveland, OH 44117
(S) Femo (Pty.) Ltd. P.O. Box 61578 Marshalltown 2107 (683.8811)	Motor spares for cars, trucks, and tractors, industrial	112	Federal-Mogul Corp. 2655 N.W. Highway Southfield, MI 48034
(S) Ferro Industrial Products P.O. Box 108 Brakpan 1540 (55.9020)	Plastics, ceramics, chemicals, and engineering equipment	209	Ferro Corp. 1 Erieview Plaza Cleveland, OH 44114
(A) Firestone SA (Pty.) Ltd. P.O. Box 992 Port Elizabeth 6000 (41.2311)	Tires, tubes, and rubber products	2687	Firestone Tire and Rubber Co. 1200 Firestone Parkway Akron, OH 44317

(S)	Fluke SA (Pty.) Ltd. P.O. Box 39797 Bramley 2018 (786.3170)	27	Electronic test and measurement instrumentation	John Fluke Mfg. Co. Inc. P.O. Box C9090 Everett, WA 98206
(S)	Fluor Engineers SA (Pty.) Ltd. 4 Verwoerd Sq., Civic Center Vanderbijlpark 1900 (6-5841)	300	Maintenance services for Natref refinery	Fluor Corp. 3333 Michelson Dr. Irvine, CA 92730
(S)	Fluor Engineers SA (Pty.) Ltd. Private Bag 1168 Secunda 2302 (01363-40-1111)	14000	Managing contractor for SASOL Two and SASOL Three	Fluor Corp. 3333 Michelson Dr. Irvine, CA 92730
(S)	Fluor Engineers SA (Pty.) Ltd. P.O. Box 9586 Johannesburg 1200 (28.3541)	3000	Design engineering procurement construction and maintenance	Fluor Corp. 3333 Michelson Dr. Irvine, CA 92730
(S)	FMC SA (Pty.) Ltd. Food Machinery Div. P.O. Box 48 Sanlamhof 7532 (94.3700)	51	Food processing, pumping, and packaging equipment	FMC Corp. 200 E. Randolf Dr. Chicago, IL 60601
(S)	Ford Motor Co. SA (Pty.) Ltd. P.O. Box 788 Port Elizabeth 6000 (39.2010)	6509	Automotive/agricultural manufacturer	Ford Motor Co. The American Rd. Dearborn, MI 48121
(S)	Fordom Factoring (Pty.) Ltd. P.O. Box 3107 Johannesburg 2000 (836.4821)	24	Factoring and leasing	Walter E. Heller Overseas Corp. 105 W. Adams St. Chicago, IL 60603

Name, Address & Tel. No. of Local Firm	Product/Service Category	No. of Employees	American Parent or Associate
(S) Foster Wheeler Energy Ltd. P.O. Box 47083 Parklands 2121 (788.0200)	Chemical engineering contractors	110	Foster Wheeler Energy Corp. S. Orange Ave. Livingston, NJ 07039
(S) Frank B. Hall (SA) (Pty.) Ltd. P.O. Box 61110 Marshalltown 1107 (833.7653)	Insurance broker	12	Frank B. Hall and Co. Inc. 261 Madison Ave. New York, NY 10016
(S) Franklin Electric SA (Pty.) Ltd. P.O. Box 39523 Bramley 2018 (793.1010)	Specialized electric motors	28	Franklin Electric Co. 400 E. Spring St. Buffton, IN 46714
(S) G A F SA (Pty.) Ltd. P.O. Box 78833 Sandton 2146 (783.7465)	Chemicals, filters, graphic films and pages	5	G A F Corp. 140 W. 51 St. New York, NY 10020
(S) Gabriel SA (Pty.) Ltd. P.O. Box 214 Tokai 7966 (72.1007)	Shock absorbers	584	Maremont Corp. 200 E. Randolph Dr. Chicago, IL 60601
(S) Gang-Nail SA (Pty.) Ltd. P.O. Box 3927 Bramley 2013 (786.8030)	Timber connector and design services for prefab. items in building industry	40	Gang-Nail Systems Inc. P.O. Box 59-2037 A.M.F. Miami, Fl 33159
(S) Gardner-Denver Co. Africa (Pty.) Ltd. P.O. Box 81 Kempton Park 1620 (975-9816)	Mining and construction equipment for blast hole drilling	282	Gardner-Denver Co. Suite 500 8585 Stemmons Parkway Dallas, TX 75247

(S) Gates SA (Pty.) Ltd. P.O. Box 38592 Booysens 2016 (630-3417)	74	Automotive and industrial rubber products	The Gates Rubber Co. 999 S. Broadway Denver, CO 80217
(S) GATX-Fuller (Pty.) Ltd. P.O. Box 50216 Randburg 2125 (789-1954)	20	Process engineering, process product suppliers	Fuller Co. GATX 2040 Ave. C Bethlehem, PA 18001
(S) GATX Lease Management P.O. Box 61049 Marshalltown 2107 (834-1761)	5	Lease packager, manufacturing equipment	GATX Leasing Corp. 4 Embarcadero Center San Francisco, CA 94111
(S) General Motors Acceptance Corp. SA (Pty.) Ltd. C.C. Box 99-356 Carlton Centre Johannesburg 2001 (21-2411)	38	Service company	General Motors Acceptance Corp. 3044 West Grand Blvd. Detroit, MI 48202
(S) General Motors SA (Pty.) Ltd. P.O. Box 1137 Port Elizabeth 6000 (48211) Johannesburg Regional Sales Office P.O. Box 81192 Parkhurst 2120 (788-2000) Johannesburg Executive Office United Towers 160 Main St. P.O. Box 260472 Excom 2023 (37-6305)	5000	Motor manufacturing	General Motors Corp. G.M. Bldg. 3044 West Grand Blvd. Detroit, MI 48202

Name, Address & Tel. No. of Local Firm	Product/Service Category	No. of Employees	American Parent or Associate
(S) Gilbarco SA (Pty.) Ltd. P.O. Box 3750 Alrode 1451 (864-7900)	Pumps, meters, and valves for the petroleum, chemical, and water industries	263	Gilbert and Barker Manufacturing Co. P.O. Box 22087 Greensboro, NC 27420
(S) Gillette SA Ltd. P.O. Box 81 Springs 1560 (813-2300)	Blades and razors, toiletries, household plastic bags and writing instruments	350	The Gillette Co. Prudential Tower Building Boston, MA 02199
(S) Goodyear Tyre and Rubber Co. SA (Pty.) Ltd. P.O. Box 5156 Walmer 6065 (51-4284)	Tires, tubes, repair materials, and industrial rubber products	2700	Goodyear Tire and Rubber Co. 1144 E. Market St. Akron, OH 44316
(S) Grace, W.R. Africa (Pty.) Ltd. P.O. Box 2256 Kempton Park 1620 (970-3985)	Chemical compounds, flexible packaging	142	W.R. Grace and Co. 1114 Ave. of the Americas New York, NY 10036
(A) Gramophone Record Co. (Pty.) Ltd. P.O. Box 2445 Johannesburg 2000 (37-2827)	Phonograph records and tapes	30	CBS Int'l. Inc. 51 W. 52nd St. New York, NY 10019
(S) Grolier Int'l. Inc. P.O. Box 19853 Johannesburg 2000 (37-1733)	Educational books	82	Grolier Inc. Old Sherman Turnpike Danbury, CT 06816

	South African Company	Employees	Product/Service	U.S. Parent
(S)	Harnischfeger SA (Pty.) Ltd. P.O. Box 4087 Alrode 1451 (864-4654)	170	Mining shovels and construction equipment	Harnischfeger Corp. P.O. Box 554 Milwaukee, WI 53201
(S)	Hay-MSL SA (Pty.) Ltd. P.O. Box 10061 Johannesburg 2000 (788-2117)	60	Consulting services	Hay Associates 229 S. 18th St. Rittenhouse Sq. Philadelphia, PA 19103
(S)	Hayes/Hill Morris (Pty.) Ltd. P.O. Box 51973 Randburg 2125 (789-1574)	5	Management consultants	Hayes/Hill Inc. Management Consultants 640 Fifth Ave. New York, NY 10019
(A)	Heineman Electric SA Ltd. P.O. Box 881 Johannesburg 2000 (36-7033)	1100	Circuit breakers (trip-switches) and earth leakage protectors	Heineman Electric Co. P.O. Box 8428 Trenton, NJ 08650
(S)	Helena Rubinstein SA (Pty.) Ltd. P.O. Box 5394 Johannesburg 2000 (609-8670)	50	Cosmetics	Helena Rubinstein Inc. 55 Hartz Way Secaucus, NJ 07094
(A)	Henred Fruehauf Trailers (Pty.) Ltd. Private Bag 5 Bergvlei 2012 (786-3500)	1400	Trailers and containers	Fruehauf International Ltd. 10900 Harper Ave. Detroit, MI 48232
(S)	Hewlett Packard SA (Pty.) Ltd. P/B Wendywood 2144 (802-5111)	247	Electronic instruments, computer systems, calculators, medical instruments	Hewlett Packard Co. 3000 Hanover St. Palo Alto, CA 94304
(S)	Honeywell (Pty.) Ltd. P.O. Box 28 Crown Mines 2025 (680-3440)	200	Process control instruments, computers, air-conditioning controls	Honeywell Inc. Honeywell Plaza Minneapolis, MN 55408

Name, Address & Tel. No. of Local Firm	Product/Service Category	No. of Employees	American Parent or Associate
(S) Hoover SA (Pty.) Ltd. P.O. Box 909 East London 5200 (46-3071)	Domestic electrical appliances	656	Hoover Worldwide Corp. 101 East Maple St. North Canton, OH 44720
(S) Hydro-Air SA (Pty.) Ltd. P.O. Box 39527 Bramley 2018 (786-4633)	Roof truss machinery	16	Hydro-Air Engineering Inc. 700 Office Parkway Suite 23 Creve Coeur, MI 63141
(S) Hyster Africa (Pty.) Ltd. P.O. Box 172 Isando 1600 (36-6544)	Fork lift trucks, mobile cranes, and heavy-duty trailers	120	Hyster Co. P.O. Box 2902 Portland, OR 97208
(S) I.B.M. SA (Pty.) Ltd. P.O. Box 1419 Johannesburg 2000 (21-4351)	Information processing in the form of office products and computers	1800	IBM Corp. Old Orchard Rd. Armonk, NY 10504
(S) IMS Int'l. SA (Pty.) Ltd. P.O. Box 11260 Johannesburg 2000 (643-3181)	Market research	87	IMS Int'l. Inc. 800 Third Ave. New York, NY 10022
(S) I.N.A. Insurance Co. Ltd. P.O. Box 6480 Johannesburg 2000 (21-7701)	Short-term insurance	70	Insurance Co. of North America P.O. Box 7723 Philadelphia, PA 19101
(S) Ingersoll-Rand Co. SA (Pty.) Ltd. P.O. Box 3720 Alrode 1451 (864-3930)	Compressed air equipment for industrial and mining industries	520	Ingersoll-Rand Co. P.O. Box 636 Woodcliff Lake, NJ 07675

(S) International Bechtel Inc. P.O. Box 3191 Johannesburg 2000 (29-5461)	35	Consultants, engineers, and constructors	Bechtel Power Corp. 50 Beale St. P.O. Box 3965 San Francisco, CA 94119
(S) International Flavours and Fragrances SA (Pty.) Ltd. P.O. Box 231 Roodepoort 1725 (763-3821)	35	Flavors, fragrances, and aroma chemicals	International Flavors and Fragrances Inc. 521 W. 57th St. New York, NY 10019
(S) International Harvester Co. SA (Pty.) Ltd. P.O. Box 12 Isando 1600 (36-2751)	501	Trucks, farm tractors, farm implements, and spare parts	International Harvester 401 N. Michigan Ave. Chicago, IL 60611
(S) ITT Africa and Middle East P.O. Box 75231 Gardenview 2047 (616-4160)	2	Liaison office for ITT products manufactured other than in South Africa	ITT 320 Park Ave. New York, NY 10022
(S) John Deere (Pty.) Ltd. P.O. Box 198 Nigel 1490 (739-2385)	530	Farm equipment	Deere and Co. John Deere Rd. Moline, IL 61265
(S) Johnson and Johnson (Pty.) Ltd. P.O. Box 87 East London 5200 (2-7340)	818	Surgical dressings and toiletries	Johnson and Johnson 501 George St. New Brunswick, NJ 08903
(S) Johnson, J.C. Controls (Pty.) Ltd. P.O. Box 4454 Johannesburg 2000 (835-1131)	110	Install environmental controls, security, and fire detection systems, computer monitoring systems	Johnson Control Int'l. Inc. P.O. Box 755 Milwaukee, WI 53201

Name, Address & Tel. No. of Local Firm	Product/Service Category	No. of Employees	American Parent or Associate
(S) Johnson, S.C. and Son SA (Pty.) Ltd. Private Bag X08 Fairland 2030 (678-6952)	Home care, auto, industrial, and personal care	168	S.C. Johnson and Son Inc. 1525 Howe St. Racine, WI 53403
(S) Joy Manufacturing Co. (Africa) (Pty.) Ltd. P.O. Box 4070 Johannesburg 2000 (613-6831)	Mining equipment	980	Joy Manufacturing Co. Oliver Bldg. Pittsburg, PA 15222
(S) Kellogg Co. SA (Pty.) Ltd. P.O. Box 309 Springs 1560 (813-2261)	Cereals, drink powders, jelly	333	Kellogg Co. 235 Porter St. Battle Creek, MI 49016
(S) Kelly Springfield Tyre Co. SA (Pty.) Ltd. P.O. Box 10600 Johannesburg 2000 (37-1420)	Rubber tires and tubes	97	Kelly-Springfield Tire Co. Cumberland, MD
(S) The Kendall Co. SA (Pty.) Ltd. P.O. Box 68 Parow CP 7500 (931-2271)	Items for thrombosis management, inhalation therapy, ECG, electrodes, electrosurgical, urological, wound management, nursing care; disposable apparel; non-woven industrial products; surgical and industrial adhesive tapes	65	The Kendall Co. 302 Park Ave. New York, NY 10022

(S) Kentucky Fried Chicken SA (Pty.) Ltd. P.O. Box 41216 Craighall 2024 (789-1192)	Fast foods	600	Kentucky Fried Chicken Co. 1441 Gardiner Lane Louisville, KY 40232
(S) Kodak SA (Pty.) Ltd. P.O. Box 39851 Bramley 2018 (736-8580)	Processing and printing of photographic products	623	Eastman Kodak Co. 343 State St. Rochester, NY 14650
(S) L & M Radiator SA (Pty.) Ltd. P.O. Box 982 Rustenberg 0300	Heavy duty radiators and cooling systems	50	L & M Radiators Inc. 1414 East 37th St. Hibbing, MN 55746
(A) Lantor Nonwovens SA (Pty.) Ltd. P.O. Box 491 Pinetown 3600 (71-4411)	Nonwoven materials and products	82	West Point Pepperell P.O. Box 298 Fairfax, AL 36854
(A) Laral Pizza Dens (Pty.) Ltd. P.O. Box 63956 Bryanston 2021 (789-2709)	Pizza restaurant chain	50	Pizza Inn Inc. 2930 Stemmons Freeway Dallas, TX 75247
(S) Laviso SA (Pty.) Ltd. P.O. Box 11561 Johannesburg 2000 (834-1651)	Chrome ore	396	International Minerals & Chemical Corp. 2315 Sanders Rd. Northbrook, IL 60062
(S) Leco SA (Pty.) Ltd. P.O. Box 1418 Edenvale 1610 (609-3306)	Analytical instruments	27	Leco Corp. 3000 Lakeview Ave. St. Joseph, MI 49085
(S) Lederle Laboratories (Pty.) Ltd. P.O. Box 58 Isando 1600 (36-1341)	Pharmaceutical and surgical sutures	127	American Cyanamid Co. Development Corp. 859 Berdan Ave. Wayne, NJ 07470

Name, Address & Tel. No. of Local Firm	Product/Service Category	No. of Employees	American Parent or Associate
(S) Leeds and Northrup (Pty.) Ltd. P.O. Box 82574 Southdale 2135 (680-5205)	Supply and servicing of industrial process control instrumentation	42	Leeds and Northrup Co. Sunneytown Pike North Wales, PA
(S) Lexington Andrews Int'l. Inc. P.O. Box 5365 Johannesburg 2000 (23-3669)	Encyclopedias	3	Macmillan Inc. 866 Third Ave. New York, NY 10022
(S) Lion Chemicals (Pty.) Ltd. P.O. Box 61436 Marshalltown 2107 (832-1622)	Calcium hypochlorite, industrial chemicals	28	Olin Corp. 120 Long Ridge Rd. Stanford, CT 06904
(A) The Lion Match Co. Ltd. P.O. Box 918 Durban 4000 (33-4101)	Matches and razor blades, packaging; scissors; kitchen, and hardware products; sunglasses; lighters	2025	Allegheny Int'l. Inc. P.O. Box 456 Pittsburgh, PA 15230
(S) Loctite SA (Pty.) Ltd. P.O. Box 543 Florida 1710 (674-1930)	Adhesives and sealants	40	Loctite Corp. 705 N. Mountain Rd. Newington, CT 06111
(S) Longyear Africa (Pty.) Ltd. P.O. Box 14189 Farramere 1518 (894-2227)	Drilling equipment sales and drilling contractors	32	Longyear Co. 925 Delaware St. SE Minneapolis, MN 55414
(B) Los Angeles Times P.O. Box 5660 Johannesburg 2000 (646-2136)	News	1	The Los Angeles Times Times-Mirror Sq. Los Angeles, CA 90053

	South African affiliate	Employees	Business	U.S. parent
(S)	Lubrizol SA (Pty.) Ltd. P.O. Box 26025 Isipingo Beach 4115 (92-1414)	43	Oil and fuel additives	Lubrizol Corp. 29480 Lakeland Blvd. Wickliffe, OH 44092
(S)	Lykes Lines Agency Inc. P.O. Box 1337 Durban 4000 (65162)	7	Shipping	Lykes Bros. Steamship Co. Inc. Lykes Center 300 Poydras St. New Orleans, LA 70130
(S)	3M SA (Pty.) Ltd. P.O. Box 10465 Johannesburg 2000 (36.3211)	1517	Adhesives and abrasives; magnetic tapes; elec- trical products; photo and printing products; copying, visual, and microfilm products	Minnesota Mining & Manufacturing Co. P.O. Box 33800 St. Paul, MN 55133
(S)	Management Placements (Pty.) Ltd. P.O. Box 47038 Parklands 2121 (788.1460)	22	Executive and manage- ment placement	
(S)	Marriott In-flight Services P.O. Box 271 Isando 1600 (35.1588)	85	Aviation and industrial catering	Marriott Corp. Marriott Dr. Washington, D.C. 20016
(S)	Masonite (Africa) Ltd. P.O. Box 671 Durban 4000 (32.3251)	2631	Hardboard and forestry	Masonite Corp. 29 N. Wacker Dr. Chicago, IL 60606
(S)	McCann-Erickson SA (Pty.) Ltd. P.O. Box 1529 Johannesburg 2000 (39.4141)	135	Advertising agency	McCann-Erickson Worldwide 485 Lexington Ave. New York, NY 10017

Name, Address & Tel. No. of Local Firm	Product/Service Category	No. of Employees	American Parent or Associate
(S) McGraw-Hill Book Co. SA (Pty.) Ltd. P.O. Box 371 Isando 1600 (36.1181)	Education books and audiovisual material	46	McGraw-Hill Int'l Book Co. 1221 Ave. of the Americas New York, NY 10020
(S) McKinnon Chain SA (Pty.) Ltd. P.O. Box 7770 Johannesburg 2000 (832.2111)	Chain, chain hoists, and attachments	438	Columbus McKinnon Corp. Audubon and Sylvan Parkways Amherst, NY 14221
(S) Metallurg SA (Pty.) Ltd. P.O. Box 61060 Marshalltown 2107 (833.1617)	Metallurgical alloys	17	Metallurg Inc. 25th E. 39th St. New York, NY 10016
(S) Metal and Chemical Industries (Pty.) Ltd. P.O. Box 575 Germiston 1400 (613.2266)	Production of nonferrous metal ingots and metal tracing	240	Associated Metals and Minerals Corp. 30 Rockefeller Plaza New York, NY 10020
(S) Meyer, Geo. J. SA (Pty.) Ltd. P.O. Box 31356 Braamfontein 2017 (39.2481)	Packaging and bottling equipment	3	Geo. J. Meyer Manufacturing 4751 S. Mayer Place Cudahy, WI 53110
(S) Miles Laboratories (Pty.) Ltd. P.O. Box 1329 Cape Town 8000 (21.7010)	Health and nutritional products	120	Miles Laboratories Inc. 1127 Myrtle St. Elkhart, IN 46515

	Company (South Africa)	Business	Employees	U.S. Parent
(S)	Mine Safety Appliances Africa (Pty.) Ltd. P.O. Box 1680 Johannesburg 2000 (942.3035/47)	Air filtration and fire protection equipment, general safety products, process instrumentation, mining cap lamps	496	Mine Safety Appliances Co. 600 Penn Center Blvd. Pittsburgh, PA 15235
(S)	Mobil Oil SA (Pty.) Ltd. P.O. Box 35 Cape Town 8000 (21.3211)	Petroleum products marketing	2519	Mobil Oil Corp. 150 E. 42nd St. New York, NY 10017
(S)	Mobil Refining Co. SA P.O. Box 956 Durban 4000 (48.3551)	Petroleum products refining	878	Mobil Oil Corp. 150 E. 42nd St. New York, NY 10017
(S)	Mohawk Data Sciences SA (Pty.) Ltd. P.O. Box 733895 Sandton 2146 (783.5075)	Computer marketing	92	Mohawk Data Sciences 7 Century Dr. Parsipanny, NJ 07054
(S)	Monarch SA Insurance Co. Ltd. P.O. Box 61115 Marshalltown 2107 (838.6711)	Non-life insurance	65	AFIA Finance Corp. 1700 Valley Rd. Wayne, NJ 07470
(S)	Monsanto SA (Pty.) Ltd. P.O. Box 73025 Sandton 2146 (783.7505)	Industrial chemicals and herbicides	33	Monsanto Co. 800 N. Lindbergh Blvd. St. Louis, MO 63166
(S)	Moore McCormack SA (Pty.) Ltd. P.O. Box 10835 Johannesburg 2000 (37.5390) P.O. Box 3677 Durban 4000 (32.9171)	Shipping lines	21	Moore McCormack Lines Inc. 2 Broadway New York, NY 10004

Name, Address & Tel. No. of Local Firm	Product/Service Category	No. of Employees	American Parent or Associate
(S) Motorola SA (Pty.) Ltd. P.O. Box 39586 Bramley 2018 (786.6165)	Two-way radio, semiconductor, and automotive products; data and control systems	250	Motorola Inc. 1303 E. Algonquin Rd. Schaumberg, IL 60696
(S) MSD (Pty.) Ltd. P/B 3 Halfway House 1685 (805.2161)	Pharmaceuticals, animal health, agrochemical products	350	Merck Sharp and Dohme Int. P.O. Box 2000 Rahway, NJ 07065
(S) Muller and Phipps Africa (Pty.) Ltd. P.O. Box 2207 Johannesburg 2000 (29.2711)	Groceries, hardware, and pharmaceuticals	350	Gatz Bros. Co. Ltd. P.O. Box 3994 San Francisco, CA 94119
(S) Nashua SA (Pty.) Ltd. P.O. Box 39524 Bramley 2018 (786.3726) (786.5303) Sales (786.3115) Service	Copying machines and related consumables, spares, and servicing	341	Nashua Corp. 44 Franklin St. Nashua, NH 03061
(B) National Public Radio Union Centre West 52 Simmonds St. Johannesburg 2001 (838.7545)	News	1	National Public Radio 2025 M St. NW Washington, DC 10036
(A) National-Standard Co. SA (Pty.) Ltd. P.O. Box 582 Uitenhage 6230 (29032)	Tire and cycle beadwire, welding wire and copper ply	149	National-Standard Co. 601 N. 8th St. Niles, MI 49120

	South Africa	Business	No.	U.S. Company
(B)	NBC News 13 Napier Rd. Richmond Johannesburg 2092 (726.2501/1405)	News	2	National Broadcasting Co. 30 Rockefeller Plaza New York, NY 10020
(S)	NCR Corp. SA (Pty.) Ltd. P.O. Box 3591 Johannesburg 2001 (833.7000)	Business systems, computers, data terminals, free-standing electronic business machines	650	NCR Corp. World Headquarters 1700 South Patterson Blvd. Dayton, OH 45479
(S)	Newmont SA Ltd. P.O. Box 5343 Johannesburg 2000 (834.3471)	Mining and exploration	72	Newmont Mining Co. 300 Park Ave. New York, NY 10022
(B)	Newsweek 7th Floor, Union Centre 31 Pritchard St. Johannesburg 2001 (34.7995)	News	3	Newsweek Inc. 444 Madison Ave. New York, NY 10022
(B)	New York Times P.O. Box 2662 Johannesburg 2000 (29-9390)	News	2	The New York Times 229 W. 43rd St. New York, NY 10036
(S)	Nielsen A.C., Co. (Pty.) Ltd. P.O. Box 5637 Johannesburg 2000 (833-7510)	Market research	300	A.C. Nielsen Int'l. Inc. Nielsen Plaza Northbrook, IL 60062
(S)	Nordberg Mfg. Co. SA (Pty.) Ltd. P.O. Box 2253 Johannesburg 2000 (642-7521)	Mining machinery	660	Rexnord Inc. Box 383 Milwaukee, WI 53201
(B)	North Carolina National Bank P.O. Box 9241 Johannesburg 2000 (836-6191)	Banking	6	North Carolina National Bank P.O. Box 120 Charlotte, NC 28255

Name, Address & Tel. No. of Local Firm	Product/Service Category	No. of Employees	American Parent or Associate
(S) Norton Co. (Pty.) Ltd. P.O. Box 67 Isando 1600 (36-5211)	Grinding wheels and coated abrasives; hand tools; polishing buffs; mining engineering	400	Norton Co. 1 New Bond St. Worcester, MA 01606
(S) N.U.S. SA (Pty.) Ltd. P.O. Box 62346 Marshalltown 2107 (833-2340)	International fuel and energy cost analysts	40	National Utility Service Ltd. 301 E. 57th St. New York, NY 10022
(S) Oak Industries SA (Pty.) Ltd. P.O. Box 1172 Pietermaritzburg 3200 (7-1451)	Electrical products and components	214	Oak Technology Inc. P.O. Box 28759 Rancho Bernardo, CA 92128
(S) O'Okiep Copper Co. Ltd. P.O. Box 17 Nababeep 8265 (no. 9)	Copper mining, milling, and smelting	2963	Newmont Mining Corp. 300 Park Ave. New York, NY 10022
(B) Opico SA P.O. Box 30116 Mayville 4058 (81-8336)	Agricultural equipment	3	Oppenheimer Intercontinental Corp. P.O. Box 849 Mobile, AL 36601
(S) Otis Elevator Co. Ltd. P.O. Box 2729 Johannesburg 2000 (28-2720)	Elevators and escalators	968	United Technologies Corp. United Technologies Bldg. Hartford, CT 06101
(S) Ottermill Switchgear SA (Pty.) Ltd. P.O. Box 32046 Braamfontein 2017 (39-1485)	Electrical switchgear	4	Westinghouse Electric Corp. Westinghouse Bldg. Gateway Center Pittsburgh, PA 15222

Company	Employees	Product	U.S. Parent
(A) Palabora Mining Co. Ltd. P.O. Box 61140 Marshalltown 2107 (833-7215)	4000	Copper, magnetite, vermiculite, and sulfuric acid	Newmont Mining Corp. 300 Park Ave. New York, NY 10022
(S) Pan American World Airways SA (Pty.) Ltd. P.O. Box 6353 Johannesburg 2000 (21-5178)	21	Airline	Pan American World Pan Am Bldg. New York, NY 10017
(S) Pandora Mining (Pty.) Ltd. P.O. Box 31198 Braamfontein 2017 (726-4216)	8	Mineral development	TexasGulf Inc. High Ridge Park Stamford, CT 06905
(S) Parker Hannifin (Africa) (Pty.) Ltd. P.O. Box 1153 Kempton Park 1420 (970.3630)	80	Components for connecting, activating, and controlling fluid power systems	Parker Hannifin Corp. 18325 Euclid Ave. Cleveland, OH 44112
(S) Parker Pen (Pty.) Ltd. P.O. Box 1046 East London 5200 (46.3135)	150	Pens	Parker Pen Co. One Parker Place Jamesville, WI 53545
(S) Penwalt Ltd. P.O. Box 48450 Roosevelt Park 2129 (782.4615)	4	Capital process separation equipment for the chemical industry	Penwalt Corp. 955 Mearms Rd. Warminster, PA 18974
(S) Pepsi-Cola Africa (Pty.) Ltd. P.O. Box 151 Bedfordview 2008 (616.3214)	600	Soft drinks	PepsiCo. Inc. 700 Anderson Hill Rd. Purchase, NY 10577
(S) The Perkin-Elmer Corp. SA (Pty.) Ltd. P.O. Box 1136 Alberton 1450 (869.7344)	8	Scientific analytical instruments	Perkin-Elmer Corp. Main Ave. Norwalk, CT 06852

Name, Address & Tel. No. of Local Firm	Product/Service Category	No. of Employees	American Parent or Associate
(S) Petrow, C.J. & Co. (Pty.) Ltd. P.O. Box 11000 Johannesburg 1000 (836.7072)	Raw asbestos	40	None—independent
(S) Pfizer Laboratories (Pty.) Ltd. P.O. Box 783720 Sandton 2146 (783.5270)	Human and veterinary pharmaceuticals and food chemicals	183	Pfizer Inc. 235 E. 42nd St. New York, NY 10017
(S) Phelps Dodge Mining Ltd. P.O. Box 31085 Braamfontein 2017 (39.6511)	Mining, processing, and export of fluorspar, mineral exploration	203	Phelps Dodge Corp. 300 Park Ave. New York, NY 10022
(S) Phillips Carbon Black Co. (Pty.) Ltd. P.O. Box 362 Port Elizabeth 6000 (4.5465)	Carbon black	185	Phillips Petroleum Co. Phillips Bldg. Bartlesville, OK 74004
(S) Playtex Africa (Pty.) Ltd. P.O. Box 3300 Durban 4000 (47.3901)	Foundation garments	255	International Playtex 45 Church St. Stamford, CT 06906
(S) Precision Valve SA (Pty.) Ltd. P.O. Box 51292 Randburg 2125	Aerosol valves and components; plastic moldings and extrusions (subsidiary companies deal in packaging machinery and materials; manufacture of polyethylene and other films for use in flexible packaging)	280	Precision Valve Corp. 700 Napperhan Ave. Yonkers, NY 10703

Company	Product	No.	Parent Company
(S) Preformed Line Products SA (Pty.) Ltd. P.O. Box 958 Pietermaritzburg 3200 (7.1520)	Fittings for overhead electric power lines	136	Preformed Line Products Co. Box 91129 Cleveland, OH 44101
Premex Asphalt Co. P.O. Box 2 Paarden Eiland 7420 (51.7388)	Ready-mix asphalt	12	None—independent
(S) Ramsey Engineering Africa (Pty.) Ltd. P.O. Box 494 Florida 1710 (674.1910)	Electronic and nuclear instrumentation for measuring and control in the materials	34	Ramsey Engineering Co. 1353 W. Country Rd. St. Paul, MN 55113
(S) Rank Xerox (Pty.) Ltd. P.O. Box 31262 Braamfontein 2017 (725-2560)	Reprographic equipment and associated products	800	Xerox Corp. High Ridge Park Stamford, CT 06094
(S) Readers Digest Assn. (Pty.) Ltd. P.O. Box 2677 Cape Town 8000 (25-4460)	Mail order publishing	396	Readers Digest Assn. Inc. P.O. Box 235 Pleasantville, NY 10570
(S) Reed Mining Tools of SA (Pty.) Ltd. P.O. Box 27141 Benrose 2011 (614-1811)	Mining tools	55	Reed Mining Tool Inc. 1600 SO Great S.W. Pkwy. Grand Prairie, TX 75051
(S) Reid & Mitchell (Pty.) Ltd. P.O. Box 9005 Johannesburg 2000	Electrical/mechanical repairs, armature welding	360	General Electric Co. 1 River Rd. Schenectady, NY 12345
(S) Revlon SA (Pty.) Ltd. P.O. Box 205 Isando 1600 (36-6951)	Cosmetics and toiletries	450	Revlon Int'l. Corp. 767 5th Ave. New York, NY 10022

Name, Address & Tel. No. of Local Firm	Product/Service Category	No. of Employees	American Parent or Associate
(S) Rheem SA (Pty.) ltd. P.O. Box 23141 Isipingo 4110 (92-1531)	Steel containers, crown closures, and tipper clips	530	City Investing Int'l. Inc. 59 Maiden Lane 37 Floor New York, NY 10038
(A) Richards Bay Minerals (Comprising Richards Bay Iron and Titanium (Pty.) Ltd. & Tisand (Pty.) Ltd. P.O. Box 401 Richards Bay 3900 (3-1171)	Heavy sand minerals, titanium, rutile zircon	1440	Standard Oil Co. of Ohio Midland Bldg. Cleveland, OH 44115
(S) Richardson-Vicks (Pty.) Ltd. P.O. Box 456 Kempton Park 1620 (970-2320)	Pharmaceuticals and toiletries	350	Richardson-Vicks Inc. World Headquarters 10 Westport Rd. Wilton, CT 06897
(S) Robbins Co. (Africa) (Pty.) Ltd. P.O. Box 995 Roodepoort 1725 (763-5696)	Mining and tunneling machines	100	Robbin Co. 7615 S 212th St. Kent, WA 98031
(S) Robertsons (Pty.) Ltd. P.O. Box 1956 Durban 4000 (31-4461)	Foodstuffs, spices, and aerosol insecticides	930	CPC Int'l. Inc. International Plaza Englewood Cliffs, NJ 07632
(S) Robins, A.H. Co. SA (Pty.) Ltd. P.O. Box 7211 Parkview 2133 (683-5111)	Pharmaceuticals	13	A.H. Robins Co. Inc. P.O. Box 26609 Richmond, VA 23261

	Company (SA)	No.	Business	U.S. Parent
(S)	Rohm and Haas SA (Pty.) Ltd. P.O. Box 78 New Germany 3620 (72-0241)	131	Chemicals	Rohm and Haas Co. Independence Mall West Philadelphia, PA 19105
(S)	Royal Planters (Pty.) Ltd. P.O. Box 29 Chloorkop 1624 (976-3150)	450	Food production	International Nabisco Brand Inc. 625 Madison Ave. New York, NY 10022
(S)	SA Cyanamid (Pty.) Ltd. P.O. Box 7552 Johannesburg 2000 (53-8830)	480	Mining, industrial, and agricultural chemicals and pharmaceuticals	American Cyanamid Co. 859 Berdan Ave. Wayne, NJ 07470
(S)	SA General Electric Co. (Pty.) Ltd. P.O. Box 5031 Benoni South 1502 (52-8111)	150	Industrial/electrical equipment	General Electric Co. 3135 Easton Turnpike Fairfield, CT 06431
(S)	SA Paper Chemicals (Pty.) Ltd. P.O. Box 47002 Parklands 2121 (783-2100)	10	Paper size and chemicals	Tenneco Inc. P.O. Box 2511 Houston, TX 77001
(S)	SA Preserving Co. (Pty.) Ltd. P.O. Box 6536 Roggebaai 8012 (21-1580)	140	Canning and exporting of deciduous fruit	Del Monte Corp. 1 Market Plaza San Francisco, CA 94119
(S)	Salsbury SA Veterinary (Pty.) Ltd. P.O. Box 1735 Kempton Park 1620 (970-1113)	55	Biological, chemical, pharmaceutical, and agricultural products	Salsbury Int'l. Inc. 2000 Rockford Rd. Charles City, IA

Name, Address & Tel. No. of Local Firm	Product/Service Category	No. of Employees	American Parent or Associate
(S) Scherag (Pty.) Ltd. P.O. Box 46 Isando 1600 (36-2966)	Pharmaceuticals	172	Schering Plough Corp. Galloping Hill Rd. Kenilworth, NJ 07033
(S) Scholl-Plough SA (Pty.) Ltd. P.O. Box 696 Isando 1600 (36-1081)	Cosmetics, toiletries, footwear, and foot care	111	Schering-Plough Corp. Inc. 2000 Galloping Hill Rd. Kenilworth, NJ 07033
(S) Searle, G.D. SA (Pty.) Ltd. P.O. Box 391157 Bramley 2018 (786-2865)	Pharmaceuticals	70	G.D. Searle and Co. P.O. Box 1045 Skokie, IL 60076
(S) Sedco Maritime Inc. P.O. Box 415 Paarden Eiland 7420 (21-6640)	Oil rigging	150	Sedco Inc. 1 Cumberland Hill Dallas, TX 75201
(S) Shulton SA (Pty.) Ltd. P.O. Box 7829 Johannesburg 2000 (36-2650)	Toiletries	85	American Cyanamid Co. 859 Berdan Ave. Wayne, NJ 07470
(A) Sigma Motor Corp. (Pty.) Ltd. P.O. Box 411 Pretoria 0001 (83-1121)	Autos	5500	Chrysler Corp. P.O. Box 1919 Detroit, MI 48231
(A) Simplicity Patterns SA (Pty.) Ltd. P.O. Box 9172 Johannesburg 2000 (836-6111)	Paper dress patterns	26	Simplicity Pattern Co. Inc. 200 Madison Ave. New York, NY 10016

Company	Description	Employees	U.S. Parent
(S) Singer SA (Pty.) Ltd. P.O. Box 38177 Booysens 2016 (683-4210)	Sewing and knitting machines	140	Singer Co. 8 Stamford Forum Stamford, CT 06904
(S) Smith Kline & French (Pty.) Ltd. P.O. Box 38 Isando 1600 (36-7011)	Pharmaceuticals	204	Smith Kline Beckman Corp. 1500 Spring Garden St. Philadelphia, PA 19101
(S) Smith Mining Equipment Companies (Africa) (Pty.) Ltd. P.O. Box 1405 Kempton Park 1620 (970-3200)	Manufacturing and marketing of mining equipment and tools	60	Smith Mining Equipment Co. Div. of Smith Int'l. 2100 Travis Suite 304 Houston, TX 77002
(S) Southern Shipping Company (Pty.) Ltd. P.O. Box 4829 Johannesburg 2000 (833-5300)	Ships charterers, exporters	6	Phibro Salomon Corp. McGraw-Hill Bldg. Rockefeller Center 1221 Ave. of the Americas New York, NY 10020
(S) Southern Sphere Mining & Development Co. (Pty.) Ltd. P.O. Box 50065 Randburg 2125 (788-1910)	Mining and exploration	135	Utah International Inc. 550 California St. San Francisco, CA 94104
(S) Sperry (Pty.) Ltd. Univac Div. P.O. Box 5981 Johannesburg 2000 (447-1243)	Supplies for Univac mainframe computer equipment	224	Sperry Corp. 1290 Ave. of the Americas New York, NY 10019
(S) Sperry (Pty.) Ltd. Sperry Vickers Div. P.O. Box 4299 Johannesburg 2000 (833-5713)	Hydraulic and pneumatic equipment fluid power accessories	80	Sperry Corp. 1290 Ave. of the Americas New York, NY 10019

Name, Address & Tel. No. of Local Firm	Product/Service Category	No. of Employees	American Parent or Associate
(S) Squibb Laboratories (Pty.) Ltd. P.O. Box 48 Isando 1600 (36-1531)	Human and veterinary pharmaceuticals	185	E.R. Squibb & Sons Inc. P.O. Box 4000 Princeton, NJ 08540
(S) Stanley Tools (Pty.) Ltd. P.O. Box 212 Maraisburg 1700 (674-1315)	Hand and hydraulic tools, hardware and door operating	22	The Stanley Works 195 Lake St. New Britain, CT 06050
(S) Stauffer Chemical SA P.O. Box 78417 Sandton 2146 (783-7520)	Industrial and agricultural chemicals; plastics and food ingredients	9	Stauffer Chemical Co. Westport, CT 06880
(S) Stein Hall SA (Pty.) Ltd. P.O. Box 520 Meyerton 1960 (01612-22340)	Chemical manufacturers	47	Celanese Int'l. Corp. 1211 Ave. of the Americas New York, NY 10036
(S) Sterling Drug SA (Pty.) Ltd. P.O. Box 2461 Durban 4000 (42-2521)	Pharmaceutical and proprietary products	390	Sterling Drug Inc. 90 Park Lane New York, NY 10016
(S) Sybron SA (Pty.) Ltd. Private Bag X2022 Pinetown 3600 (72-0726)	Marine, industrial, and textile chemicals		Sybron Corp. 1100 Midtown Towers Rochester, NY 14606
(S) TAC National (Pty.) Ltd. P.O. Box 5034 Benoni South 1502 (54-5964)	Industrial adhesive for packaging and woodworking	70	National Starch & Chemical Corp. 10 Finderne Ave. Bridgewater, NJ 08807

	South African Operation	No.	Product/Activity	U.S. Parent
(S)	Tampax SA (Pty.) Ltd. P.O. Box 137 Brakpan 1540 (55-8476)	50	Tampons	Tampax Inc. 5 Dakota Dr. Lake Success, NY 11040
(S)	Taylor Instrument (Pty.) Ltd. P.O. Box 9895 Johannesburg 2000 (618-3340)	23	Process control instrumentation	Sybron Corp. 110 Midtown Tower Rochester, NY 14604
(S)	Technicon Autoanalyzer (Pty.) Ltd. P.O. Box 39390 Bramley 2018 (786-4630)	14	Automated chemical analyzers	Technicon Instruments Corp. 511 Benedict Ave. Tarrytown, NY 10591
(S)	T.G. Exploration Ltd. P.O. Box 31838 Braamfontein 2017 (726-4216)	13	Mineral exploration	TexasGulf Inc. High Ridge Park Stamford, CT 06504
(A)	Thomson, J. Walter Co. SA P.O. Box 8735 Johannesburg 2000 (21-9271)	111	Advertising	J. Walter Thomson Co. 466 Lexington Ave. New York, NY 10017
(B)	Time Magazine News Bureau P.O. Box 52630 Saxonwold 2:32 (41-8224)	4	News	Time Inc. Time Life Bldg. Rockefeller Center New York, NY 10020
(B)	Time Life Int'l. P.O. Box 783701 Sandton 2146 (783-7565)	7	Magazine, books	Time Inc. Time Life Bldg. Rockefeller Center New York, NY 10020
(S)	Timken SA (Pty.) Ltd. P.O. Box 5050 Benoni South 1502 (892-2986)	251	Tapered roller bearings	Timken Co. 1835 Dunber Ave. SW Canton, OH 44706

Name, Address & Tel. No. of Local Firm	Product/Service Category	No. of Employees	American Parent or Associate
(S) Titanium Industries SA (Pty.) Ltd. P.O. Box 1311 Alberton 1450 (903-3102)	Titanium marketing and fabricating	4	Titanium Industries 110 Leigh Drive Fairfield, NJ 07006
(S) Tokheim SA (Pty.) Ltd. P/B 2 Wendywood 2144 (802-1130)	Petroleum dispensing equipment	45	Tokheim Corp. 1602 Wabash Ave. Fort Wayne, IN 46801
(S) Tran Systems (Pty.) Ltd. P.O. Box 39194 Booysens 2016 (683-6842)	Switchboard network systems	50	Amdahl International Corp. 1250 East Arques Ave. Sunnyvale, CA 94086
(S) Trane SA (Pty.) Ltd. P.O. Box 38649 Booysens 2016 (835-3031)	Air-conditioning, heating, ventilation, heat transfer equipment; transport refrigeration products	52	The Trane Co. 3600 Parmel Creek Rd. La Crosse, WI 54601
(A) Trans World Airlines Inc. P.O. Box 9564 Johannesburg 2000 (23-4023)	Airline sales office	4	Trans World Airlines Inc. 605 3rd Ave. New York, NY 10016
(A) Trochem (Pty.) Ltd. P.O. Box 14032 Wadeville 1422 (34-2457)	Specialized chemicals for the mining industry	56	Eenkal Corp. 4620 W. 77th St. Minneapolis, MN 55435
(A) Tsumeb Corp. Ltd. P.O. Box 40 Tsumeb, Namibia/SWA 9000 (0671-3061)	Mining, milling, smelting of copper	6500	Newmont Mining Corp. 300 Park Ave. New York, NY 10022

(S)	Tubatse Ferrochrome Ltd. P.O. Box 46 Steelpoort 1133 (013239)(no. 311)	Ferrochrome	544	Union Carbide Corp. Old Ridgebury Rd. Danbury, CT 06817
(S)	Tupperware Div. of Dart Ind. (Pty.) Ltd. P.O. Box 89 Constantia 7843 (74-1023)	Polythene household containers	160	Dart & Kraft Inc. 2211 Sanders Rd. Northbrook, IL 60062
(S)	Twentieth Century Films SA (Pty.) Ltd. P.O. Box 1100 Johannesburg 2000 (37.5708)	Film distributors	3	20th Century-Fox International Corp. Box 900 Beverly Hills, CA 90213
(S)	Twin Disc SA (Pty.) Ltd. P.O. Box 75140 Gardenview 2047 (613.5717)	Power transmission equipment	9	Twin Disc Inc. 1328 Racine St. Racine, WI 53403
(S)	UCAR Chrome Co. SA (Pty.) Ltd. P.O. Box 8194 Johannesburg 2000 (21.7387)	Chrome mining	340	Union Carbide Corp. Old Ridgebury Rd. Danbury, CT 06817
(S)	UCAR Minerals Corp. P.O. Box 282 Brits 0250 (01211 5746/68/88; 5699/56773)	Vanadium products	792	Union Carbide Corp. Old Ridgebury Rd. Danbury, CT 06817
(A)	UIP Warner (Pty.) Ltd. P.O. Box 5423 Johannesburg 2000 (29.2123)	Film distributors	50	Warner Bros. Int'l. 4000 Warner Blvd. Burbank, CA 91522

Name, Address & Tel. No. of Local Firm	Product/Service Category	No. of Employees	American Parent or Associate
(S) UNBRAKO (Pty.) Ltd. P.O Box 7202 Johannesburg 2000 (37.5441)	High tensile threaded socket fasteners manufactured by parent company	17	Standard Pressed Steel Co. Benson East Jenkintown, PA 19046
(S) Union Carbide SA (Pty.) Ltd. P.O Box 8194 Johannesburg 2000 (21.7387)	Chemicals and plastics	52	Union Carbide Corp. Old Ridgebury Rd. Danbury, CT 06817
(B) Union Carbide SA (USA), Inc. P.O. Box 8194 Johannesburg 2000 (21.7387)	Regional office	28	Union Carbide Corp. Old Ridgebury Rd. Danbury, CT 06817
(S) Uniroyal (Pty.) Ltd. P.O. Box 4945 Johannesburg 2000 (21.2721)	Tires, chemicals, and industrial rubber goods	204	Uniroyal Inc. Oxford Management and Research Center Middlebury, CT 06749
(S) Unit Rig and Equipment Co. SA (Pty.) Ltd. P.O. Box 1477 Edenvale 1610 (609.2014)	Heavy-duty off-highway trucks spare parts	9	Unit Rig and Equipment Co. P.O. Box 3107 Tulsa, OK 74191
(B) United Press Int'l. P.O. Box 2385 Johannesburg 2000 (29.8328)	News	3	UPI Inc. 204 E. 42nd St. New York, NY 10017
(S) Upjohn (Pty.) Ltd. P.O. Box 246 Isando 1600 (36.2271)	Human and veterinary pharmaceuticals	151	Upjohn Co. 7000 Portage St. Kalamazoo, MI 49001

	Company (South Africa)	Product/Service	No.	U.S. Parent
(S)	Valenite-Modco (Pty.) Ltd. P.O. Box 405 Kempton Park 1620 (975.9572)	Tungsten carbide and special purpose engineering tooling	70	Valeron Corp. Box 899 Royal Oak, MI 48068
(S)	Valvoline Oil Co. SA (Pty.) Ltd. P.O. Box 14053 Wadeville 1422 (34.2444)	Lubricants, greases, automotive chemical products, and rust preventatives	14	Valvoline Oil Co. P.O. Box 1400 Lexington, KY 40591
(S)	Van Dusen Aircraft Supplies Co. SA (Pty.) Ltd. Box 18033 Rand Airport Germiston 1419 (34.8954)	Aircraft spares	5	Van Dusen Air Inc. 2801 E. 78th St. Minneapolis, MN 55420
(S)	Warner Brothers Music (Pty.) Ltd. P.O. Box 17356 Hillbrow 2033 (643.3143)	Music/Publishing	3	Warner Communications Inc. 75 Rockefeller Plaza New York, NY 10020
(B)	Washington Post Union Centre W. 52 Simmonds St. Johannesburg 2001 (838.7545)	News	1	The Washington Post 1150 15th St. NW Washington, DC 20005
(5)	WEA Records (Pty.) Ltd. P.O. Box 17356 Hillbrow 2033 (643.3143)	Records and tapes	34	Warner Communications Inc. 75 Rockefeller Plaza New York, NY 10020
(S)	Westinghouse Electric SA P.O. Box 31224 Braamfontein 2017 (37.1487)	Representative for U.S. office for Westinghouse Electric Corp, Pittsburgh, USA	7	Westinghouse Electric Corp. Westinghouse Building Gateway Center Pittsburgh, PA 15222

Name, Address & Tel. No. of Local Firm	Product/Service Category	No. of Employees	American Parent or Associate
(S) Whitehall Products SA (Pty.) Ltd. P.O. Box 7131 Johannesburg 2000 (618.4110)	Pharmaceuticals, toiletries, and household products	107	American Home Products Corp. 685 3rd Ave. New York, NY 10017
(S) Wilbur Ellis Co. (Pty.) Ltd. P.O. Box 4258 Cape Town 8000 (55.2965)	Foodstuffs; engineering, and marine goods	60	Wilbur-Ellis Co. 320 California St. San Francisco, CA 94104
(S) Wilson Learning SA (Pty.) Ltd. P.O. Box 78423 Sandton 2146 (789.1993)	Human performance systems	12	Wilson Learning USP Corp. 6950 Washington Ave. S Minneapolis, MN 55344
(S) Wyeth Laboratories (Pty.) Ltd. P.O. Box 42 Isando 1600 (36.3631)	Pharmaceuticals and infant nutritionals	300	Wyeth Int'l. Ltd. P.O. Box 8616 Philadelphia, PA 19101
(S) Zets Exploration (Pty.) Ltd. P.O. Box 31198 Braamfontein 2017 (726.4215)	Explores for, holds, and evaluates certain gold properties	13	TexasGulf Inc. High Ridge Park Stamford, CT 06904

Appendix C
Disinvestment

The most frequently heard—and perhaps the most deeply felt—response to American corporate involvement in South Africa has been the call for disinvestment. Withdrawal, proponents argue, can hasten the end of apartheid by strengthening internal resistance, by forcing the government to change, or at a minimum by removing the economic stake that may inhibit the U.S. government from imposing economic sanctions. The term *disinvestment*, as used here, refers to the withdrawal of U.S. capital from South Africa. We use the term *divestment* (see appendix D) to mean the sale of stock in companies doing business in South Africa.

Supporters of the disinvestment movement argue for the withdrawal of U.S. investments in South Africa on both moral and economic grounds. The moral argument is that it is simply wrong to maintain economic relations with a country whose economy has been built, and continues to rely, on the state-enforced exploitation of black labor. Any involvement with the morally abhorrent system of apartheid is, in this view, unjustifiable, and both individual companies and the United States as a nation have a moral obligation to sever economic ties with South Africa.

The essence of the economic argument supporting disinvestment is that the presence of American business can do little to aid the progress of South African blacks, but does a great deal to support the white regime. This argument turns on the nature of U.S. investments in South Africa. On the whole, U.S. business in that country is capital-intensive. And U.S. firms employ less than 2 percent of the black work force. Yet U.S. firms are concentrated in the computer, petroleum, automotive, and financial services industries, which are vital to the apartheid system and to the South African economy as a whole and which often involve technology that South Africa could not duplicate on its own.

Thus, supporters of disinvestment contend that U.S. investments and loans serve as a more important support for the white minority government than the size of such investments might otherwise indicate. Removing that support would therefore also have a greater effect than the size of U.S. investments might suggest. Not only would key sectors of the economy be harmed, but withdrawal of U.S. investments might also have a dramatic psychological impact on other foreign investors, thereby making it more difficult for the South African government to attract foreign capital.

The goal sought through weakening of the economy by disinvestment is, of course, to force rapid economic and social change in South Africa. Proponents of disinvestment believe that the abolition of apartheid and the establishment of true power-sharing will occur only through such pressure, that subtle methods will produce only cosmetic changes.

Importantly, the legal restrictions on removing capital from South Africa have recently been relaxed. In February 1983, the South African government abolished the system of exchange controls for nonresidents. The former requirement that capital be withdrawn only through the so-called financial rand market had provided a major disincentive to the withdrawal of investments from South Africa, since the financial rand traded at an exchange rate as much as 40 percent lower than the ordinary commercial rand. Firms withdrawing their investments will therefore no longer suffer a penalty due to exchange controls.

A charge commonly leveled at the disinvestment movement is that it has no realistic chance of success in the near future, the reason being that few companies will withdraw from South Africa unless there are economic reasons to do so, and the political climate of the United States is such that legislated disinvestment is unlikely anytime soon. Importantly, the disinvestment movement need not be completely successful in order to affect events in South Africa. The fear of legislated withdrawal or of shareholder resolutions on withdrawal has probably been an important stimulus for initiatives such as the Sullivan Principles, for various types of social development expenditures, and, at a minimum, for raising corporate consciousness of the evils of apartheid. Indeed, some would argue that disinvestment is most effective as a threat—that actual withdrawal would reduce the ability of Americans to influence change in South Africa, but that the threat of mandated withdrawal increases corporate willingness to improve the working conditions, pay, and living conditions of the black employees of U.S. corporations. If U.S. businesses truly want to continue their operations in South Africa, they may have to become responsive to black demands. Thus, by maintaining the pressure for withdrawal, proponents of disinvestment improve the effectiveness of those working for change from within U.S. corporations.

For further discussion of the arguments for disinvestment, see L. Litvak, R. DeGrasse, and K. McTigue, *South Africa: Foreign Investment and Apartheid* (Washington, D.C.: Institute for Policy Studies, 1978); and G. Hovey, Questions and Answers on Disinvestment (pamphlet published by the American Committee on Africa, 1981).

For further information, contact the American Committee on Africa or TransAfrica (see appendix H for addresses).

Appendix D
Divestment

The divestment movement seeks to bring about a change in the corporate policies of U.S. firms with operations in South Africa by encouraging individuals, universities, and pension funds, among others, to sell their shares of stock in corporations that fail to take certain steps with regard to their South African operations. Such steps may include total withdrawal, signing of the Sullivan Principles, or investment in certain social development expenditures. The ultimate goal of most persons active in the divestment movement, however, is the withdrawal of U.S. corporate investments from South Africa.

Proponents of divestment have employed a number of means to achieve their goals. Student protests have resulted in the review of university investment policies and the divestment of various university endowments, including those of the University of Wisconsin, Michigan State University, Ohio University, University of Massachusetts, University of Oregon, Antioch College, Indiana Central University, and Hampshire College.

Union activists have secured divestment of several union pension funds. Some of the unions that have sought to sever economic ties to South Africa are the International Longshoremen and Warehousemen's Union, United Auto Workers, United Electrical Workers, and Service Employees' International Union.

Various churches and church groups have taken similar action, including the National Council of Churches, the United Methodist Board of Global Ministers, the American Lutheran Church, the Reformed Church in America, and the American Friends Service Committee. Some of these groups have also been active in legislative efforts to mandate divestment. As a result, various states and municipalities have passed legislation requiring divestment of public employee pension funds and restricting government contracts with companies involved in South Africa (see appendix F).

Prior to divesting their stock, some groups have attempted to influence change from within the corporation. Stockholder resolutions have functioned as a form of private legislation seeking changes in a company's activities in South Africa. Such proposals have encountered strong opposition from management and have rarely attracted a large percentage of votes. See D. Schwartz and E. Weiss, "An assessment of the SEC shareholder proposal rule," *Georgetown Law Journal* 65 (1977): 635, 643–44, 678–80. Nevertheless, the "hassle factor" of such resolutions undoubtedly has increased the attention corporate executives pay to their South African operations.

It is difficult to assess the effectiveness of the divestment movement, because divestment is often a means rather than an end. Proponents of divestment, however, sometimes chart their success in terms of the amount of stock sold as part of a divestment campaign. Although it is impossible to calculate total figures, a few examples may prove useful. Massachusetts approved legislation requiring divestment of about $90 million worth of investments; similar legislation in Connecticut required divestment of $100 million of pension fund assets. Legislation also resulted in divestment of $79 million by Philadelphia and about $75 million by Washington, D.C. The Investor Responsibility Research Center estimates that, between 1976 and 1983, approximately $150 million worth of stock was sold by churches and universities in response to calls for divestment. For more information, contact the American Committee on Africa, the American Friends Service Committee, or the Investor Responsibility Research Center (see appendix H for addresses).

Appendix E
The Sullivan Principles

The Sullivan Principles are a set of equal opportunity guidelines for employers in South Africa intended to "promote racial equality in employment practices for U.S. firms operating in the Republic of South Africa to promote programs which can have a significant impact on improving the living conditions and quality of life for the non-white population, and to be a major contributing factor in the end of apartheid." The principles were promulgated by the International Council for Equality of Opportunity in 1977, at which time twelve corporations agreed to abide by them. The principles have been signed by just over one-third of the U.S. corporations with operations in South Africa, including many of the largest firms: The 125 firms that are currently signatories to the principles employ 70 percent of all workers in American companies. Compliance with the principles is monitored by the Arthur D. Little Company, of Cambridge, Massachusetts, which publishes an annual report summarizing the progress of U.S. corporations in adhering to the principles.

The Sullivan Principles have undergone four "amplifications" since 1977. The latest revision came in November, 1984, in response to growing support for what came to be known as the "Tutu Principles." In his address to the national conference of the South African Council of Churches in June, 1983, Bishop Desmond Tutu declared that as a minimal condition of their continued presence in South Africa, multinationals should be prepared "to help ensure that workers' families should be allowed to live with them; to permit union organization by black workers; to promote labor mobility by opposing influx control; and to make 'massive' investments in education and training programs for blacks of the sort that have credibility in the black community." Reverend Sullivan responded by amplifying the sixth principle to call on signatories actively to oppose all apartheid laws, in particular, the laws restricting black mobility.

The Sullivan Principles call for:

Nonsegregation of the races in all eating, comfort, and work facilities

Equal and fair employment practices for all employees

Equal pay for all employees doing equal or comparable work for the same period of time

Initiation of and development of training programs that will prepare, in substantial numbers, blacks and other nonwhites for supervisory, administrative, clerical, and technical jobs

Increasing the number of blacks and other nonwhites in management and supervisory positions

Improving the quality of employees' lives outside the work environment in such areas as housing, transportation, schooling, recreation, and health facilities.

The latest amplification of the Sullivan Principles (November 1984) reads as follows:

Principle I: Nonsegregation of the races in all eating, comfort and work facilities. Each signator of the Statement of Principles will proceed immediately to:

Eliminate all vestiges of racial discrimination.

Remove all race designation signs.

Desegregate all eating, comfort and work facilities.

Principle II: Equal and fair employment practices for all employees. Each signator of the Statement of Principles will proceed immediately to:

Implement equal and fair terms and conditions of employment.

Provide non-discriminatory eligibility for benefit plans.

Establish an appropriate and comprehensive procedure for handling and resolving individual employee complaints.

Support the elimination of all industrial racial discriminatory laws which impede the implementation of equal and fair terms and conditions of employment, such as abolition of job reservations, job fragmentation, and apprenticeship restrictions for Blacks and other non-whites.

Support the elimination of discrimination against the rights of Blacks to form or belong to government registered and unregistered unions and acknowledge generally the rights of Blacks to form their own unions or be represented by trade unions which already exist.

Secure rights of Black workers to the freedom of association and assure protection against victimization while pursuing and after attaining these rights.

Involve Black workers or their representatives in the development of programs that address their educational and other needs and those of their dependents and the local community.

Principle III: Equal pay for all employees doing equal or comparable work for the same period of time. Each signator of the Statement of Principles will proceed immediately to:

Design and implement a wage and salary administration plan which is applied equally to all employees, regardless of race, who are performing equal or comparable work.

Ensure an equitable system of job classifications, including a review of the distinction between hourly and salaried classifications.

Determine the extent upgrading of personnel and/or jobs in the upper echelons is needed, and accordingly implement programs to accomplish this objective in representative numbers, insuring the employment of Blacks and other non-whites at all levels of company operations.

Assign equitable wage and salary ranges, the minimum of these to be well above the appropriate local minimum economic living level.

Principle IV: Initiation of and development of training programs that will prepare, in substantial numbers, Blacks and other non-whites for supervisory, administrative clerical and technical jobs. Each signator of the Statement of Principles will proceed immediately to:

Determine employee training needs and capabilities, and identify employees with potential for further advancement.

Take advantage of existing outside training resources and activities, such as exchange programs, technical colleges and similar institutions or programs.

Support the development of outside training facilities, individually or collectively—including technical centers, professional training exposure, correspondence and extension courses, as appropriate, for extensive training outreach.

Initiate and expand inside training programs and facilities.

Principle V: Increasing the number of Blacks and other non-whites in management and supervisory positions. Each signator of the Statement of Principles will proceed immediately to:

> Identify, actively recruit, train and develop a sufficient and significant number of Blacks and other non-whites to assure that as quickly as possible there will be appropriate representation Blacks and other non-whites in the management group of each company at all levels of operations.

> Establish management development programs for Blacks and other non-whites, as needed, and improve existing programs and facilities for developing managing skills of Blacks and other non-whites.

> Identify and channel high management potential Blacks and other non-white employees into management development programs.

Principle VI: Improving the quality of employees' lives outside the work environment in such areas as housing, transportation, schooling, recreation and health facilities. Each signator of the Statement of Principles will proceed immediately to:

> Evaluate existing and/or develop programs, as appropriate, to address the specific needs of Black and other non-white employees in the areas of housing, health care, transportation and recreation.

> Evaluate methods for utilizing existing, expanded or newly established in-house medical facilities or other medical programs to improve medical care for all non-whites and their dependents.

> Participate in the development of programs that address the educational needs of employees, their dependents, and the local community. Both individual and collective programs should be considered, in addition to technical education, including such activities as literacy education, business training, direct assistance to local schools, contributions and scholarships.

> Support changes in influx control laws to provide for the right of Black migrant workers to normal family life.

> Increase utilization of and assist in the development of Black and other non-white owned and operated business enterprises including distributors, suppliers of goods and services and manufacturers.

Increased dimensions of activities outside the workplace.

> Use influence and support the unrestricted rights of black businesses to locate in the urban areas of the nation.

> Influence other companies in South Africa to follow the standards of the equal rights principles.

> Support the freedom of mobility of black workers to seek employment opportunities wherever they exist, and make possible provisions for adequate housing for families of employees within the proximity of workers' employment.

> Support the end of all apartheid laws.

With all the foregoing in mind, it is the objective of the companies to involve and assist in the education and training of large and telling numbers of blacks and other nonwhites as quickly as possible. The ultimate impact of this effort is intended to be of massive proportion, reaching and helping millions.

Periodic Reporting. The Signatory Companies of the Statement of Principles will proceed immediately to:

> Report progress on an annual basis to Reverend Sullivan through the independent administrative unit he has established.

> Have all areas specified by Reverend Sullivan audited by a certified public accounting firm.

> Inform all employees of the company's annual periodic report rating and invite their input on ways to improve the rating.

Some argue that the principles provide a screen behind which U.S. corporations can hide without engaging in truly progressive measures in South Africa. Others argue that the Sullivan Principles have prompted real, if limited, improvements in the living and working conditions of black employees of U.S. firms. In either case, the Sullivan Principles have increased the information available to stockholders and the general public about the practices of many U.S. firms in South Africa and have provided a benchmark against which to measure the progress of the signatory firms (and thus, at least indirectly, nonsignatory firms as well). The following is an alphabetical listing of signatories as of October 1983, with their progress ratings.

Rating Categories

I   Making good progress
II   Making progress
III Needs to become more active
     IIIA Low point rating on principles 4–6
     IIIB Has not met basic requirements of principles 1–3
IV Endorsors (companies with few employees or little equity)
     IVA No employees
     IVB Fewer than ten employees
     IVC Less than 19 percent equity in South African operation
V   New signatories
VI Nonreporting signatories

Alphabetical List of Signatories

AFIA Worldwide Insurance	IIIA
Abbott Laboratories	II
American Cyanamid Company	I, VI
American Express Company	IVB
American Home Products Corporation	V
American Hospital Supply Corporation	II
American International Group, Inc.	IIIB
Armco, Inc.	II, IVB
Ashland Oil, Inc.	IIIA, IVA, VI
Borden, Inc.	I
Borg-Warner Corporation	II
Bristol-Myers Company	II
Burroughs Corporation	I
Butterick Company, Inc.	IIIA
CBS, Inc.	IIIA
CIGNA Corporation	II
CPC International, Inc.	II, IVA
Caltex Petroleum Corporation	I
Carnation Company	IIIB
Carrier Corporation	V
J.I. Case Corporation	IIIA, IVA
Caterpillar Tractor Company	II
Celanese Corporation	IIIA
The Chase Manhattan Corporation	II
Chicago Bridge and Iron Company	V
Citicorp	I, IVC
The Coca-Cola Company	I, II
Colgate-Palmolive Company	I
Control Data Corporation	I
Cooper Industries, Inc.	II
Cummins Engine Company, Inc.	IVB
D'Arcy MacManus & Masius Worldwide, Inc.	IIIB
Dart & Kraft, Inc.	VI
Deere & Company	II, IVA
Del Monte Corporation	II
Deloitte Haskins & Sells	IVC
Dominion Textile, Inc.	VI
Donaldson Company, Inc.	IIIA
The Dow Chemical Company	IV, IVB

E.I. DuPont De Nemours and Company	II
The East Asiatic Company, Ltd.	VI
Eastman Kodak Company	I
Englehard Corporation	VI
Exxon Corporation	I
FMC Corporation	VI
Federal-Mogul Corporation	IIIA
Ferro Corporation	IIIA
The Firestone Tire and Rubber Company	IIIB, IVA
John Fluke Manufacturing Company, Inc.	IIIA
Fluor Corporation	II
Ford Motor Company	I
Franklin Electric Company, Inc.	VI
General Electric Company	II, VI
General Motors Corporation	I
The Gillette Company	I
Goodyear Tire and Rubber Company	II
W.R. Grace and Company	IIIA
Walter E. Heller International Corporation	IVC
Heublein, Inc.	II
Hewlett-Packard Company	II
Honeywell, Inc.	II
Hoover Company	IIIA
Hyster Company	II
International Business Machines Corporation	I
International Harvester Company	IIIA, IVB
International Minerals and Chemicals Corporation	IIIA
International Telephone and Telegraph Corporation	I, IVC, VI
The Interpublic Group of Companies, Inc.	VI
Johnson Controls, Inc.	VI
Johnson and Johnson	I
Joy Manufacturing Company	VI
Kellogg Company	II
Eli Lilly and Company	I, II, IVA
Marriott Corporation	IIIA
Marsh and McLennan Companies	VI
Masonite Corporation	IIIB
McGraw-Hill, Inc.	I
Measurex Corporation	VI
Merck & Company, Inc.	I, II
Mine Safety Appliances Company	IIIB
Minnesota Mining and Manufacturing Company	I
Mobil Oil Corporation	I
Monsanto Company	I
Motorola, Inc.	IIIA
NCNB Corporation	IVB
NCR Corporation	IIIA
Nabisco Brands, Inc.	II
Nalco Chemical Company	IIIB
Norton Company	II, IIIA, IVB
Norton Simon, Inc.	IVA
Olin Corporation	IIIA, IIIB, VI
Oshkosh Truck Corporation	IVA
Otis Elevator Company	II
The Parker Pen Company	II
Pfizer, Inc.	I, II
Phelps Dodge Corporation	IIIA, VI

Phillips Petroleum Company	II
Reader's Digest Association, Inc.	IIIA, IVA
Rexnord, Inc.	IIIA
Richardson-Vicks, Inc.	IIIA
Rohm and Haas Company	IIIA, IVB
Schering-Plough Corporation	II
Sentry Insurance—A Mutual Company	IIIA
Smith Kline Beckman Corporation	II, V
Sperry Corporation	I
Squibb Corporation	IIIA
The Standard Oil Company (Ohio)	II, IIIA
The Stanley Works	II
Sterling Drug, Inc.	IIIA
Tampax, Inc.	I
J. Walter Thompson Company	VI
Time, Inc.	IVB
The Trane Company	IIIB
Union Carbide Corporation	I, II, IVB
The Upjohn Company	II, IIIA
Warner Communications, Inc.	I, IIIA
Warner-Lambert Company	II, IIIA
Westinghouse Electric Corporation	I
Wilbur-Ellis Company	IIIA
Xerox Corporation	I

For a comprehensive examination of the Sullivan Principles, see D. Hauck, M. Voorhes, and G. Goldberg, *Two Decades of Debate: The Controversy over U.S. Companies in South Africa* (Washington, D.C.: Investor Responsibility Research Center, 1983), pp. 97–121.

Appendix F
Federal and State Actions

In recent years, federal and state governments have taken a variety of actions relating to U.S. business involvement in South Africa. An even larger number of actions remain under consideration.

Export Restrictions

In 1976 the U.S. government prohibited sales of American computers and computer technology to the South African military, police, and atomic energy agencies. The following year this restriction was extended to agencies administering the system of influx control. In 1978 the federal government proscribed the sale of any American-made goods or technology to the South African military and police.

The Reagan administration has relaxed some of these restrictions and has permitted sales of several "general purpose items" including food, clothing, chemicals, industrial equipment, and photocopying equipment to the military and police. Moreover, sales of medical supplies to the military and police and sales of computers to certain government agencies have been approved on a case-by-case basis.

There is no government policy restricting loans by U.S. commercial banks to South African firms or the South African government. The 1978 "Evans Amendment" to the Export-Import Bank Act, however, restricts the Export-Import Bank from promoting certain commercial activities in South Africa. The Evans Amendment provides:

> (9) In no event shall the Bank guarantee, insure, or extend credit or participate in the extension of credit (a) in support of any export which would contribute to enabling the Government of the Republic of South Africa to maintain or enforce apartheid; (b) in support of any export to the Government of the Republic of South Africa or its agencies unless the President determines that significant progress toward the elimination of apartheid has been made and transmits to the Congress a statement describing and ex-

plaining that determination; or (c) in support of any export to other purchasers in the Republic of South Africa or its agencies unless the United States Secretary of State certifies that the purchaser has endorsed and has proceeded toward the implementation of the following principles: nonsegregation of the races in all work facilities; equal and fair employment for all employees; initiation and development of training programs to prepare nonwhite South Africans for supervisory, administrative, clerical, and technical jobs; increasing the number of nonwhites in management and supervisory positions; a willingness to engage in collective bargaining with labor unions; and improving the quality of life for employees in such areas as housing, transportation, schooling, recreation, and health facilities.

Finally, following the Reagan administration's vote in favor of a $1.1 billion loan to South Africa from the International Monetary Fund in 1982, the U.S. Congress passed the International Monetary Fund Replenishment Act in 1983. This statute directs the U.S. representative to the International Monetary Fund to vote against all loans to countries that practice apartheid. The new law reads as follows:

(b) The Congress hereby finds that the practice of apartheid results in severe constraints on labor and capital mobility and other highly inefficient labor and capital supply rigidities which contribute to balance of payments deficits in direct contradiction of the goals of the International Monetary Fund. Therefore, the President shall instruct the United States Executive Director of the Fund to actively oppose any facility involving use of Fund credit by any country which practices apartheid unless the Secretary of the Treasury certifies and documents in writing, upon request, and so notifies and appears, if requested, before the Foreign Relations and Banking, Housing and Urban Affairs Committees of the Senate and the Banking, Finance and Urban Affairs Committee of the House of Representatives, at least twenty-one days in advance of any vote on such drawing, that such drawing: (1) would reduce the severe constraints on labor and capital mobility, through such means as increasing access to education by workers and reducing artificial constraints on worker mobility and substantial reduction of racially-based restrictions on the geographical mobility of labor; (2) would reduce other highly inefficient labor and capital supply rigidities; (3) would benefit economically the majority of the people of any country which practices apartheid; (4) is suffering from a genuine balance of payments imbalance that cannot be met by recourse to private capital markets. Should the Secretary not meet a request to appear before the aforementioned Committees at least twenty-one days in advance of any vote on any facility involving the use of Fund credit by any country practicing apartheid and certify and document in writing that these four conditions have been met, the United States Executive Director shall vote against such program.

For a more detailed discussion of U.S. export restrictions to South Africa, see D. Hauck, M. Voorhes, and G. Goldberg, *Two Decades of Debate: The Controversy over U.S. Companies in South Africa* (Washington, D.C.: Investor Responsibility Research Center, 1983), pp. 31–40.

U.S. Aid to South Africa

In recent years, the United States has initiated several programs to aid black South Africans. Under Secretary of State Lawrence S. Eagleburger outlined these programs in a June 1983 speech:

—A $4 million-a-year scholarship program which brings approximately 100 black South African students a year to the United States for undergraduate and graduate degrees. The majority of these students are studying in the hard sciences. By 1985 there will be some 400 black South Africans enrolled in U.S. institutions of higher education, and we will begin graduating more black engineers, chemists, and computer engineers than now exist in South Africa.

—In cooperation with the AFL-CIO, programs of support are being initiated to train labor leaders in South Africa in skills which will improve the collective bargaining ability of black and mixed trade unions and enhance the dialogue between the American and South African labor communities. The U.S. contribution to this program will increase from $190,000 this fiscal year to $875,000 next year.

—In cooperation with the National African Federated Chamber of Commerce of South Africa, we are beginning this year a project to support small business development in the black community. Over the next two years, some $3 million will be invested in this project designed to enhance the economic leverage of the black community.

—In conjunction with black community groups throughout South Africa, we have underway a tutorial program to assist black high school students preparing for the matriculation examination which will determine their professional futures. Over the next two years this $2 million project should significantly boost the number of blacks eligible for university admission.

—Moreover, the U.S. Senate has recently expressed its interest in setting aside $5 million for an internal scholarship program as a counterpart to the program now bringing black South African students to the United States. This program, implemented through private South African institutions, could provide scholarship support to some 400 black South African students per year.

Congressional Legislation

Both houses of Congress have held hearings on U.S. business involvement in South Africa, but legislative activity on this issue has largely been concentrated in the House of Representatives. Even in the House, most legislation has not even been reported out of committee. There are a few exceptions.

In 1977, following the death of Steven Biko, the House passed a resolution denouncing South Africa's treatment of opponents of apartheid. As noted above, in 1978, both houses of Congress passed the "Evans Amendment" to the Export-Import Bank Act of 1945, which restricted government-subsidized loans to South Africa. And more recently, Congress passed the IMF Replenishment Act of 1983 quoted previously.

Perhaps the most significant congressional legislation is the proposed Export Administration Amendments Act. In 1984 members of the House Foreign Affairs Committee and the Senate Banking Committee were considering bills passed by each house. The House version, H.R. 3231, included several amendments that would impose far-reaching economic sanctions against South Africa. The text of H.R. 3231, as passed by the House, reads as follows:

United States Policy Toward South Africa Act of 1983

Subtitle 1 — Labor Standards: Endorsement and Implementation of Fair Employment Principles

Sec. 311. Any United States person who (1) has a branch or office in South Africa, or (2) controls a corporation, partnership, or other enterprise in South Africa, in which more than twenty people are employed shall take the necessary steps to insure that, in operating such branch, office, corporation, partnership, or enterprise, those principles relating to employment practices set forth in section 312 of this Act are implemented.

Statement of Principles

Sec. 312(a). The principles referred to in section 311 of this Act are as follows: [Act lists the Sullivan Principles].

Subtitle 2 — Prohibition on Loans and Importation of Gold Coins

Loans to South Africa

Sec. 321(a). No bank operating under the laws of the United States may make any loan directly or through a foreign subsidiary to the South African Government or to any corporation, partnership, or other organization which is owned or controlled by the South African Government, as determined under regulations issued by the Secretary. The prohibition contained in this subsection shall not apply to loans for educational, housing, or health facilities which are available to all persons on a totally nondiscriminatory basis and which are located in geographic areas accessible to all population groups without any legal or administrative restriction.

(b) The prohibition contained in subsection (a) of this section shall not apply to any loan or extension of credit for which an agreement is entered into before the date of the enactment of this Act.

Gold Coins

Sec. 322. No person, including any bank operating under the laws of the United States, may import into the United States any South African krugerrand or any gold coin minted in South Africa or offered for sale by the South African Government.

Subtitle 3 — Investment in South Africa Prohibition

Sec. 331. The President shall, not later than 90 days after the date of the enactment of this Act, issue regulations prohibiting any United States person from making any investment in South Africa. For purposes of the preceding sentence, the term "investment" means—

(1) establishing or making a loan or other extension of credit for the establishment of a business enterprise in South Africa, including a subsidiary, affiliate, branch or office in South Africa; and

(2) investing funds in an existing enterprise in South Africa, including making a loan or other extension of credit, except that this paragraph shall not be construed to prohibit—

(A) an investment which consists of earnings derived from an enterprise in South Africa established before the date of the enactment of this Act and which is made in that enterprise; or

(B) the purchase of securities on a securities exchange. The President may issue such licenses or orders as are necessary to carry out this section.

Termination of Prohibition

Sec. 333. If the President determines that the Government of South Africa has made substantial progress toward the full participation of all the people of South Africa in the social, political, and economic life in that country and toward an end to discrimination based on race or ethnic origin, the President shall submit that determination, and the basis therefore, to the Congress. The regulations issued pursuant to this subtitle, and any license or order issued under this subtitle, shall terminate upon enactment of a joint resolution approving such determination.

For additional discussion of the history of congressional legislation concerning South Africa, see D. Hauck, M. Voorhes, and G. Goldberg, *Two Decades of Debate: The Controversy over U.S. Companies in South Africa* (Washington, D.C.: Investor Responsibility Research Center, 1983), pp. 41–47.

State and Municipal Legislation

State legislatures and municipal governments have become increasingly involved in the divestment debate in recent years. Legislation seeking to cut economic ties with South Africa has been introduced in more than twenty states and many cities. Several of these initiatives have been successful.

The Massachusetts legislature, in early 1983, passed a bill (over the veto of Governor King) which requires divestment of all pension fund monies invested in corporations and banks doing business in South Africa. Approximately $100 million of investments will be affected by the law, which states:

> (vi) After January 1, 1983, no public pension funds under this subsection shall remain invested in any bank or financial institution which directly or through its subsidiaries has outstanding loans to the Republic of South Africa or its instrumentalities, and no assets shall remain invested in the stocks, securities or other obligations of any company doing business in or with the Republic of South Africa. Any proceeds of sales required under this paragraph shall be invested as much as reasonably possible in institutions or companies which invest or conduct business operations in Massachusetts so long as such use is consistent with sound investment policy.
>
> (vii) Notwithstanding the provisions of the preceding paragraph, if sound investment policy so required, the investment committee may vote to spread the sale of such investments over no more than three years so that no less than one-third the value of said investments is sold in any one year. So long as any funds remain invested in any bank, financial institution or firm referred to in paragraph (vi), the investment committee shall annually, on or before January thirty-first, file with the clerk of the senate and the clerk of the house of representatives a report listing all South Africa-related investments held by the fund and their book market value as of the preceding December first.
>
> *Mass. Gen. L. Anno. Ch. 32 § 23(d)(1) (Supp. 1983).*

Michigan has enacted two laws concerning U.S. firms doing business in South Africa. In 1980 the Michigan legislature mandated that no state funds be deposited in banks making loans to the South African government, South African corporations, or U.S. corporations with South African operations. In 1982, the legislature required the endowments of all state universities and colleges to divest any investments in corporations doing business in South Africa.

Connecticut has enacted into law a measure that requires the divestment of all state funds invested in corporations that do not demonstrate that they are meeting certain standards in South Africa. Specifically, the law provides:

Sec. 3–13f. State investment policy in relation to corporations doing business in South Africa.

(a) In carrying out his fiduciary responsibility, the state treasurer shall, within a reasonable period of time, disinvest all state funds currently invested in any corporation doing business in South Africa and invest no new state funds in any such corporation unless such corporation satisfies all the following minimum requirements: (1) Such corporation has adopted the Sullivan principles and has obtained a performance rating in the top two categories of the Sullivan principles rating system prepared by Arthur D. Little, Inc., (2) such corporation does not supply strategic products or services for use by the government of South Africa or for use by the military or police in South Africa and (3) such corporation recognizes the right of all South African employees to organize and strike in support of economic or social objectives, free from the fear of dismissal or blacklisting. The state treasurer shall consult with the investment advisory council in developing, interpreting and administering any policy relating to these requirements. For the purposes of this section the term "doing business in South Africa" shall mean conducting or performing a manufacturing, assembly or warehousing operations within the Republic of South Africa or, if a bank or other financial institution, lending money to the Republic of South Africa or any agency or instrumentality thereof, and the term "strategic products or services" shall mean articles designated as arms, ammunition and implements of war in 22 Code of Federal Regulations Part 121, and data processing equipment and computers sold for military or police use or for use in connection with the pass system as practiced in the Republic of South Africa.

(b) In determining whether or not to invest state funds in any corporation, the state treasurer, in administering this section, may require a social audit of any corporation doing business in South Africa.

Gen. Stat. Conn. Ch. 32, section 3–13f (1983).

Municipalities that have passed legislation similar to that of these states include Washington, D.C., Philadelphia, Berkeley, and Hartford.

For a more complete discussion of such state and municipal actions, see D. Hauck, M. Voorhes and G. Goldberg, *Two Decades of Debate: The Controversy over U.S. Companies in South Africa* (Washington, D.C.: Investor Responsibility Research Center, 1983), pp. 47–59; M. Boyer, "Divesting from Apartheid: A Summary of State and Municipal

Legislative Action on South Africa" (pamphlet published by the American Committee on Africa, March 1983).

For more information, contact the following organizations (see appendix H for their addresses).

American Committee on Africa

Interfaith Center on Corporate Responsibility

Subcommittee on Africa, U.S. House of Representatives Committee on Foreign Affairs

TransAfrica

Appendix G
U.S. Corporate Contributions to Black South African Development

In response to outside pressure—in the form of the Sullivan Principles, shareholder resolutions, threatened or actual divestment by private institutions, and, more recently, legislative action—many American corporations in South Africa have begun to devote a share of their revenues to projects aimed at helping not just their black employees but the larger black community. These projects have focused on two critical areas: education and housing.

One popular form of corporate assistance to community education is the Adopt-A-School program, which is affiliated with the International Council for Equality of Opportunity, sponsors of the Sullivan Principles. Seventy-six U.S. corporations have "adopted" 150 South African primary and secondary schools, to which they help provide facilities, teachers' salaries, and classroom and library materials. Last year, contributions to the Adopt-A-School program totaled nearly R865,000.

U.S. corporations contributed $6 million to build the Pace Commercial College, a modern, private high school in Soweto. Tuition and fees for most Pace students are donated by the American and South African private sector. American corporate contributions to Pace and to basic educational programs in communities near U.S. facilities exceeded R1.3 million last year.

About 20 percent of the black employees of American companies in South Africa are engaged in some form of skills training. At most companies this consists of efforts to upgrade job skills and functional literacy. Some larger employers are training blacks for technical positions requiring English language fluency and science or business expertise.

U.S. corporations in South Africa have begun efforts to assist black business development. Some American corporations are currently sponsoring blacks in management courses in the United States. Other corporations have set up black franchises and have begun soliciting suppliers from among black-owned businesses.

A number of U.S. companies have provided their black employees with home ownership and home improvement assistance. Often such assistance involves low-interest or no-interest loans to help employees purchase their own homes. Similar efforts have been made to improve the quality of health clinics serving black communities.

Many firms are also among the supporters of the United States-South Africa Leader Exchange Program (USSALEP). USSALEP was founded in 1958 to facilitate visits by educators, journalists, professionals, and others between the United States and South Africa. In 1977 USSALEP initiated the Careers Development Project in order to provide advanced training for promising African, "colored," and Indian men and women. USSALEP is financed by gifts from foundations, corporations, and individuals.

For more information, contact the American Chamber of Commerce in South Africa, the International Council for Equality of Opportunity Principles, or USSALEP (see appendix H for their addresses).

Appendix H
Organization Address List

American Chamber of Commerce in South Africa
Anglo American Life Centre
27th Floor
45 Commissioner St.
Johannesburg 2001
South Africa

American Committee on Africa
198 Broadway, Room 401
New York, NY 10038
(212) 962-1210

American Friends Service Committee
1501 Cherry St.
Philadelphia, PA 19102
(215) 241-7169

Interfaith Center on Corporate Responsibility
475 Riverside Dr., Room 566
New York, NY 10115
(212) 870-2295

International Council for Equality
  of Opportunity Principles
1501 Broad St.
Philadelphia, PA 19102
(215) 236-6757

International Defense and Aid Fund for Southern Africa
P.O. Box 17
Cambridge, MA 02138
(617) 491-8343

Investor Responsibility Research Center
Suite 900
1319 F Street, NW
Washington, D.C. 20004
(202) 833-3727

South Africa Foundation
Suite 620
1225 19th St., NW
Washington, D.C. 20036
(202) 223-5486

Subcommittee on Africa
Committee on Foreign Affairs
House of Representatives
Washington, D.C. 20515
(202) 226-7807

TransAfrica
545 8th St., SE
Suite 200
Washington, D.C. 20003
(202) 547-2550

United Methodist Church Office for the United Nations
777 United Nations Plaza
New York, NY 10017
(212) 682-3633

United Nations Center Against Apartheid
One United Nations Plaza
New York, NY 10017
(212) 754-2110

United States-South Africa Leader Exchange Program
1700 17th St., NW
Washington, D.C. 20009
(202) 232-6720

Washington Office on Africa
110 Maryland Ave., NE
Washington, D.C. 20002
(202) 546-7961

Index

145–149; shortage of skilled, xxiv, 5–8, 42–43, 50; statistics of, 158–159. *See also* Sullivan Principles; Trade unions
Labanization, xiii, 46, 61
Lebowa, 157. *See also* Homelands
Legal Resources Centre, 74
Legislation, state and federal, 225–232
Liaison committees, 9–10
Lijphart, Arend, 48. *See also* Confederalism

Mabuza, Enos, 15
Mandela, Nelson, 61. *See also* African National Congress
Marais, Jaap, 43, 44
Market economy. *See* Neoclassical liberalism
Marxism, 49. *See also* Neo-Marxism
Metal and Allied Workers' Union, 77
Migrant labor. *See* Labor, migrant
Military, xiv, xv, 13–14, 118
Mosala, Leonard, xxxv, 123
Motlana, Nthato, xxi
Movimento Popular de Libertacao de Angola (MPLA), 59
Mozambique, xiii–xiv, xv, 19, 58, 130
Mugabe, Robert, xv, 19, 46, 141
Mulder, Connie, 134
Mutual security treaties. *See* Security agreements
Mvubelo, Lucy, 138

Namibia, 58
Nation: definition of, xix–xxi, 21, 115
National African Federated Chamber of Commerce (NAFCOC), 74
National Forum, 20
National party (NP), xvii–xviii, xxi, 42, 43, 47–51, 114, 124, 144
National Union of Textile Workers, 77
Nationalist. *See* National party
Nattrass, Jill, 153
Neo-Marxism: view of corporation, xxvii, xxviii, 149–151
Neoclassical liberalism: view of corporation, xxvi, xxx
Nickel, Herman, 132, 138
Nigeria, xvii

Nonaggression pacts. *See* Security agreements
Northern Ireland, xix, 142–143

Oppenheimer, Harry, 49, 56, 132, 153
Orderly Movement and Settlement of Black Persons Bill, 27, 35. *See also* Riekert Report; Influx control
Orthodox Ideologues, 44–47. *See also* Conservative party

Pass laws. *See* Influx control
Pluralist view of corporation, xxvii, xxx
Polstu, 51
Population, 30, 103, 115, 157–158
Power-sharing. *See* Constitution
Progressive Federal Party (PFP), 41, 43, 51–52, 56–57
Promotion of Bantu Self-Government Act, xvii–xviii, 22

Quoboza, Percy, 138
QwaQwa, 30, 157. *See also* Homelands

Recession, 3–4, 131
Removals, population. *See* Resettlement
Resettlement, xxii, 3, 28–29, 32, 91, 127
Retief, Piet, 124
Rhoodie, Eschel, 34
Riekert Report, 25–27, 29, 31, 32, 35, 144, 149. *See also* Influx control
Rockefeller Commission, xii, 39, 40, 140
Ruling Technocrats, 47–51, 60. *See also* National party
Rural development, 35–36, 98–100, 101–105. *See also* Homelands
Rural Foundation, proposal for a, 101–102, 104
Rural outsiders. *See* Urban–rural division
Rural service centers, 102–103

Sabotage. *See* Guerrilla activity
Sampson, Anthony, 151, 155
Sanctions: against South Africa, xxv, xxvi, 4–5, 12–13, 39, 40, 52–53, 109–112. *See also* Disinvestment; Arms embargo

About the Contributors

Heribert Adam is professor of sociology at Simon Fraser University, Canada. He is the author of numerous books and articles on the structure of white power in South Africa, including *Modernizing Racial Domination* (1971) and, with Hermann Giliomee, *Ethnic Power Mobilized: Can South Africa Change?* (1979).

Tony Bloom is chairman of the Premier Group, one of the largest manufacturing corporations in South Africa. He has become a leader in the South African business community through his consistent and public opposition to certain government policies.

Gatsha Buthelezi is chief minister of KwaZulu, the largest of the black "homelands;" president of Inkatha Yenkululeko yeSizwe, a national cultural liberation movement with over 360,000 members; and chairman of the South African Black Alliance, an alliance of black organizations in South Africa.

Halton Cheadle is assistant director of the Centre for Applied Legal Studies, University of the Witwatersrand, Johannesburg. He is editor of the *Industrial Law Journal* and the *South African Labour Bulletin*. During 1972–73 he assisted in the formation of the predominantly black Trade Unions Council, and later served as Acting Secretary of the National Union of Textile Workers and Metal and Allied Workers Union. He currently provides legal counsel to several black trade unions.

Oscar Dhlomo is minister of education and culture of KwaZulu. He is currently implementing a massive development program in KwaZulu that encompasses education, agriculture, housing, and health care.

Fred Ferreira is director of industrial relations for Ford Motor Company of South Africa. Under his leadership, Ford became the first company in the country to train unindentured black apprentices (1976), to recognize an unregistered trade union (1977), and to employ full-time black shop stewards (1980). Since the historic strike at Ford's Struandale Plant in 1979, Ferreira has been widely recognized as an authority on labor relations in South Africa.

Hermann Giliomee is professor of political science at the University of Cape Town. He is author and editor of numerous historical and political studies of South Africa including, with Heribert Adam, *Ethnic Power Mobilized: Can South Africa Change?* (1979) and, as coeditor, *The Shaping of South African Society, 1652–1820* (1979).

John Kane-Berman is director of the South African Institute of Race Relations. He formerly worked as a senior editor of the *Johannesburg Financial Mail* and as a freelance journalist and consultant. He is the author of *South Africa: The Method in the Madness* (1978) and *Apartheid and Business* (1980).

Leonard Mosala is former treasurer of the Soweto Committee of Ten, a committee of community leaders that rose to prominence during the Soweto riots in 1976. He is former chairman of the African Chemical Workers Unions.

Griffiths Zabala is director of Self-Help Associates for Development Economics. Through this organization and others, he initiates and advises community development projects in South Africa.

About the Editors

Jonathan Leape is on the staff of the Economics Department at Harvard University. He received an A.B. in American History and Literature from Harvard College and a B.A. in Philosophy, Politics, and Economics from Oxford University. He is a National Science Foundation Graduate Fellow and is currently completing a Ph.D. in Economics at Harvard University. In the summer of 1981, he and Bo Baskin traveled to South Africa and interviewed over a hundred journalists, scholars, businessmen, students, and political leaders from every major political organization and ethnic group.

Bo Baskin is an associate in the Mergers and Acquisitions Department of a major investment bank in New York City. He received his B.A. in Economics from Davidson College. He attended Oxford University on a Rhodes Scholarship and received a B.A. in Philosophy, Politics, and Economics. He returned from England to complete his Masters in Public and Private Management at the Yale University School of Management. Before the 1981 trip with Jonathan Leape, he spent a year in Africa as the headmaster of a school in Kenya.

Stefan Underhill is a law clerk to the Honorable Jon O. Newman of the United States Court of Appeals for the Second Circuit. He received a B.A. in Government from the University of Virginia, where he was an Echols Scholar. He attended Oxford University on a Rhodes Scholarship and received a B.A. in Philosophy, Politics, and Economics. He received a J.D. from the Yale Law School where he was Articles and Book Reviews Editor of the *Yale Law Journal*.